Praise for *Fatal Storm*

Whatever else Mundle may write, this is likely to be his master work
—and it deserves to be ranked a master work of reportage. . . . He's
done himself, the offshore sailing community, the rescuers and the
memory of the dead men—to which he has dedicated the book
proud."

—*The Mercury*

Fatal Storm can be recommended to everyone who has a thirst for
adventure. It is a story of survival under the most horrific conditions.
. . . You will not be able to put the book down."

—*Geelong Advertiser*

Mundle rivals the endeavour of author Sebastian Junger, who wrote
the international best-seller *The Perfect Storm*, but also surpasses
it in that Junger recreated portions of his narrative drawing upon
informed supposition. [Mundle] takes the reader inside the storm,
inside the yachts, and into the cockpits of the helicopters. Anyone who
has been caught offshore in foul weather will recognize the authenticity
of Mundle's account. For most of the past 70 years, the standard text for
sailors contemplating making ocean passages has been K. Adlard Cole
work *Heavy Weather Sailing*. It now has a rival."

—*Daily Telegraph*

Rob Mundle's book is a riveting and harrowing story of the storm
which devastated a sporting nation."

—*Daily Telegraph*

It is hard to grasp the sheer power of the raging sea—even harder to
imagine so few casualties. . . . This book is a fitting testament to all
rescuers involved in tragic events—and a warning to all those who
want to sail offshore of the perils of the sea."

— *Herald Sun*

You don't need to be an offshore racer to enjoy this book. Without
question, thousands of people who have never been on a sailboat will
buy this book and enjoy it immensely. But those of you who have
sailed offshore should run—not walk—to your nearest bookstore and
pick up a copy, right now!"

—*Scuttlebutt*

FATAL STORM

THE INSIDE STORY OF THE TRAGIC SYDNEY-HOBART RACE

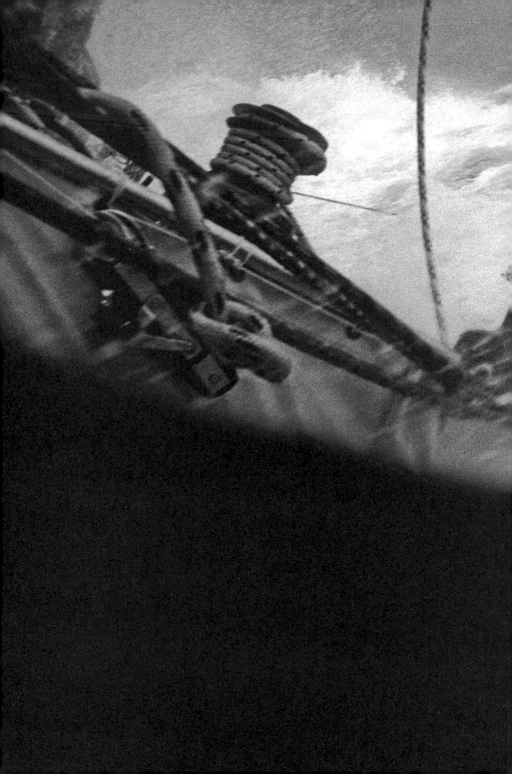

FATAL STORM

THE INSIDE STORY OF THE TRAGIC SYDNEY–HOBART RACE

ROB MUNDLE

INTERNATIONAL MARINE/MCGRAW-HILL
Camden, Maine • New York • Chicago • San Francisco • Lisbon
London • Madrid • Mexico City • Milan • New Delhi • San Juan
Seoul • Singapore • Sydney • Toronto

The **McGraw·Hill** Companies

1 2 3 4 5 6 7 8 9 10 DOC DOC 0 9 8 7
© 1999, 2000, 2007 Rob Mundle
Published in Australia in 1999 as *Fatal Storm: The 54th Sydney to
Hobart Yacht Race* by HarperCollins *Publishers* Pty Limited.
This edition published by arrangement with HarperCollins.
All rights reserved. The name "International Marine" and the
International Marine logo are trademarks of The McGraw-Hill
Companies. Printed in the United States of America.

The Library of Congress Catalog Card Number for the cloth edition of this book is 99-73354

2000 paperback ISBN 0-07-136140-5

2007 paperback ISBN-13: 978-0-07-148770-2
2007 paperback ISBN-10: 0-07-148770-0

I dedicate *this book to the memory of the six sailors who perished and to the rescue crews, without whose valiant efforts many more lives would surely have been lost.*

Yachts that experienced problems or encountered difficulties, and even those that continued racing, reported that "exceptional" waves were responsible for inflicting the damage or causing severe knockdowns. These waves were always a minimum of 20 percent and up to 100 percent bigger than the prevailing seas and always came from a direction other than the prevailing wave pattern. . . . Whether or not a yacht was hit by an extreme wave was a matter of chance.

PETER BUSH, Chairman
The 1998 Sydney to Hobart Race Review Committee
Cruising Yacht Club of Australia
from his summary of key findings and recommendations

Contents

Foreword

I clearly remember Rob Mundle's late-night television update on the Sydney to Hobart race on December 26, 1998. He had spoken with meteorologist Roger Badham and reported that the Sydney to Hobart race fleet, which was then flying down the New South Wales coast, could find themselves sailing into a severe depression forming in Bass Strait. It had the signature of a hurricane, but worse still, the westerly winds it would generate would oppose a strong current.

I knew that could only mean huge waves and horrific sailing conditions. My mind immediately went back to August 1979, when I was the helmsman on the Australian Admiral's Cup yacht *Impetuous* in the disastrous Fastnet Race out of Cowes, England. That race claimed the lives of fifteen fellow yachtsmen. After we rounded Lands End—the southwest tip of England—we received a weather forecast saying we could "expect a northwesterly change with wind gusts of 30 to 40 knots." The first gusts, which came in at around 10 P.M., were at 60 knots. They later rose to 80.

It appears that the same might have happened in the Sydney to Hobart—gusts of around 92 knots were registered at Wilsons Promontory, due west of the fleet.

The carnage that resulted seemed unbelievable until we saw on television the size of the waves and the strength of the wind. The rescue effort was remarkable, and I say without hesitation that Australia is deeply indebted to those who took part. At the same time, my deepest sympathy goes to the families and friends of those who died in this tragic event. Hopefully the lessons learned will be studied well and applied to all future offshore races.

Australia is an island continent founded by seafarers, and even to this day is largely dependent on sea trade. It is because ours is a sport that fosters the qualities of our forebears—daring, comradeship, endurance, and the risk-taking demanded by the ocean—that so many of us enjoy offshore sailing.

For me, the most fitting epitaph to this tragedy comes from the great Australian poet Adam Lindsay Gordon:

No game was ever worth a rap

for a rational man to play

Into which no accident, no mishap

could possibly find its way.

SIR JAMES HARDY
five-time America's Cup skipper

Preface

Sailors have always known that the ultimate storm might descend on the Sydney to Hobart yacht race one day. And that is exactly what happened in the fifty-fourth staging of the race.

Since its inception in 1945 the race has stood as an Australian sporting icon. Each year, from the start on Boxing Day, December 26, until the yachts reach the finish line 630 nautical miles away, Australians devour news of its progress via television, newspapers, and radio.

Like so many other extreme sports, ocean racing contains an element of danger. That is part of its special appeal to a world stripped by proliferating rules and regulations of much of its primitive spirit of adventure. That the notorious waters of the Tasman Sea and Bass Strait are part of the challenge only adds to the excitement for competitors and "spectators."

Having been a sailor all my life, and having covered the Sydney to Hobart thirty times, I knew soon after the start that a potential for disaster existed. The next morning, when a weather station at Wilsons Promontory, a knuckle of land that juts out into Bass Strait, registered more than 90 knots of wind from the west, my fears were confirmed.

This book details what happened in the ensuing maelstrom: a weather bomb exploded over the fleet. It led to the largest peacetime search-and-rescue effort ever in Australia. Of the fleet of 115 yachts, only 44 reached Hobart, 55 sailors were winched to safety, and 5 yachts sank. Six sailors died.

I have deliberately avoided the controversies that some have associated with the race. It was not my object to ascribe blame. Instead, I have told the story of what happened in the hope that, if necessary, others might ask questions. It must be stressed that there were 1,135 competitors in this race. Almost every one of those sailors could tell a unique and compelling story. *Fatal Storm*, however, deals with the major incidents. It is the result of more than 300,000 words collected in 124 interviews. My research leaves me in no doubt that nothing short of a miracle could have saved at least forty competitors who did *not* die in this race. Heroic rescues, superb seamanship, the location of the storm, the air and sea temperature, and, perhaps, divine intervention all reduced the final toll.

Acknowledgments

To create a book of this magnitude in just sixteen weeks was a massive effort that I could not have completed alone.

I am deeply indebted to many people, none more than the large number of sailors, search-and-rescue participants, families, friends, and race officials who took time to tell me their story.

On the production side, no one made a greater effort than my assistant, Nicky Ronalds. She was tireless in her coordination of interviews, research, and reading—and in keeping me organized. My media mate Mark Rothfield kept me on course with the writing, while Carmel Paterson put in an inordinate number of hours at the computer transcribing interviews. Photographers Richard Bennett and Ian Mainsbridge were also important contributors.

On the personal side, I must thank Lindsay "The Duck" Walker for being such a great mate and providing the ideal writing environment at his waterfront home—"The Duck Pond." Peter Sutton gave invaluable advice when it was needed most, while a host of other friends gave me exceptional moral support over what was a very demanding period in my life.

Introduction to the 2007 Edition

by John Rousmaniere

The first thing that must be said about *Fatal Storm* is that Rob Mundle's portrayals of courageous sailors and heroic rescuers fighting for their lives are as vivid as any I have read. Whether seen through the eyes of helicopter crews searching the vastness of the deeps for solitary boats hidden among the waves, or viewed from the unstable perspective of the sailors on (and too often beneath) the tumultuous sea's surface, the action is breathless and ceaseless.

Fatal Storm is such a terrific read because the right person told it. An experienced Australian sailor and professional writer, Rob Mundle knows the race, the course, and the people intimately. Yet when it fell upon his shoulders to write what must have been the most difficult story of his career—a story of six deaths, hundreds of incidents of destruction, and thousands of fearful hearts—he was not content to coast on his contacts and experience but performed a mighty feat of legwork. The results of the 124 interviews he conducted are displayed on every page in vivid, telling quotations. Take, for example, these three sentences from three pages toward the end of Chapter 11: "Our whole world exploded," "He too ended up underwater, under the boat, without air," and "The yacht was making no move to come upright." Any one of those declarations is startling in its own right. Racing in on each other's heels, they are devastating.

Sensitive readers may think that, considering the circumstances, some of the sailors' comments in these pages are flippant. A fundamental rule of Australian slang—"Strine," as it is called—is that that the closer disaster looms, the more understated the participants must be. The owner of a boat blasting through the night under razor-thin control turns to a shipmate and, as though they are out for a gentle evening sail, asks if he wants to "have a drive." A survivor of the tragic *Winston Churchill* (which lost three sailors) describes the maelstrom as an "absolute shemozzle." And so on, including the conversation between the extraordinarily composed sailors in Chapter 17 who, though desperately clutching a shredded life raft, engage in a comic byplay that would not be out of place in an Abbott and Costello routine. Not many disaster accounts feature a running dialogue whose punch line is, "Mate, who gets to eat who first?"

I mention this with all due respect to the humanity and experience of these sailors. There is no frivolity here. People who crack jokes as their heads are drawn into a lion's mouth very likely have considerable experience wrestling with lions. Australians have been dealing with a hostile sea for far too long to expend energy making profound observations about it.

The Aussies in these pages know two truths about nasty weather. The first is that in naturally tempestuous places like Bass Strait, discomfort is regular and must be expected. In 2000 the fleet had a brutal 600-mile beat to windward through a snowstorm. A year later some boats encountered a waterspout that one astonished sailor described as looking "like a gigantic vacuum cleaner coming down to suck away all the tiny boats littering the water." And in 2006 a gale on the first night sank a 40-year-old wooden boat, brought about several dismastings, and caused enough other grief for a sizable 12 percent of the 78-boat fleet to withdraw. Injuries were numerous. "I was steering the boat when it launched off a huge wave," reported one casualty. "The boat became airborne. When it crashed back down I was catapulted onto the deck hardware." A police launch took him ashore with a fractured wrist, a broken hand, and a cracked sternum.

The second truth that Australians and other seafaring folk know about the sea and weather was voiced by the poet Byron: "Man marks the earth with ruin, his control stops with the shore." It is no coincidence that after the 1979 Fastnet Race storm (in which fifteen sailors died, 5 boats sank, and 25 boats were abandoned) the only person to quote that line publicly was Jim Hardy, an Aussie and Sydney–Hobart veteran. A great American sailor, Carleton Mitchell, once made the point differently when he quoted a Bahamian saying about the weather: "You eats what the cook serves."

On December 27, 1998, Bass Strait served up a phenomenal meal. Winds in the 70-knot range blasted into the teeth of a 4-knot contrary current to kick up a seaway of grim proportions and absolute confusion. Fortunately for the sailors and for us, the blow came in daylight. In the dark, nobody could have found a path around what someone called "the white-capped mountains," and without sunlight, the photographers could not have taken the remarkable photographs that illustrate this book. *Fatal Storm* confirms four lessons that I have painfully learned from bad weather. One is that the sound of a storm is usually more frightening than its appearance. Another is that while bad weather always threatens to come between people—"a great wind isolates one from one's own kind," wrote Joseph Conrad in *Typhoon*—well-led crews unite rather than fracture. A third conclusion is that blame-finding and finger-pointing are usually wrongheaded after storms; dirty weather needs no human cooperation to beat up crews. Finally, there is the look of a storm: in each hard chance there appears at least one moment of astonishing beauty. The photographers captured more than one of those moments.

When I asked Rob Mundle how he was affected by writing *Fatal Storm*, he replied, "The fact that I was an offshore sailor led me to really appreciate the depth of the trauma that these men and women faced. I shed tears as sailors related their horrendous stories, their fears, and their fight to survive. I think that, because I shared emotions with so many people, I came out the other side feeling as shell-shocked as they did.

"It certainly took me a long while to get my head back to normal, but at the time, all this fired my adrenaline and my determination to make sure some amazing stories were not lost. And the book certainly changed my attitudes for the better when it came to racing offshore. It's a big reminder: be prepared!"

I had experienced much the same thing eighteen years earlier when writing a book about the 1979 Fastnet Race storm, *Fastnet, Force 10.* I vividly remember the dawning awareness, as my fellow crewmembers and I reached shore, that our own experiences in the storm we had just sailed through comprised only a footnote to a large and tragic story. Just how tragic became clear as we surveyed a wharf crowded with solemn women and men staring mournfully out to the English Channel. The existential fear that began to sink in at that moment spread and deepened during my interviews with survivors and my long nights of writing. The acute sense of vulnerability invited new religious feelings and experiences that changed my life.

I meanwhile discovered, as Mundle later would, that the effort to make sense of the disaster was helping others. The skipper of a boat that had been rolled over in a storm off the New Jersey coast told me that he decided against abandoning ship because "I remembered what I'd read in that book about the Fastnet Race, and that was good enough for me." There is no question in my mind that these two books have been effective because their authors set out not to preach or point fingers, but rather to tell stories with as much detail as they could gather. We presented our accounts in all their variety and occasional confusion, and with the understanding that readers were capable of forgiving the inevitable human error and smart enough to draw their own conclusions about the many important questions that arose.

One of those questions concerns whether the start of the Sydney–Hobart should have been postponed. When the Cruising Yacht Club of Australia, the race's sponsor, said in its report (summarized in this book's Afterword) that "No one cause can be identified as being responsible" for the catastrophe, they were engaging in predictable bureaucratic mumbo jumbo. *Obviously* there was a cause: it was the catastrophic storm into which 115 yachts sailed. The issue that is begged is why the boats were there in the first place.

Mundle describes a cataract of contradictory prerace weather forecasts, the most pessimistic of which was true but, alas, not believed.

We now know, post-Hobart disaster, that any such intense disagreement among forecasters offers a sound rationale for postponing the start of an ocean race until everybody is on the same page. But in 1998 there was little precedent for such a thing. Of the approximately 150 starts in the combined histories of the world's "big four" long-distance races (Sydney–Hobart, Fastnet, the Los Angeles–Hawaii Transpac, and Newport–Bermuda), to my knowledge only two starts have been postponed. Both were for the Bermuda Race, whose organizers, not coincidentally, are both unusually obsessed with safety and unusually authoritative, if not authoritarian, in race management. They believe it is *their* race, not the sailors'.

The usual guiding principle in ocean racing has been that the ultimate decision to race lies with the crews themselves. While some races have established and enforced a high standard for qualifying to participate, others appear to have been guided by faith in this principle and belief that a record of regular bad weather, as in the Sydney–Hobart, would separate the sheep from the goats by discouraging weak boats and inexperienced crews from entering. That does not always happen. Mundle takes pains to show how deeply people of all abilities care about sailing in the Sydney–Hobart. The only one of the big four races run every year, it is a day-after-Christmas Boxing Day ritual for hundreds of sailors. Participants relish the gathering of old friends of ages ranging from teens to eighties, the morning prerace beer at a waterfront bar, the fancy lunch, the start with all boats at the same gun, the crowds of spectators, the television coverage. All that and more show us something about Australians' love of tradition, just as Super Bowl rituals say something about Americans'.

Much in this book suggests that this challenging, much-loved race was regarded with a "business as usual" attitude. Just five years earlier, after only 38 of the 104 starters finished a brutal Hobart, the official post-race inquiry recommended that onboard safety equipment be improved and that the sailors practice using it. Yet those good recommendations were not backed up by consistently enforced rules. As *Fatal Storm* makes clear, old or recently rebuilt boats that had sailed many races were allowed to enter, evidently without careful inspection, only to be beaten up, torn apart, and sunk. And sailors who had made the trip countless times were flattened by seasickness, surprised by faulty safety gear, or confused by emergency routines.

Any or all of those problems could occur in any big blow. Reports from such nonrace calamities as the Queen's Birthday Storm north of New Zealand in 1994 taught many lessons, but the events that attract the most attention and stimulate the most changes are the big ocean races. The unexpectedly violent storm that swept through the 303 boats in the 1979 Fastnet Race brought more information about the behavior of boats and sailors in extreme weather, and more improvements in boats, equipment, techniques, and attitudes about seamanship, than any event in the entire history of pleasure sailing. New regulations were written, a definition of unstable boats was drawn up, new safety equipment was developed, and training programs were created as safety-at-sea seminars. Sometimes these new policies and rules were effective—safety seminars have become extremely popular in the United States—and sometimes they took awhile to catch hold—until another crisis got everybody's attention.

That crisis was the 1998 Sydney–Hobart. Well before the coroner of New South Wales issued the report of the official government inquest two years later, a rigid regulatory regime was put into place throughout international sailing. (The coroner's instructive report may be found with related materials at www.ussailing.org/safety/studies/1998_sydney_hobart.htm.)

Of course, regulations cannot solve every problem. Alongside sound equipment and thorough crew training there must be the honest caution, even fearfulness, that lies at the heart of the word "forehandedness." In this area, one of the most instructive anecdotes I know concerns Sir Edmund Hillary, the New Zealand mountaineer who was one of the first climbers to summit Mt. Everest. In his autobiography he describes a period of deep discouragement during a slog to the South Pole. Lying in his sleeping bag one night, kept awake by his faltering confidence, he took a personal inventory of his aptitudes and came up with this: "Slightly crazy, frequently terrified, and not a bad navigator—and that about summed it up."

Reassured of his fundamental competence and his instinctive caution, Hillary slept like a baby. He had succeeded in making healthy fear into his dear companion, and in treating his adventures as anything but business as usual.

NEW YORK
JANUARY 1, 2007

John Rousmaniere sailed in the 1979 Fastnet Race, in which fifteen sailors were lost, and wrote the definitive book about it, Fastnet, Force 10. *His other books include* After the Storm: True Stories of Disaster and Recovery at Sea; A Berth to Bermuda: 100 Years of the World's Classic Ocean Race; *and* The Annapolis Book of Seamanship, *the textbook for many American sailing schools. He edited a book about lessons learned from the Fastnet storm,* Desirable and Undesirable Characteristics of Offshore Yachts. *He has sailed more than 35,000 miles.*

Part One

One
Are You Doing the Hobart This Year?

Christmas 1998 was fast approaching, and the long talons of an icy winter were creeping across the northern United States. While families were busy preparing for the festive season, John Campbell's mind was on the warmth he would soon be experiencing almost half a world away. It was going to be tough not spending Christmas with his loved ones; fortunately, they all understood why he wouldn't be home.

Campbell was due to fly out of Seattle, Washington, on December 23 on a frog-leap trip to Vancouver, Honolulu, then Sydney. The day he would lose crossing the international dateline meant he would arrive in Sydney soon after sunrise on Christmas Day. That didn't matter. December 26 was far more important.

He couldn't take much gear with him; there would be no room for excess baggage aboard the yacht he'd be joining. He knew, though, that he must take his seaboots. Bulky though they were, the boots were essential for keeping warm should cold conditions prevail off the coast of Tasmania. His thoughts turned to the old yellow boots he had worn on the odd occasion sailing Puget Sound. They were too tight. Over the years Campbell had learned that one of the many safety factors you apply to your personal equipment for ocean racing is oversize seaboots, which are relatively easy to remove if you fall overboard. If they are too tight and can't be taken off, you might as well be treading water with a brick on each foot. New boots were indispensable for this adventure, and Campbell's first priority for his dwindling time at home was to get to the marine store in downtown Seattle and buy them. He did just that. He bought size 12s—one-and-a-half sizes larger than he would normally wear.

At only thirty-two years of age, John Campbell had tried but failed to complete the Sydney-to-Hobart yacht race on two previous occasions. On the way to the airport, John and his father mused that the third time would be the charm. John had been assured by his Melbourne-based sailing friend, Peter Meikle, that the yacht in which they would be racing, the 42-foot sloop *Kingurra*, was one of the more robust of the 115 entrants. *Kingurra*'s owner, Peter Joubert, was the boat's designer, and the yacht's long racing record included no fewer than fourteen Hobarts.

With nearly twenty hours of travel behind him, Campbell exited Sydney's international air terminal bleary-eyed and jet-lagged. The sky was clear, the new day already warm. As he traveled to the Cruising Yacht Club of Australia on the eastern outskirts of the city's business district, he was reminded that Christmas is a very different beast in the Southern Hemisphere. The 28 degrees Celsius (82°F) day didn't jibe with the artificial snow and winter Christmas scenes painted on shop windows. There was one familiar thing, though: effervescent children clutching new toys.

The docks at the Cruising Yacht Club (CYC) were among the busiest places in Sydney at that early hour on Christmas Day. The atmosphere was carnivalesque. Race yachts flying colorful battle flags bobbed at the docks like impatient thoroughbred horses tethered to a rail. Crewmembers from out of town, who were berthing aboard, were shuttling to and from the clubhouse showers. Breakfast was serving on the wooden deck extending over the harbor—a hearty feed of bacon and eggs for most. Many were hoping it would soak up the liquid excesses of the Christmas Eve celebrations at the club.

John Campbell felt at home as he made his way along the narrow timber dock to *Kingurra*'s berth. He was warmly welcomed: old as well as new friends appreciated his effort in joining the crew for the big race. As he stepped aboard he quickly realized what Meikle had meant; *Kingurra* should get them to Hobart, all right. Campbell took his bag below, and the dark wood interior, just like the exterior, said "solid." This was a sea boat. He noted the sturdy bunks, the sensibly sized navigation area, and the compact overall layout. There was always something within arm's length to hang onto in rough weather. Even the toilet—the "head," in nautical terms—was as comfortable as it was well designed.

Seventy-four-year-old Melburnian Peter Joubert was taking part in his twenty-seventh Sydney to Hobart. Around midmorning he and his crew guided *Kingurra* away from the dock and headed for a secluded bay on the harbor. Once the yacht was anchored, Joubert disappeared below to the galley and began preparing the massive roast meal he had been planning the previous two days. While the crew relaxed on deck and absorbed the peaceful surroundings—a tree-lined bay dotted with impressive terra-cotta-roofed homes—they talked about the great race that would commence in just over twenty-four hours. The forecast suggested it would be a bit rough the first night out, but that was nothing unusual.

Wonderful aromas wafted from the galley, reassuring the regular crewmembers that this would once again be a memorable Christmas feast. John Campbell knew it would be a heck of a lot better than airline food.

A few miles from where the *Kingurra* crew was anticipating a Christmas repast and praising their chef, another Hobart race crew was enjoying a similar day afloat. Bruce Guy's *Business Post Naiad*, a fourteen-year-old Farr 40-footer from Port Dalrymple Yacht Club in northern Tasmania, was one of many yachts at anchor in busy Quarantine Bay, just inside North Head at the entrance to Sydney Harbour. The yacht had arrived a few days earlier, and Guy had been joined by regular crewmembers Rob Matthews, Phil Skeggs, Peter Keats, and Jim Rogers. Greg Sherriff hooked up with them for the passage across Bass Strait and up to Sydney, where Greg's brother Matt would replace him for the race.

"We had a southerly buster on the way up. It was a great ride," said Matthews. "We hit 20 knots a couple of times. At one stage we were going so fast that Bruce, who was up forward in the toilet, was hit by a fountain of water forced up through the vanity basin. For a second he couldn't work out where it was coming from."

It was the first trip to Sydney for thirty-four-year-old Phil Skeggs, an athletic former footballer working as a locksmith in Launceston. He and his wife, Stephanie, were back-fence neighbors of Bruce and Ros Guy. The Skeggs had been married fourteen years and had two children—Joshua, aged six, and nine-year-old Kirsty. Skeggs had been sailing only five years, but his physical prowess made him a valuable member of the experienced *Business Post Naiad* crew. The Launceston media was abuzz with the news that one of their own had entered the Sydney to Hobart. The stories were accompanied by photographs showing the crew on deck and Bruce and Ros Guy at home in front of a Christmas tree, preparing for the adventure.

"Phil was ecstatic about being in such a big city," said Matthews. "He had an absolutely fabulous few days. He went around taking 'happy snaps,' as he called them, of the Harbour Bridge, the ferries and Darling Harbour. We plunked him on the train and let him go off by himself sightseeing for the day. He loved it."

Christmas Day was a chance for family reunions for some of the Tasmanians. Bruce Guy had Ros, their children, and their nephew aboard. Crewmember Peter Keats, whose children Karen and David were living in Sydney, grabbed the opportunity to treat them to something special.

"It was a great day," said Keats. "Lots of laughing. Everyone really enjoyed it. We all jumped in the water and swam around. It was beautiful and warm—a bit different to home. We even gave the bottom of the boat one last scrub. Then someone jokingly suggested there might be sharks around—so that was it. Everyone got out of the water. It was time for lunch and a couple of quiet drinks."

That evening, with *Business Post Naiad* tucked safely away back at the CYC dock, the crew headed for the crowded outdoor bar to relax over a few beers. The mood was buoyant yet anticipatory, and almost inevitably, the conversation turned to the weather forecast.

"Go easy on the Christmas dinner if you don't like sailing to windward." That was the early advice from leading yachting meteorologist Roger "Clouds" Badham in the *Australian* on December 17, 1998. "It all depends on a low that looks like forming off the New South Wales south coast late next week." Badham was basing his predictions on the most recent American model—a long-range weather forecast developed from a computer analysis of existing world weather patterns. "Any forecast outside six days for these things can only be described as 'fuzzy' at best," Badham said. "There have been intense and sometimes cyclonic [hurricane-strength] lows active in the Tasman Sea over the past six weeks."

It was mid-November 1998 when prominent Australian sailor David Witt went to Rarotonga, the capital of the Cook Islands and Witt's newly adopted home. He had an agreement to train young local sailors, in return for which he would represent the Pacific island nation in the Sydney Olympics. He also had a sponsor for the entry of a maxi yacht in the Sydney to Hobart, and he wanted the yacht to represent the Cooks. Witt and his Olympic crewman, Rod Howell, headed to the home of "Papa Tom"—the man who had opened their door to Olympic competition. His real name is Sir Thomas Davis, and he had been the nation's prime minister from 1978 to 1987. He claims he still does not know why the Queen knighted him.

Papa Tom, a big, powerful, gray-haired man, is, to say the least, a colorful character. He has two passions: sailing and riding his Harley Davidson motorcycle. Everyone knows him and everyone waves each time he blasts down the dusty roads. When not riding his Harley he drives an old Jaguar, the only one on the island. His home is at the edge of the foothills on what the locals call "the back of the island." Built chalet-style with a high-pitched roof, it occupies a large, lush green lawn dotted with tall, coconut-heavy palms. The interior of the home is spacious and open, and surrounding it is a wide verandah, features that maximize ventilation while minimizing heat.

On the day of their visit, Witt and Howell were warmly welcomed by Papa Tom onto the verandah. The trio settled into comfortable chairs, and within seconds the loquacious Witt was divulging his plan. Papa Tom liked the idea.

Witt then took it to the next stage, recalls Papa Tom.

"He said, 'If this plan succeeds, will you sail with us?' I was stunned. I said, 'Hey, I'm eighty-one years old. I'd only get in the way. I can't pull any ropes.' But inside me the sailor said, 'Do it.' If you have the ocean and sailing in your blood, you can't refuse an invitation to sail in a great race like the Sydney to Hobart—even if you are eighty-one. For me it was a dream come true."

Papa Tom was educated in New Zealand and Australia. In the winter of 1952 he sailed a small yacht with his wife, two children, and two crew across the Pacific from New Zealand to South America, en route to Boston where he was to become a lecturer and researcher at Harvard.

"That was a horrendous trip. It was in a 44-foot ketch and we were sailing in midwinter—the first small yacht ever to sail west to east in the roaring forties at that time of year. It was a 7,000-mile voyage and we had fourteen days of hell."

He spent twenty years in America, becoming a civilian researcher for the military, closely aligned with the American space program. He pioneered much of the research into life-support systems for America's first astronauts.

"In the early 1970s I was asked by the chiefs of the Cook Islands to come back home and straighten up the place, because they were in all sorts of trouble. They had enormous social and economic problems, and I decided that I definitely had to do something about it. I went on to become prime minister.

"I say with pride that I took the country from near the bottom of the economic barrel among the independent states of the Pacific to the very top. Then the chiefs decided they could do it all themselves—so I went out. Now they've gone all the way back to where they started. That's life."

Papa Tom built two large Polynesian sailing canoes between 1992 and 1995 and sailed them extensively around the Pacific. The voyages were designed to prove his theories on the migratory and trading routes taken by his ancestors centuries before.

On December 18, 1998, Papa Tom flew into Sydney and began preparing for his newest adventure—the Sydney-to-Hobart race.

After representing Great Britain in the Star class two-man keelboat in the 1996 Olympics in Atlanta, Glyn Charles and crewman Mark Covell turned their attention to Sydney and the 2000 Olympic Games. They were proud of their eleventh place on the Olympic course off Savannah, a historic and beautiful city on Georgia's Atlantic coast. They had taken third and fourth places in two of the heats against some of the very best sailors in the world, and were encouraged to mount a strong campaign for the year 2000.

Charles was an accomplished yachting coach who dreamed of one day winning an Olympic medal, and his life was going exactly the way he wanted. He was one of the fortunate few able to carve out a career in the sport he enjoyed so much. He was born in landlocked Winchester in 1965, and it was on Chichester Harbour, southwest of London, that he learned to sail. His racing prowess emerged in the Royal Yachting Association's Youth Squad. Charles was considered a late starter in the world of competitive sailing, having adopted the sport at the advanced age of thirteen.

Although ranked nationally in the top three, his desire to be selected for the British team in the World Youth Championship was at first frustrated by other talented sailors. Undeterred, Charles pushed himself even harder, and eventually won a national championship in one of the world's most competitive Olympic classes: the 14-foot singlehanded Laser dinghy. It was his first major step up the international sailing ladder.

The Olympic Games were his target, but in 1988 and 1992 his efforts to represent Britain in the three-man Soling keelboat class were foiled by his arch rival Lawrie Smith. In 1996, Charles finally beat Smith for the Olympic Star class berth.

His ability to win in a wide range of boats—from dinghies to dayboats and ocean racers—brought Charles to the attention of yacht owners. His was a talent they craved. But Charles wasn't into sailing just any old boat, and he raced according to a time-honored adage: finishing second in a yacht race was like finishing second in boxing. "It's no use sailing some crummy old shitter," he explained to British journalist Bob Fisher in 1998. "That gets nobody anywhere." He wanted to race boats with some potential.

Olympic class sailing and offshore racing yachts soon became the mainstay of his life. He sailed for Britain four times in the Admiral's Cup, the unofficial ocean racing team championship. In 1997, however, he would change camps and race for Australia.

Steve Kulmar, skipper of an Australian Admiral's Cup team yacht, the Mumm 36 *Sea*, and a finisher of sixteen Sydney to Hobarts and five Fastnet Races (across the Irish Sea), got to know Charles through prominent Sydney sailmaker and yachtsman Grant Simmer.

"I knew that the Australian team would need local knowledge for the waters of the Solent and off the coast of England," said Kulmar. "The perfect solution would have been to carry both a local navigator and a local tactician, but the weight of two extra people would have dulled our performance. So we looked for somebody who could navigate and also had strong local knowledge and great tactical skills.

"Grant mentioned Glyn Charles and gave me his number. I called him. It was about two months before the 1997 Admiral's Cup series. After a bit of to-ing and fro-ing, he decided he would join us. He was an absolutely terrific person to have on the boat in that he worried all the time about making it go fast. He was always putting his heart and soul into it. We had a terrific series. Glyn was a very energetic guy on the yacht but laid-back in an almost Australian sort of way on shore."

Glyn Charles's partner, Annie Goodman, was equally passionate about sailing. The comfortable cottage they shared in Bosham, on the shores of Chichester Harbour, reflected a lifestyle closely attuned to the sea. It was a perfect base for both, central to much of England's sailing activity.

Checking his e-mails one day, Charles found one from Steve Kulmar. Kulmar had committed to sailing on *Sword of Orion* in the 1998 Sydney to Hobart, and during some lead-up races it had become clear the crew needed more depth—someone who could comfortably slip into the role of tactician or supervisor.

"Ironically, I was talking to Grant Simmer again and he said Glyn was planning to come to Sydney to coach the British Olympic Soling contender, Andy Beadsworth, in preparation for the world championship," Kulmar recollects. "So I e-mailed Glyn immediately and asked 'Are you interested in doing the Hobart?' He said he'd have a think about it. Information went backwards and forwards, and in the end he said, 'OK, subject to final discussions in Sydney.'"

Charles met with Kulmar and *Sword of Orion*'s owner Rob Kothe at the CYC the morning he arrived from London: December 10. They talked at length and outlined their plans for the race. About two days later Charles agreed to race—but only in the Hobart, because he had coaching commitments from December 11 to 22.

Glyn Charles already had four Fastnet Races to his credit. He had now committed to his first Hobart.

Well-known sailing figure John "Steamer" Stanley had done it all. Fifty-one years old, he had been a champion in the famous 16- and 18-foot skiffs that race on Sydney Harbour. His keelboat experiences included Admiral's Cup racing in England, sixteen Sydney to Hobarts, and the oldest trophy in the history of sport, the America's Cup. He had also had the pleasure of indulging a sailor's dream: a cruise around the planet on a small yacht.

Steamer was a remarkable battler both on and off the water. There was a touch of irony in his nickname, which came from the legendary "Stanley Steamer" steam engine, a machine known for its strength and reliability. He was born with two dislocated hips, and for much of his life he hobbled. His condition improved greatly after a dual hip replacement, but still he moved with a noticeable limp. More recently, his left kidney had been removed after a cancerous tumor was found, and then a malignant melanoma was taken from his arm. That would have been enough to slow most people, but just when things seemed to be taking a turn for the better—only months before the 1998 Hobart race, in fact—asbestosis was found on one of Steamer's lungs—a direct result of his years working as a builder. "All I can say is that life can only get better," he commented after learning of his latest medical ailment.

His plan was to do another Hobart race, once again aboard the classic 55-foot cutter *Winston Churchill*, a yacht built in Hobart in 1942 by the legendary Percy Coverdale. It took its name from the great man himself, but only after Coverdale wrote to Churchill and received his written permission. After servicing Tasmanian lighthouses during World War II, the yacht contested the inaugural Sydney to Hobart.

In 1959 a Bass Strait storm almost claimed *Winston Churchill*. As the yacht crashed off a large wave, the mast jumped from its step and speared through the bottom of the hull. Owner Arthur Warner, a Victorian Government minister, saved the vessel by wrapping sails around the damaged hull and beaching it at the aptly named Wreck Beach, near Wonthaggi.

Steamer was an authority on sailing in Australia, and the vintage *Winston Churchill* held a special place in the history he loved to recount. That tie was strengthened when he worked on its restoration for six months in Sydney after it was purchased by Richard Winning in 1997. It took a labor of love to return the traditionally planked wooden hull to pristine condition, the huon pine planks stripped bare, then repainted, and the heavy wooden mast replaced by a considerably lighter and slightly taller aluminum section. When *Winston Churchill* was relaunched she was nothing short of a magnificent tribute to yachting and yacht builders of a bygone era.

Steamer saw *Winston Churchill* as "a real boat, a classic yacht; a yacht designed to go across the ocean." It was the style of yacht he enjoyed: "Ocean racing as such is something I'm not really interested in these days. I'm not into sitting on the rail anymore—those days are long gone. I like to enjoy my sailing with a bunch of mates."

Richard Winning decided to enter his gleaming, meticulously restored yacht in the 1997 Sydney to Hobart for the thrill of it. "We look at it as a bit of recreation," he told the *Business Review Weekly*. He added that *Winston Churchill* "will be here long after we have all gone." John "Steamer" Stanley was at the head of the queue for a crew position. Winning didn't hesitate; after all, Steamer was a racing yachtsman, a seaman, and a boatbuilding craftsman.

They were justifiably proud of their result in 1997, given that they raced with only one large headsail that had to be rolled up like a blind when the wind piled on. *Winston Churchill* was the seventy-ninth finisher in a fleet of 110, including numerous arch rivals of similar vintage. *Winston Churchill*'s capabilities had been greatly enhanced with new sails for the 1998 race. When Winning confirmed right on the knock of closing date for entries that he did want to compete, Steamer gathered the crew together.

"I entered again just for the fun of doing it," Winning said. "We planned to do it every year until we got too old." Steamer assembled a group of sailors with considerable offshore experience. The crew included Jim Lawler and Bruce Gould, plus an enthusiastic nineteen-year-old, Michael "Beaver" Rynan, who worked weekends as a tender driver delivering crews to the yachts moored off Sydney's Middle Harbour Yacht Club. Racing to Hobart aboard *Winston Churchill* with the likes of John Stanley was, he told friends, "the chance of a lifetime."

Once more the grand old yacht was painstakingly prepared, and by Christmas Eve all that remained was to provision the galley. Winning and Steamer met at the marina in the northside suburb of Woolwich, borrowed a small motor launch, and headed for the waterfront supermarket at nearby Birkenhead Point. They loaded shopping cart after shopping cart with provisions for the nine-man crew. As the little launch chugged back across the bay with its cargo, the two men chatted idly about the race and their plans for Christmas Day. Both intended to spend it with family and friends. Winning said he would go to the yacht late in the afternoon and touch up a couple of spots of varnish; he wanted the boat positively glistening for the start.

More than twenty plastic bags filled with food and the essential utensils for cooking were stowed in *Winston Churchill*'s galley. This done, Winning and Steamer motored the grand old lady gently across to the CYC's marina, attracting considerable attention on the way. This was, after all, the famous *Winston Churchill*, replete with gleaming cream topsides, wood made bright with many liberal coats of varnish, and a trim and tidy rig.

Docking completed, Winning and Steamer headed for the bar on the club's lower deck. It was packed with families, friends, and excited sailors. Many wore caps indicating that they'd raced overseas, done the Hobart before, or simply that their yacht had a major sponsor; faded red Mount Gay Rum caps were among the real collector's items. Present also were a large group of "punters" who had come to ogle, and several young ladies—"racer chasers"—who were keen to meet the competitors.

Winning and Steamer met up with sailing rival Don Mickleborough and some of his crew and enjoyed a few beers and plenty of laughs. Later, the pair headed for Winning's Vaucluse home, where they would enjoy a Christmas Eve dinner with his wife, Stephanie, and the children.

After dinner, Steamer headed back to the yacht to sleep. He would take a cab home the next morning, then go on for Christmas Day drinks at Richard "Sightie" Hammond's home with Mickleborough and other competitors, followed by a Christmas lunch with his mother, Eve, and "all the mob."

Julie Hodder had wanted an ocean racing yacht while her husband, Garry, wanted a Porsche. The end result was that Julie was about to set sail in the fifty-fourth Sydney to Hobart as one of three owners of the 50-foot *Foxtel-Titan Ford*. Her husband was still driving a family sedan.

"He tolerates the yacht," remarked the forty-five-year-old. "I think he likes keeping me happy. When we discussed our options—the yacht or the Porsche—we figured there's not a lot you can do with the car. Mind you, he's now starting to wonder about the yacht. The first ocean race he did with us was the Brisbane to Gladstone race not long after we bought the yacht. We almost sank. Then the yacht was just about wrecked when it hit a reef in the Whitsunday Islands."

The couple had returned to Australia a few years earlier after a successful business foray in Hong Kong and had bought a comfortable home with alluring waterviews in Clontarf, in Sydney's north side. It wasn't long before Julie was back among the familiar faces at the local Middle Harbour Yacht Club, eager to get into sailing once again.

She came from a sailing family, and one of her prized possessions was a fading black-and-white photograph of herself with her father sailing across the English Channel when she was just six months old. Soon after that photo was taken, the family moved to Australia and established a home near the shores of Lake Macquarie, north of Sydney. Few women were actively involved in offshore racing when Julie began. She soon outgrew the sailing dinghy scene on Lake Macquarie and leaped at the chance to join the crew of a small Junior Offshore Group racer.

Years later, Julie Hodder returned to sailing in England in grand style—as the only female among a crew of twenty-nine aboard the maxi yacht *Condor* for the Fastnet Race. That was 1981—two years after the disastrous 1979 event in which an Irish Sea gale took the lives of fifteen sailors.

"It was a wonderful life aboard the maxi for two great years. I really loved it. Mind you, cooking for twenty-eight guys when we were racing was quite a challenge. I enjoyed the long delivery trips more than the racing. Two months at sea is an ideal thing. You get into your own regime . . . great camaraderie; no traffic jams; no hassled people; no news." The long trips also allowed Julie to expand and consolidate her navigational skills. She envisioned one day being the navigator on an oceangoing yacht, and dreamed of owning an offshore racer.

Back in Australia, Julie served her apprenticeship as an understudy navigator and general crewmember aboard *Diamond Cutter*, one of the more competitive yachts out of Middle Harbour Yacht Club. She was rewarded with wins in the club's offshore championship and a Brisbane to Gladstone race.

"Navigating was certainly the way to go for me," said Julie. "I love ocean racing, but I hate sitting on deck and getting wet. I like doing anything on the yacht where I can actually move. Even the cooking appeals. You don't need big, strong muscles to navigate, and there are two other pluses for me: I don't get seasick and I love dabbling with computers and electronics. So navigating's my ideal job."

Almost inevitably, the Sydney to Hobart entered her offshore sailing agenda, and by 1998 she had participated no fewer than five times.

After returning from Hong Kong, Julie sailed on a number of yachts, mainly in distance events. She also participated along with hundreds of other sailors in the summer midweek twilight "beer can" races. It was during these Wednesday night races that she and former world 18-foot skiff champion Peter Sorensen began discussing the possibility of buying an offshore race yacht.

"I always wanted a boat, but I could never figure out why people would want to own one by themselves. It's better to share the costs and the fun. Pete and I always got along well. I liked the way he ran a boat, the way he used it all the time: Wednesdays, Thursdays, and weekends, Pete was always out there. I thought a 40-footer might be something we could handle physically and financially. Then I realized he was thinking more along the lines of a 50- or 60-footer. That became a little easier to accept when he brought Stan Zemanek into the equation."

Zemanek, Australia's most successful nighttime talk radio host, had known Sorensen since they raced skiffs on Sydney Harbour decades earlier. With the syndicate formed, Hodder, Sorensen, and Zemanek purchased the 50-footer *Morning Mist III* from Melbourne in 1998. Their desire was straightforward: race hard and have a good time. Their initial target was the exclusive, invitation-only Big Boat Series at Hayman Island in Queensland's Whitsunday region in August. *Morning Mist III* collected first prize in her division. The trio had a winner.

They were hoping their good fortune would continue the following week at Hamilton Island Race Week, but just eight miles out of Hayman their luck ran out. *Morning Mist III* plowed into a reef while traveling at a speed of 8 knots. The structural damage to the hull and keel was so extensive that the insurers almost declared a total loss. Chastened but by no means defeated, Hodder, Sorensen, and Zemanek trucked the yacht back to Sydney for major surgery and turned their attention to the Hobart race.

"The damage was massive," said Julie. "The hull had to be stripped of everything, then turned upside down in a shed at McConaghy's boatyard. Almost the entire bottom had to be cut out and rebuilt."

The work took longer than anticipated. Plans to test *Morning Mist III*—now named *Foxtel-Titan Ford*—in feeder races in late December evaporated. The keel was bolted back on and the yacht relaunched only days before the start.

The Hobart race would be its first sea trial.

In August 1979 Paul "Tanzi" Lea was one of many people hailed as a hero in Britain. For three days he piloted a Royal Navy Sea King helicopter through a vicious storm over the Irish Sea, searching for disabled and sinking yachts and plucking survivors from the decimated fleet in the Fastnet Race. Fifteen competitors died that year, along with two sailors who were accompanying the fleet on a nonrace yacht.

"I was actually on leave . . . summer leave because it was August. I was sitting at home in the garden talking to some friends when the phone call came. They said, 'Look, there's a problem with the Fastnet Race. Can you come on out and help?' Off I went, and I think we were about the third Sea King to launch out of the air station at Culdrose."

The rescue effort was a distressing yet poignant climax to an impressive career, which had begun at the age of seventeen. Lea had joined the Royal Navy in 1964 despite harboring a desire to head for the skies rather than the sea. Eight years later his dream was realized when he was assigned to train with a Sea King squadron. In 1981 he moved to Australia with his wife, Gill, and their two young children, Daniel and Joanne.

"I came on an exchange posting for just over two years," he said. "It was an opportunity we really looked forward to. I did ten months on the Sea Kings and then fifteen months as an instructor with 723 Squadron. It was a very enjoyable period in our lives, so much so that when we went back to the U.K. the lifestyle I'd experienced in Australia began to nag at me. In the end it got to me so much that I had no alternative but to sit down with my wife and children and talk about living in Australia."

Lea reestablished contact with the Royal Australian Navy and, after two years of negotiation, was offered a permanent job with the primarily land-based Sea King squadron at HMAS *Albatross* at Nowra, south of Sydney. He went on to become the chief pilot and commanding officer.

In mid-1990, when they arrived in Australia, Lea and his wife were feeling confident about their new life. The children weren't so sure.

"After a few months, however, my eldest son, Daniel, said, 'Dad, I want to stay here now.' Australia was home."

Just three years after arriving in Australia, Lea was called on to act as a guardian over the Sydney-Hobart fleet in the punishing 1993 event. Having enjoyed considerable dinghy sailing over the years, Lea found that the Sydney to Hobart rekindled his interest, and he began to follow the race each year. For the Christmas 1998 holidays Lea was on leave, not standby, from HMAS *Albatross*.

"I remember hearing that the yachts might meet a bit of dodgy weather, but I thought, oh, we're covered, even though we only get twelve hours' notice in an emergency. Sunday [December 27] was a normal day for me. I went kayaking on the local river in the morning, as I often do. In the afternoon it was the usual gardening . . . that sort of stuff. At around seven o'clock the phone rang. The message was simply 'come on in.' Luckily, I hadn't had a drink . . . so I was at the base by 7:30 P.M."

Lieutenant Commander Tanzi Lea was again on his way to becoming a hero.

Rob Kothe was a relative newcomer to the Grand Prix level of ocean racing, but that didn't stop him from wanting to be a winner.

"I was always interested in sailing, so much so that in the fifties and sixties I was one of the young kids who listened to everything on the radio that had anything to do with sailing. I always listened to the call of the America's Cup on radio. You've got to be nutty to do that. The problem was that I lived out in the bush, on the other side of the Great Dividing Range, at Tumbarumba, down toward Canberra. I couldn't go sailing in the seventies, so I was a sail plane competitor—a glider pilot. When I came to Sydney I realized that sail planing was out and sailing was in."

Kothe would later discover, as he increased his profile at the CYC, that he and fellow member George Snow, the owner of the maxi yacht *Brindabella*, used to share the same airspace gliding over the Brindabella Ranges near Canberra.

After a year away, Steve Kulmar had decided it was time to return to offshore racing.

"I needed a year away from the sport after sailing in the Admiral's Cup in England in 1997," Kulmar said. "I'd sailed boats every year of my life since I was eight. There had been little else in just about all of my social life and available time. I needed a break. I told a friend, Ron Jacobs, I was thinking about doing some casual sailing again. He encouraged me to meet with himself and Rob Kothe at the Oaks Hotel at Neutral Bay in late September. I found Kothe to be a nice enough bloke and as keen as mustard. I thought, 'Well, I'll do a couple of races with them and see.'

"I made it clear that I wasn't available all the time because I didn't want to get caught up in the full-on racing scene and immediately find myself back where I was a year earlier. If we thought we all liked each other, well, then I'd commit to a Hobart. It was a pretty casual arrangement." Kothe, Kulmar, and the *Sword of Orion* crew did strike a chord, and Kulmar committed to do the Hobart as a principal helmsman.

Kulmar and his wife, Libby, had been childhood friends in the Sydney waterfront suburb of Hunters Hill. Both sailed out of the local sailing club. Friendship blossomed into romance, and they married in 1983—but not before Steve sailed in the Admiral's Cup that year. Libby knew she was marrying a man and his sport.

"I never had any qualms about Steve going ocean racing," she said. "Never. Not even in 1984 when I was pregnant with Pip and it was a rough race did I worry. I'd lie in bed at night, listen to the storm outside, and say, 'Yeah, it's windy,' but that was it. [Steve was aboard the eventual race winner, *Indian Pacific*, that year.] I didn't even worry about the 1998 race when we heard what it was going to be like."

It was the Kulmar family's turn to host Christmas lunch at their modern, flat-roofed home overlooking Manly and the waters of northern Sydney Harbour. The huge ceiling-to-floor windows afforded spectacular views, and large doors admitted summer sea breezes to keep the occupants cool. A large swimming pool, aside from providing instant relief from the summer heat, was also a great benefit to daughters Pip, thirteen, and Madeline, ten, who were competitive swimmers.

"We had thirty-three people for lunch—family, friends, and some sailors," recalls Libby. "It was glorious. The kids were in the pool all day having a great time. Everyone was talking about the race. They were keen to follow it, especially with Steve racing again."

Mindful that he probably wouldn't get much sleep in the ensuing days, Steve Kulmar slipped quietly away from the Christmas celebrations around midafternoon and went to bed. When he returned to the party after his "power nap," there were few guests remaining. The day wound down in a relaxed and convivial fashion, and before long the entire Kulmar clan, including Libby's parents, who were staying over, turned in as well.

Just forty-eight hours later Steve Kulmar would be part of Australia's largest ever peacetime search and rescue operation.

Two
History of
the Great Race

Shortly after VJ Day—Victory in the Pacific Day for the Allies in 1945—a small group of offshore sailing enthusiasts held a dinner at Usher's Hotel in Sydney. About twelve months earlier they had formed the Cruising Yacht Club of New South Wales (later the Cruising Yacht Club of Australia). Before and during World War II, Usher's was one of the classiest hotels in bustling downtown Sydney. Successful businessmen relaxed there over a chilled ale at the end of a hectic day and ladies enjoyed being wined and dined in the plush dining room. The five-story, well-proportioned building was located on one of the city's busy thoroughfares, Castlereagh Street. Its robust design, with windows, doorways, and awnings heavily ornate against the dark brick building, was a typical example of colonial architecture.

One of the CYC's founders, Peter Luke, knew Captain John Illingworth, the Royal British Navy's Chief Engineer at its wartime Sydney Harbour base at Woolloomooloo, to be a preeminent ocean racing yachtsman. A prominent Sydney magazine had enthusiastically described Illingworth as "perhaps the greatest exponent of sailing and ocean racing yet to visit Australia," noting that the Englander had "greatly impressed Australian yachtsmen with knowledgeable lectures substantiated by victories in leading offshore and harbour events." Little wonder Luke invited Illingworth to be the dinner speaker.

In the early days of the CYC, members would hold what they described as "very informal and low-key" club meetings in the photographic studio owned by Peter Luke's father, Monty. It was next door to Usher's Hotel. When members gathered over dinner, it was usually at a small place near Wynyard, the midcity rail and bus terminus. "The name of the place was Sue's Café," Peter Luke recalled, "but the food they served was sufficiently bad for us to call it the Greasy Spoon."

That the dinner was to be at Usher's made it a very special occasion. Captain Illingworth captivated his small audience with vivid stories of offshore racing in England. Later, as they relaxed over port and fine cigars, Bert Walker, the club's first president, casually remarked to Illingworth, "Jack Earl and I are cruising down to Hobart after Christmas. Why don't you join us?" (Earl, who became a marine artist of international acclaim, was also the first Australian to cruise around the world.) Finding it a splendid idea, Illingworth accepted. Enthusiastic conversation followed until someone in the group ventured, "Let's make a race of it."

And so the great race was conceived.

Once the decision had been made, there was no slowing the momentum. The start date was set as December 26, Boxing Day, placing the race in the height of summer while allowing competitors and their families to enjoy Christmas Day at home.

The general public first learned of the event in a brief article in the October 1945 issue of *Australian Power Boat and Yachting Monthly Magazine*, in an addendum so small it could easily have gone unnoticed.

YACHT RACE TO TASMANIA; IT IS EXPECTED THAT AN OCEAN YACHT RACE MAY TAKE PLACE FROM SYDNEY TO HOBART PROBABLY STARTING ON DECEMBER 26, 1945. YACHTSMEN DESIROUS OF COMPETING SHOULD CONTACT VICE PRESIDENT MR. P. LUKE, 62 CASTLEREAGH STREET, SYDNEY, FOR INFORMATION. ENTRIES CLOSE DECEMBER 1, 1945.

The article itself announced the results of a race conducted by the "Cruising Yacht Club of NSW" over 17 nautical miles from Sydney Harbour to Palm Beach. The sturdy 35-foot cutter *Maharani* (later abbreviated to *Rani*), skippered by Captain J. Illingworth, was the winner.

The Notice of Race for the Sydney to Hobart soon appeared. It reminded competitors that the "setting of spinnakers is not permitted," in keeping with the cruising attitudes of those first entrants. The CYC devised a method of measuring and handicapping yachts and chose a starting line "from Flagstaff Point, off Quarantine Bay, 200 yards in length, with the starter's boat identified by a white CYC flag." The use of the white CYC flag remains a club tradition to this day. The line was actually just inside the entrance to Sydney Harbour to the north. In later years the race started on the south side, closer to the downtown area.

The Royal Yacht Club of Tasmania, in Hobart, agreed to manage the finish line and the Royal Australian Air Force agreed to schedule "flying exercises" for Catalina flying boats over the course so they could report the position of any yacht sighted.

Word of the race was greeted with great enthusiasm by the daily press. Weary after five years of war, the Australian public was eager for fresh excitement and adventure. This was it: a perfect panacea in the form of a daring 630–nautical mile voyage from New South Wales to Tasmania. Brave men, and at least one woman, would be fighting unpredictable and often tempestuous seas aboard small boats—for *fun*.

With the start date approaching, ten yachts registered to compete. At the last minute the Livingston brothers advised that their yacht, *Warrana*, was unable to leave Melbourne in time to reach Sydney for the race's start. In future races, however, the Livingstons would leave an indelible mark on the history of the classic. They raced their famous *Kurrewa* yachts with considerable success, and they also donated a magnificent perpetual trophy, the F. & J. Livingston Trophy, for the first yacht south of Tasman Island at the entrance to Tasmania's Storm Bay.

That first race provided avid Australian newspaper readers and radio listeners all the high drama and exhilaration they wanted. Front-page headlines reported a fast-approaching southerly gale bearing down on the fleet and the possibility that the storm had claimed *Rani*,

Captain Illingworth, and his crew. The Catalina flying boats could locate only the 56-footer *Winston Churchill* at the front of the fleet. There was no sign of *Rani*. The flight crew didn't realize that Captain Illingworth had pushed on into the storm while his rivals had slowed or even stopped. Lashing themselves to the mast, Illingworth and his crew pressed on and sailed out of the blue into Storm Bay, 44 miles from the finish. They reached Hobart unscathed and received a tumultuous welcome. *Rani* claimed both the line honors trophy and the prize for being first on handicap.

Jack Earl saw that first race this way:

"We had a wonderful sail down the coast until we got to Montagu Island, when a southerly buster hit us. Illingworth, we heard later, had reefed down and fore-reached *Rani* through it. He just refused to take any of the gear off her. His attitude was, 'We will only have to put it back on again.' We reefed down and nursed our ship along in a very conservative fashion, and hove-to through that gale. Some of the boats actually put into the south coast ports. The crews of *Saltair* and *Abermerle* are supposed to have spent time ashore shooting rabbits and going to the movies.

"Illingworth just kept plugging away. He was out of radio contact for quite a few days, and at one stage we all presumed he'd been lost. Well, of course, the rest is history. Illingworth won by a day. We were still mooching down the Tassie coast when we heard that he had suddenly popped up in Storm Bay. When we got right up into the Derwent, there was a tremendous northwesterly gale. It blew 74 knots and really knocked the fleet about. We had a triple reefed main, a jib, and a mizzen. But within a quarter mile of the line, the breeze suddenly dropped and the Derwent was as flat as a millpond. It wasn't worth putting all that gear back on again, so we just concentrated on getting across the finish. We came in third just behind *Winston Churchill*. We learned a few tricks from that first race, and when I went down the following year as mate in Bob Bull's *Christina*, we pulled out all stops and won."

Illingworth's remarkable effort in plowing through the worst of the gale and trouncing his opponents stimulated an enormous tide of public interest in the event. *Australian Power Boat and Yachting*

Monthly noted: "The hope that an ocean race would be held annually was expressed at a civic reception given by the Lord Mayor (Mr Soundy, MHA) at the Hobart Town Hall on January 8, 1946."

Responding to a speech by the Governor of Tasmania, Admiral Sir Hugh Binney, Captain Illingworth said he and his crew had been "deeply impressed by the welcome given us in Hobart, which was an ideal place at which to end an ocean race."

The race report continued: "The Cruising Yacht Club at Sydney and the Royal Yacht Club of Tasmania have launched the sport of ocean racing on a firm basis. A next step is for an Australian yacht to visit Great Britain and 'take the ashes away.' Every other branch of Australian sport has been represented in contests in Britain. The president of the CYC (Mr Walker), who sailed *Saltair*, said that nowhere else could yachtsmen have received a better welcome."

Walker was quoted as suggesting that the next race was likely to attract between thirty and forty boats. "At no far distant time Australia should challenge the U.S.A.," he said. "We have the men in Hobart now who can steer a boat as well as and better than Mr Vanderbilt [the famed America's Cup defender]."

The Sydney–Hobart was soon confirmed as an annual event, and it took only a few years for it to be acclaimed, along with the Fastnet Race out of England and America's Newport to Bermuda, as one of the world's three "majors" in offshore racing. All three events demanded the highest skill and endurance, regardless of the conditions.

In many respects the Sydney to Hobart is perhaps the greatest of them all. From the colorful start within the natural amphitheater that surrounds Sydney's magnificent harbor, to the finish at the waterfront dock area of the beautiful and historic city of Hobart, it is a race of guts, determination, majesty, and splendor.

The 630-mile course has four distinct and always challenging components. There is the unpredictable and often savage Tasman Sea off the New South Wales south coast; the notorious Bass Strait crossing between mainland Australia and the island state of Tasmania, where wild winds and shallow water can compress waves into massively powerful, foaming liquid mountains; the challenging stretch down the Tasmanian east coast and across the often appropriately named Storm Bay, where bitterly cold winds can sweep in from the Antarctic region, bringing a freezing winter chill even in summer; and finally there's the test presented by the last stretch, the 11 nautical miles up the Derwent River to the finish line. Anywhere on this course the whim of the wind gods can take a crew from calm to calamity in a flash—even on the river.

The Sydney to Hobart is an unpredictable race, at times serene, at others terrifying. A gentle spinnaker ride down the coast with the sun warming the crew's backs is like a sleigh ride across smooth new snow. The first light of the new day, where the darkest of nights gives way to dawn's palette of pastels, offers an experience few forget.

Roger Hickman, an experienced offshore racer and race veteran, sees the appeal of ocean racing in general, and the Hobart race in particular, this way: "Ocean racing takes place in the stadium of life. It's not as though you're inside some artificially heated and lit stadium. It's got all the features of 'why do people climb Mount Everest.' It's something you just have to do. There is this wonderful challenge to complete the race and be safe. Thrown in with this is the most romantic environment in the world. You get all the benefits of the wind, the sea, the sun, the moon, and the stars plus the spectacle of marine life. It's all rolled into something competitive. It's the absolute classic situation where man, or woman, is pitted against the elements.

"It is certainly an 'on-the-edge' sport like skydiving, motor racing, football, and so many others. You can't be under the illusion at any time that it is safe. Like any other 'on-the-edge' sport, ocean racing can be extremely dangerous. That's an aspect we all accept. Unbridled dangers have always been a vital part of life. Ocean racing delivers those dangers as well as moments of beauty that will be with you the rest of your life."

Although Nature makes the rules and decides the result, the competitors, the camaraderie, the teamwork, and the stamina ultimately make the race what it is. Some sailors, like Sydney's Richard "Sightie" Hammond, cannot get enough of the Sydney to Hobart. The 1998 race was his fortieth start, a record. For him and so many others, Christmas Day is more like Boxing Day Eve—the eve of the start of the Hobart. Hammond has a host of Hobart race stories, but the one he recalls with the most clarity is his first race in 1952. It was baptism by fire—or, more specifically, ice. Aboard the aging Tasman schooner *Wanderer* that year, he remembers that both the yacht and its owner, Eric Massey, were very old. "I went for the adventure. To race to Hobart was something just about every young sailor wanted to do. I was one of the lucky few to secure a ride."

Hammond thought his initiation was complete when a howling southerly buster with winds gusting up to 40 knots swept across the fleet off the New South Wales south coast. Massey deemed the conditions so bad at the height of the storm that he ordered the yacht to ride it out with all sails lowered.

Worse was to come.

First it was torment. *Wanderer* had made such slow progress south that on New Year's Eve it was caught in a windless hole just off the coast at St. Helens, near the northeast corner of Tasmania. The crew could only listen to the celebrations on shore. The torment turned to torture soon after *Wanderer* entered Storm Bay and was blasted by a wild southwesterly gale.

"It was blowing 60 knots, the seas were raging, and the spray was near horizontal," Hammond said. "To say it was bitterly cold is an understatement—there was bloody ice on the mast. Without doubt it was the most memorable Hobart race I have ever done, partly because it was my first and partly because it was so rugged and cold."

It wasn't enough to turn Hammond away from the sport, however. He became one of Australia's best ocean racing navigators, earning the nickname "Sightie" because he could so often be seen taking sun sights with a sextant.

Another yachtsman who wasn't deterred from returning to the Hobart race after a horrific experience was Jim McLaren of Sydney. In 1956 he competed for the second time, on this occasion aboard his own yacht, the 30-footer *Vailima*, a tiny double-ender that had been built by its original owner in a suburban backyard. According to McLaren, it was a race in which "not much happened." For most sailors it would have been a race where plenty happened. "We had a southerly when we cleared Sydney Heads, another southerly change off the New South Wales south coast, then a third, a beauty, as we entered Bass Strait. Three bloody fronts before we got halfway.

"The last one was from the southwest. The wind got to 86 knots—bloody hard. I don't think the seas were as big as what they experienced in the 1998 race, but the same wind and rain were certainly there. You couldn't sail in it. We had to go down to bare poles. We did manage to set the sea anchor, but it took only one big wave to break the rope attached to it. The same wave took out the forward hatch. After that we could only run with it. We felt as if we were heading for New Zealand. I was getting a bit worried because we could only hang on and hope. We were like that for twenty-four hours."

McLaren and his crew set sail again and eventually crossed Bass Strait unscathed. Then, off Tasmania's eastern coast, they suffered the indignity of having the wind evaporate completely. Finally they reached Hobart, almost eight days after leaving Sydney. But they weren't last to finish: P. S. Parry's *Renene* took almost ten days. McLaren declared he would never race south again.

His love of the sea made him relent, however, and he returned to racing. It must have been in his blood: in June 1988, his daughter, Kay Cottee, became the first woman to sail single-handed, nonstop, and unassisted around the world.

The Sydney to Hobart has attracted a vast cross-section of competitors over its long history. It has fascinated a prime minister and a premier, numerous media magnates, millionaires, billionaires, and countless average "Joes" from Struggle Street. Edward Heath, who later became Britain's Prime Minister, won the race in 1969 with his 34-foot sloop *Morning Cloud*. Heath thought it was appropriate that on the twenty-fifth anniversary of Illingworth's victory, another Briton had taken the honors. Three years later, American media magnate Ted Turner posted a rare double in being both first to finish and then being awarded outright victory—the corrected time, or handicap, trophy.

Rupert Murdoch competed with his own yacht, *Ilina*, in the

early 1960s but had to wait until 1995 to savor victory. He was aboard the sleek, white-hulled maxi *Sayonara* owned by friend and business associate Larry Ellison, head of the Oracle software company. Murdoch's son, Lachlan, was aboard the same yacht for the 1998 race.

While an addiction for some, the Sydney to Hobart has cured many sailors of the desire to ocean race. It dishes up an abundance of seasickness, discomfort, and fear. There is, of course, only one certain cure for seasickness: sitting under a tree.

The 1998 race was the thirty-fourth pilgrimage south for seventy-four-year-old Sydneysider Don Mickleborough. When asked why so many people keep going back, he had trouble explaining the allure. "I'm buggered if I know why we keep doing it—I guess it's the camaraderie. It's just that you're out there with your friends. You face the best and the worst of the conditions and have to work hard to get through. I suppose if I couldn't sail to Hobart with my mates, I wouldn't bother going." Then, after pondering awhile longer, "OK. Yes. It's the parties. Sure, the race is there as a race. But it also gets you from one good party to an even better one."

Standing out in the memories of many is a 1962 party, back when the Sydney to Hobart first went international. Wealthy New York ship broker Sumner A. Huey Long had brought what was then the world's ultimate racing yacht, *Ondine*, to challenge Australia's best. Dubbed the "Yankee yawl," this truly exceptional boat sported a unique aluminum hull painted pale blue. Huey Long was justifiably confident.

But much to his dismay, and to the surprise of almost all observers, *Ondine* didn't get it all her way. Only after the massive wooden spinnaker pole on the big Sydney schooner *Astor* splintered was Long able to bring his state-of-the-art yacht from behind to win. He made it home by just 100 yards. It was a sweet victory indeed for Long because *Ondine* also established a new mark for the 630-mile course: three days, three hours, forty-six minutes, and sixteen seconds. But Long's hope for the double victory died when Vic Meyer's powerful steel racer, *Solo*, sailed in to claim the ultimate handicap trophy, the prize for the best corrected time.

Long was not happy. He was certain *Solo* had broken race rules. He flew to Launceston in northern Tasmania to find aerial photographs he thought existed. He was sure these photographs would show *Solo*'s life raft was not, as required under race rules, carried on deck. At five o'clock the morning after Long left for Launceston, there was a party still in full swing aboard *Astor* on Hobart's historic waterfront. It included a young Rupert Murdoch—who had just moved to Sydney from Adelaide and taken over the ownership of the *Daily Mirror* newspaper—and many of the crew who had been with him for the race aboard his yacht *Ilina*: "Thunder," "Rawmeat," "Curley," and Don (known as "Don Two" because there already was a "Don Juan"). As they partied, *Ondine* floated silently nearby.

Long's actions became the subject of much debate among the revelers aboard *Astor*. The consensus was that instead of trying to dethrone *Solo*, Long should be enjoying life as a hospitable host in postrace celebrations aboard his yacht. From there it was an easy leap for some of those aboard *Astor* to decide they would help out. An *Ondine* party would happen, with or without Huey Long.

Murdoch, ably assisted by one of his newspaper managers, "Curley" Brydon, convinced a local printer he was *Ondine*'s owner and on that authority had a thousand impressive party invitations printed. The "Ondine blue" invitations announced a celebration to take place aboard the yacht the next evening. The self-proclaimed planning committee retired to the local hotel that afternoon to continue their work. There Murdoch, Mickleborough, Brydon, and friends hand-addressed invitations to everyone from Hobart's Lord Mayor to the local pipe band; the Marine Board, the nurses' quarters of the Hobart hospital, and owners of other competing yachts.

"They were signed 'hope you can make it, Huey,'" Mickleborough recalled. "And just to cover our bases I had my brother in Launceston send a telegram to *Ondine*'s sailing master, Sven Joffs, in Hobart, asking him to ready the yacht for the party. He signed it 'Huey.'"

By 8 P.M. the scene around Constitution Dock was spectacular. Murdoch and company had sufficient 18-gallon kegs of beer delivered to the area in front of *Ondine* to satisfy the considerable thirst of the assembled guests. With no sign of Huey Long, Joffs, the dedicated yacht manager, stood on the deck looking bemused, if not bewildered. All the time he was easing out the dock lines to make it impossible for those onshore to board. As the pipe band played, the Lord Mayor's car slowly made its way through the crowd. The Lord Mayor alighted, greeted by the call for "three rousing British cheers."

It became apparent this was to be a "no-host party." But in Hobart you don't need a host, and in fact you don't need a reason for a party. Eventually Huey Long arrived and immediately realized what was happening. He retreated to his hotel and spent the next few hours trying unsuccessfully to charter an aircraft out of town.

"Sadly, Huey missed a great party," Mickleborough said. "Even the police joined in."

Huey Long suffered no long-term effects after the 1962 post-race celebrations, and the magic of Hobart brought him back again and again with successively bigger yachts in the years that followed.

The second Sydney to Hobart, in 1946, attracted a fleet of nineteen starters and confirmed the race's future. Once again the colorful comments and plaudits flowed following its completion. *Seacraft* magazine's headline read, "Small Yacht Wins Again . . . *Christina*'s great victory proves that the present generation can provide its full quota of iron men to sail the wooden ships."

The following year the fleet expanded to 28, but further growth stalled until 1956. From that year on the Sydney to Hobart grew steadily until 1985, when a fleet of 180 vessels set sail. Nothing could compare with the fiftieth anniversary race in 1994, however, when a staggering 371 yachts lined up on Sydney Harbour. It was one of the greateast assemblies of ocean racing yachts and talent the world had seen.

Accompanying the growth of the race over more than five decades has been the steady development of one of the best safety and communication networks covering any of the world's major offshore events. Due to the probability of inclement, if not downright ferocious, weather, the Sydney to Hobart has become an annual testbed for race organization, yacht design, and hull construction. Top international sailors such as New Zealander Geoff Stagg do this race as often as possible "for a reality check." Stagg, the representative-at-large for the world's most successful ocean racing yacht designer, Bruce Farr of Annapolis, Maryland, was aboard 1997 race winner *Beau Geste*. He reckons the Sydney to Hobart stresses just about everything—the structure, rig, sails, and crew. "The Hobart is a bloody great race. I think it's actually tougher than an around-the-world race because I don't think the around-the-world racers get anything like the extreme conditions you get in a Hobart race. The Hobart race also demands a good all-round boat. One-way machines rarely do well. In fact, very few of them actually finish." Stagg said that one of the most difficult aspects lies with the crew and what is demanded of them.

"You need a real balance. It's hard for the crew in the middle of the boat to understand that in a race like the Hobart they have to stay on the rail [sitting on the windward side of the deck] around the clock when you are belting upwind. Their weight is crucial to the performance of the yacht. It doesn't matter how tired you are—you have to stay there. At the same time, we have to get the helmsman and [sail] trimmer who are off watch down below to rest. Having them rested for their next watch is just as crucial as having the remaining crew on the rail. When the moment presents itself, when we crack off or set spinnakers, that's when the bulk of the crew can catch up on a lot of sleep. That's the key to winning races. It's a team effort. If you don't do that, you're not serious about winning."

The Sydney to Hobart has garnered many impressive statistics. Prior to the 1998 event, a total of 4,230 yachts carrying more than 35,000 competitors had faced the starter. Considering the extreme dangers, it was remarkable that only two sailors had lost their lives from injuries. Incredibly, no one had been lost overboard and not recovered—a fact that many saw as evidence of solid safety procedures and rigid race organization—as well as good fortune.

The most remarkable stories of survival emerged from the 1993 event, one of the toughest on record before the 1998 race. A southerly gale with winds gusting up to 50 knots and a fast-flowing opposing current whipped up mountainous waves off the New South Wales south coast. Conditions were so severe that 66 of the 104 starting yachts were forced out.

Around midnight on the second night, a huge breaking wave overwhelmed the 35-foot sloop *MEM*. As the yacht capsized, owner-skipper John Quinn's safety harness broke, hurling him into the sea. Quinn surfaced, only to see his yacht sailing away. The crew knew he'd gone overboard and were desperately searching, but they couldn't see him. Other race yachts and ships rushed to the area to search, but Quinn was thought to have little chance of surviving. Every fifteen minutes or so a colossal breaking wave more than 40 feet high would sweep the area. After four unsuccessful hours of searching, the worst was feared. Race officials discussed writing his obituary. But Quinn, aided by a light buoyancy vest, was still alive and was duck-diving under each immense breaking wave.

"The only time I got a bit desperate was right at the end, and that was for a very short period of time," Quinn said. "At that stage, my vest was losing some of its buoyancy and I was starting to take in water and get tired. A while later, as I rode to the top of one big wave, I saw it—the most beautiful Christmas tree you've ever seen. It was a bloody big ship with all lights blazing, coming ever so slowly toward me. At one moment I thought the ship was going to pass without anyone spotting me because it was coming down the drift at an angle and the stern, where all the lookouts were gathered on the bridge and using searchlights, was the most distant point from me. My heart began to sink.

"Then a big wave picked up the stern and knocked it sideways toward where I was. Suddenly the ship was right there, just meters away. I started to yell my lungs out 'Hey, hey, hey!' Brent Shaw, who was manning a searchlight, was fantastic. After hearing me shout, he got the searchlight on me and started to shout out 'I've got you! I can see you!'"

While the searchlight was trained on Quinn, the race yacht *Atara*, which was just astern and damaged but still searching, moved in to drag him aboard. It had been five freezing hours since he'd fallen overboard. He was 50 miles offshore.

The Quinn rescue prompted yet another review of race safety standards and search-and rescue-operations. And again the Hobart race led the world toward new standards.

Former Sydney–Hobart race director Gordon Marshall told of one big change that the Hobart race brought to international yacht design: "We heard alarm bells in the early to mid-1970s when the lightweight, skiff-type yachts arrived on the scene. In one race only one of six of these lightweights reached Hobart. It was apparent they couldn't handle rough conditions. In fact they were dangerous because they carried the minimum amount of ballast and the maximum amount of crew weight to keep them upright. The yachts were also extremely wide so the crew could sit out on the side, their weight contributing to keeping the yacht as level as possible. At one stage the hulls were becoming so wide and the keels so small they probably would have stayed upside down had they capsized.

"We had no option but to introduce stability factors into race rules. Yachts had to prove they were stable and self-righting before being allowed to compete. It was one rule that became universally accepted around the world, and in turn ocean racing became safer."

Even in the early 1990s, some people didn't like the trend in yacht design. In December 1990 the late Alan Payne, a legendary Australian yacht designer, published some thoughts in the *Weekend Australian* under the headline, "Bad weather could turn Sydney–Hobart into a racing catastrophe. Modern yachts not safe in heavy seas." He referred ominously to the "hundred-year storm."

"I'm not talking about the blows they normally experience in a race where the wind gets up for a few hours then abates and everyone gets to Hobart and says how tough it was," Payne said. "I'm talking about extreme conditions where huge seas break. These waves can really happen in the worst conditions on these race courses [he was referring to the Sydney to Hobart and Melbourne to Devonport races]. These are the conditions where the yachts will fail structurally, where they will be capsized and where rigs break. The problems are that they aren't strong enough, or in the event of a capsize are so stable in the inverted position that they don't want to come upright."

Eight years later, in the 1998 race, much of what Payne predicted could happen did happen. His theories were based on careful research into what sea conditions would be developed by a 35-knot gale in Bass Strait over a twenty-four-hour period. He said that it was inevitable in those conditions that every yacht would see a wave at least 33 feet (10 meters) high on the 150-mile fetch from Gabo Island, off the mainland, across to Flinders Island, off Tasmania's northeast corner. In fact many in the 1998 Hobart fleet saw winds of around 70 knots—twice as strong as those on which Payne based his predictions. His calculations suggested three yachts would completely disappear, taking twenty-two people with them; six crew would be lost overboard; three life rafts containing twelve people would never be found; and a rescue helicopter would crash while on mission.

It was apparent after the 1998 race that if it hadn't been for the Herculean rescue effort and the fact that much of the drama occurred in relatively close proximity to the southeast corner of the Australian mainland, Alan Payne's predictions could well have come true. While generally accepting his comments, ocean racing authorities have been quick to stress that the standards covering design, construction, communications, and safety equipment are among the most stringent in the world.

In the early days of racing to Hobart, the oft-heard comment was "wooden yachts and iron men." Today, the sailors who manned those heavily timbered craft could look at the modern yachts made of fiberglass and space age materials and mumble "plastic yachts and plastic men." One of the greatest sailors to emerge from the Hobart race, Magnus Halvorsen (who with brother Trygve won three consecutive races aboard *Freya* in 1963 to 1965), refers to contemporary offshore yachts as "cocktail shakers."

But modern ocean racing yachts represent the latest in design technology, materials, and equipment. Instead of starting life as a series of pencil sketches, drawings, and half models eyeballed by the builder, the yachts more often than not originate in the "mind" of a powerful computer. Working within basic parameters determined by the owner (primarily length and budget), the designer and design team begin formulating a shape based on the limitations of the handicapping rule and the optimum performance attainable for a yacht of the desired size. The rule of thumb is that the greater the waterline length of the yacht and the larger the sail area, the faster the boat will be. Hull shapes are usually computer analyzed, then tank-tested before a decision is made on the final shape.

Engineers must design the structure using proven laminate information and calculations generated by a computer that tests the loads, the hull, deck, keel, and rudder. Apart from fiberglass, other exotic materials such as carbon fiber, Kevlar, and honeycomb or foam cores are used. Often the hulls are baked in huge ovens to achieve maximum strength.

Indeed, boatbuilding technology and techniques are not that different from those used in spacecraft construction. Almost the entire vessel, from hull to rig to sails, is handcrafted, a painstaking process that can take up to six months. Because of the intricate nature of the construction, the yachts are extremely vulnerable if not built to precise specifications. Modifications that disregard the very nature of a one-piece structure—a monocoque—are usually catastrophic. This type of structure is literally only as strong as its weakest part, a principle clearly illustrated in the 1988 race.

Rod Muir's new spare-no-expense, space-age maxi *Windward Passage II* was deemed to have a mortgage on line honors and probably the course record. On the Bass Strait approach the boat was doing everything expected of it: leading the fleet and bettering the record pace set by *Kialoa* in 1975. But a howling southwesterly gale turned that around. Initially, the *Windward Passage II* crew answered the challenge of the rising seas and howling winds and kept the race record in their sights. Then, in the middle of the night, the entire crew heard a sickening crack. Across the deck near the cockpit, a split had developed that could expand and led to total structural failure at any moment.

Windward Passage II had gone from brilliant to busted in an instant. It turned out someone had cut a small hole in the laminate deck to accommodate a compass, hadn't reinforced the area, and thus had inadvertently compromised the structural integrity of the hull. As one crewmember put it, if *Windward Passage II* had continued in the race, there was a chance the "back half of the boat would have fallen off."

Compare that incident with *Rani*'s problems in the first race.

Her crew stuffed a blanket into a gap in the planks to slow a leak so they could continue!

Improvements in design, construction, and materials have seen a steady increase in the speeds at which yachts travel. Interestingly, it took twenty-one years for the record set by the now vintage American maxi ketch *Kialoa* in 1975—two days, fourteen hours, thirty-six minutes and fifty-six seconds—to be bettered. In 1996 the German giant, *Morning Glory*, owned by Hasso Plattner, scraped a mere thirty minutes off the record. *Kialoa* and the rest of the fleet had a dream run in 1975: the crews set spinnakers as soon as they cleared Sydney Heads, and from there on it was smooth sailing all the way down to Hobart. Such ideal conditions are rarely encountered.

A telling comparison can be drawn between the first race in 1945 and the gale-lashed 1993 event, where only 38 of the 102 starters finished. The 1993 fleet struggled against head winds and mountainous seas all the way south in what was considered a slow race. Of the 1945 fleet, only the fastest yacht, *Rani*, had an elapsed time that would have positioned it before the slowest yachts in 1993—it would have crossed the line thirty-fourth. Compared to the 1992 race, *Rani* would have finished a day and a half behind the slowest yacht.

International media interest in the Sydney to Hobart race has always ensured it receives prominent publicity. At the same time, Australian television, newspapers, and radio have elevated the event to the status of prime-time, compulsory Boxing Day entertainment. Its start is the subject of a two-hour national live television coverage; it is always front-page and headline news; and hundreds of thousands of spectators watch from home, headlands, and beaches on the harbor shores or cram the omnipresent and colorful flotilla of boats that gather to see the fleet off.

The media's enthusiasm for procuring first-hand and exclusive information from the fleet began with the earliest races. There have been many industrious, almost ingenious efforts, to get the "scoop," and none more so than the scheme hatched by the Sydney *Sun* newspaper's yachting writer, Lou D'Alpuget (Blanche D'Alpuget's father), and the then-young journalist Frank McNulty in 1947.

D'Alpuget, who wanted an exclusive, saw McNulty, crewing on the yacht *Moonbi*, as his source. D'Alpuget didn't want to use radio communications, which could have been easily overheard. So, when *Moonbi* set sail on Boxing Day that year, it had on board three small guests—homing pigeons. After two days at sea, McNulty did as planned. He penciled onto cigarette papers a report on the yacht's progress and attached them to the legs of the birds.

"I took the pigeons onto the deck and released them, but they refused to leave," he said. "I think they were seasick. I held them up and they just fluttered back to the deck. Eventually I took a bird in my cupped hands and began swinging it toward the sky. After a few swings I let the bird go and sure enough it flapped off toward the coast."

And so D'Alpuget got his scoop.

The media's thirst for Hobart race news still hasn't abated. It starts weeks before the event every year. The official television network treats viewers to a one-hour special on preparations about ten days before Boxing Day.

In 1998 the Christmas Eve prerace briefing was big news. Roger Badham had been quoted in the *Australian* as saying there was plenty of wind brewing for the fleet.

"A high casualty rate is the likely scenario when a forecast southerly buster hits the fleet within twenty-four hours of the start of the Telstra Sydney to Hobart yacht race on Boxing Day." He then reported that the approaching front originally expected on Christmas Day had slowed dramatically. It now appeared it would pummel the fleet during the first night at sea or early the next morning.

"I'm beginning to wonder how God knows it's time for a Hobart race," Badham said. "The pattern looks like it will be very similar to what we have seen in most of the recent Hobart races. That means a northeasterly wind for the start and a fast spinnaker run down the coast before the fleet hits a brick wall in the form of a southerly buster. It's still a little early to make an accurate prediction on whether or not the conditions will give the frontrunners a shot at the race record, but if I had to stick my neck out now I'd say it won't happen. The indications from all the computer models we have avail-

able say that it looks like the wind will be quite soft off the Tasmanian coast. That will slow the leaders for some time."

Badham said the southerly buster was likely to deliver winds
between 25 and 30 knots for twelve to twenty-four hours. The wind
was then likely to change direction toward the east and abate.

The forecast conditions for the first twenty-four hours of the
1998 event were uncannily similar to those experienced two years earlier. In 1996 George Snow's maxi *Brindabella* led Hasso Plattner's
Morning Glory for the first three hours of the race before losing its
mast soon after the southerly hit. *Morning Glory's* crew reacted conservatively: fearing dismasting or structural problems, they lowered
the mainsail completely and set a headsail. It was a wise move, and
they survived under that configuration until the wind began to ease—
then they went on to set the record.

At the 1998 prerace briefing the official weatherman, Ken Batt,
injected some Christmas spirit when he appeared before his eager
audience wearing a Santa Claus hat. He was short on weather "gifts,"
however, and admitted the pattern was becoming a little difficult to
predict. It appeared the southerly buster would certainly hit the first
night out, but there was also a low lurking off the east coast that
showed signs it might move south. The competitors and the media
left the briefing room faced with a lot of "ifs and maybes."

"It was really the first Hobart race that I'd done in a number of
years where I felt there was an unresolved—an absolutely unresolved—
weather pattern," recalls Steve Kulmar. "There was a divergence of opinion. Ken had started by saying the three models disagreed. The only
thing they could agree upon was that we'd run into the change in the
first twenty-four hours. The computer models were saying 'We think
there's a low-pressure system somewhere up off Coffs Harbour, which is
going to have an influence over here, but we can't agree on the direction it will travel.' I think the European model was saying there's a low
pressure in the [Great Australian] Bight, and it's the major influence. So
I guess I left that weather briefing thinking we'll just have to catch up
and look at it in detail on Boxing Day morning."

Unknown to everyone, a trap was being laid.

Three
The Anticipation

A magnificent summer day dawned over Sydney Harbour on December 26, 1998. Steve and Libby Kulmar awoke around 6:30 to the first silver shafts of sunlight dancing on the glassy waters of the harbor off Forty Baskets Beach. Steve noticed that a heavy dew had settled on the lawn during the night. In Sydney that could only mean that a strong northeasterly sea breeze would develop in the afternoon, a breeze that would make for great racing under spinnaker.

As always, Steve's mother had made a boiled fruitcake for the crew. While breakfast was being prepared, Libby cut this moist and dark homemade treat into sections so everyone on board could enjoy two slices each. She was tempted to taste it but resisted out of superstition and tradition. Meanwhile Steve methodically packed his gear, and went to great lengths to ensure everything would stay dry.

Libby's parents, John and Nerolie—"Noo" to everyone—were also up. John planned to go to the club to enjoy the sights and bid farewell to Steve. Then he and Noo would head north to the central coast for a vacation at picturesque Avoca Beach.

"Why don't you come up for a few days while Steve's away?" Noo asked Libby over breakfast.

"Oh, I don't think I'll come up. I think I'm going to have to pick up Steve." Libby's response shocked her after she'd said it. In recalling those comments Libby did not know what prompted her. "I've never ever said anything like that before Steve had gone to do any other ocean race. We've always expected him to finish in Hobart and he has. I can't explain why I said it."

The latest weather forecasts confirmed that nothing had changed. There would be a nice northeasterly for the start, then a south to sou'westerly change during the night—a typical southerly buster for what was shaping up as a typical Hobart race. There was, however, still an element of uncertainty about the intentions of a low lingering off the New South Wales coast and what impact an upper air disturbance might have on conditions in Bass Strait. Roger Badham was already well on his way to the CYC from his home at Coledale, south of Sydney. He had been up almost the entire night analyzing the very latest local and international computer models of the developing weather patterns.

Badham had outlined what he expected to happen, what to watch for and what other potential scenarios might occur. Most of the race's high-profile competitors were relying on him to provide the answers to the mysteries of meteorology--answers that would give them the best possible chance of winning. Badham's briefcase was filled with folders marked with the name of each yacht he was servicing: *Sayonara, Brindabella, Wild Thing, ABN AMRO Challenge, B-52,* and many others.

"This is a typical Hobart race—with the southerly change—but this is one of the most difficult in recent years to accurately pinpoint the wind changes due to an intense low that looks set to develop near Tasmania," he said. "The low is associated with an upper cold air trough [and fast-moving fronts] that will produce heaps of breeze south of Tasmania, and things look pretty reasonable on the Tassie coast. Over Bass Strait—well, it depends exactly where the low develops—how close to Tasmania . . . but best guess is not too far south, and the forecast [in the early hours of December 26] is for quite strong winds across Bass Strait on the 27th and slowly moderating winds on the 28th.

"This afternoon/tonight, 26 December: northeasterly sea breeze in the afternoon ahead of a southerly front expected around midnight. This is a sou'westerly change through Bass Strait and a southerly (180°) change along the NSW [New South Wales] coast. This is a trough system, and thunderstorms are likely. Late yesterday, storms gave short wind-squalls of 50 to 60 knots across Victoria—this will be the case again this afternoon, so be prepared. A low in the Tasman looks like being absorbed into the trough/front and sliding down the front to be off Tasmania tomorrow.

"Sunday 27 December: high pressure must wait over the Great Australian Bight while a low-pressure system spins up southeast of Tasmania. The high will ridge along the Victorian coast and north Bass Strait around the New South Wales corner, but if the low really spins up, it will be the cyclonic circulation around this that will dominate Bass Strait."

The one word that stood out was "cyclonic." Americans call it a hurricane.

There was plenty already happening when Badham and his wife, Margaret, arrived at the CYC to deliver the eagerly awaited forecasts. His weather predictions would determine sail inventory for the race, the yacht's course, and tactics for the first twelve hours, and how the yacht might be configured for maximum performance. The docks were jammed with sailors, supporters, spectators, and media. Wheelbarrows laden with supplies, ice, crew bags, and equipment were deftly guided through the crush. High in the forest of masts and what seemed to be the tangle of rigging supporting them, crewmembers were swinging around like monkeys on strings, scanning for potential problems. Television crews with bulky cameras on their shoulders panned, tilted, and zoomed in and out to capture the prerace atmosphere. Reporters were busy interviewing race personalities.

Tom Sobey, a seventeen-year-old from Albury on the New South Wales–Victoria border, attracted much attention. His efforts the previous day to hitch a ride aboard a race yacht had failed. Undaunted, he decided to give it one more shot on Boxing Day. From 7 A.M. he had walked the docks at the CYC with signs pinned to the front and back of his shirt. The scrawled red writing read CREW AVAILABLE. Sobey had just finished his final year of high school and had come to Sydney on the off-chance he might snaffle a ride to Hobart. Like so many young sailors raised in a world of dinghy racing, Sobey regarded the Hobart as the ultimate event. But 1998 was not his year, and as the fleet set sail, Tom Sobey watched from shore.

As Steve Kulmar was leaving for the CYC on Boxing Day morning, he stopped by his daughter Pip's room, kissed her cheek, and whispered good-bye. A muffled grunt from a head firmly buried in a pillow was Pip's only response. Later, as Steve and the other family members drove toward the Sydney Harbour Bridge, a personal concern unrelated to the race or the weather niggled him. He hated the fact that the yacht was at the crowded club on race day and much preferred it when the preparations were done elsewhere. He didn't enjoy struggling with his bags through a crowd to get to the yacht. But like the weather conditions, this was out of his control.

Sailors, wannabes, socialites, media types, and countless curious spectators had been gathering at the club since early morning. For some, navigating through the throng had become a tricky business. Paul Borge, from Mooloolaba in Queensland, confidently made his way along the dock with a white cane in one hand and a friendly arm to hang onto. He was heading for *Aspect Computing*—the yacht manned by the group competing under the banner "Sailors with Dis-Abilities." Borge had lost his sight two years earlier yet was determined to continue sailing. Also in the *Aspect Computing* crew was twelve-year-old Travis Foley, a dyslexic from Mudgee and the race's youngest competitor.

The smell of breakfast—bacon and eggs cooking on the club's outdoor barbecue, toast, and freshly brewed coffee—filled the air as sailors clad in their colorful T-shirts and shorts mingled with the punters in their best summer attire. In the small parking lot at the side of the club, crewmembers waited anxiously for representatives from the Bureau of Meteorology to arrive with the official race forecast. On the street, others were paying $10 and throwing their excess baggage, cruising sails for the trip home, inflatable dinghies, and spare equipment into the back of the large truck that was heading to Hobart.

Excess weight would slow a yacht, so only the bare essentials could be taken on board.

George Snow, property developer and owner of Australia's glamour maxi, *Brindabella*, was having his hand shaken and his back slapped as he struggled through the crowd to his 75-foot racer at the end of the marina.

"Good luck, mate. Make sure you beat those Americans," came a call from the crowd. It was a nice thought, but deep down Snow and his enthusiastic supporter both knew that the odds were against his "old girl" beating the triple world champion *Sayonara*. A few hundred meters to the north, at d'Albora Marinas, *Sayonara*'s owner, the trim, fit, and energetic Larry Ellison, had arrived and was attracting a fair amount of attention. But one of his crewmembers was stealing the show. Lachlan Murdoch, the twenty-seven-year-old CEO and Chairman of News Corporation in Australia, stood with his fiancée, Sarah O'Hare. Needless to say, the photographers were having a field day.

Sayonara was an impressive piece of yachtbuilding and a beautiful boat. From its sleek white hull and aerodynamic carbon-fiber mast to the crew's crisp white T-shirts—complete with the bold red-and-black *Sayonara* logo—it was arguably one of the finest yachts in the world and was wholly justified in being the odds-on favorite. A spare-no-expense campaigner, Ellison had assembled an experienced and highly accomplished crew. It was headed by New Zealand ace and principal helmsman Chris Dickson, an America's Cup, match racing, and around-the-world racer who had come straight from taking his marriage vows in Auckland. Californian Mark Rudiger, the navigator, had guided Paul Cayard's *EF Language* to a crushing victory in the Whitbread round-the-world race earlier in the year.

Steve Kulmar and family arrived at the club, squeezed their car into the packed temporary parking lot, unloaded gear, then prepared themselves for the annual dock dance, ducking, weaving, and dodging to reach the yacht.

"We'd never been aboard *Sword of Orion,* so we all hopped on and had a bit of a look around," recalls Libby Kulmar. "I hadn't met

Glyn [Charles] and some of the crew, so we chatted while they were getting ready."

The family didn't want to stay for the start, preferring to be home in time to watch it live on television. They decided to go to the clubhouse with Steve, but not before Madeline photographed her father with the new waterproof camera he'd been given for Christmas. They met up with friends, Bob and Sue and Matt Fraser. Bob had an update on the weather—the southerly buster was definitely brewing and would likely greet the fleet off the south coast of New South Wales between 2 A.M. and dawn. He confirmed the anticipated wind strength in the change was around 35 knots and added that it might back to the west. The looming low was still an unknown quantity. Kulmar thought they would probably have a quick beam reach for the crossing of Bass Strait. But he was getting impatient. It was time to go. He walked Libby, Maddie, and John back to the car.

"We wanted to get back home, cool off with a swim, then watch the start on television," said Libby. Steve was about to say good-bye to Maddie when she produced a surprise gift for him.

"Dad, I got this in the Christmas stocking. It's a good luck charm for you. I've got one and this one's yours."

She handed him a loop of thin luminous yellow cord. Hanging on it like a pendant was a pink piglet's head, about one third the size of a golf ball. When you squeezed it, the piglet's mouth opened and shut and made a clacking sound.

"You have to wear it," Maddie said.

Steve bent down and Maddie put it over his head.

"Maddie, it's beautiful. Thank you, darling," he said as he kissed her good-bye. He waved as they drove off, and then, with the piglet pendant secured around his neck, battled his way back to *Sword of Orion*.

The CYC was not the only hive of prerace activity Boxing Day morning. All around the harbor, other yacht clubs, marinas, and private docks were buzzing with last-minute preparations. In pretty Mosman Bay, two well-known and well-respected yachting figures were getting their charges set for sea.

Ian Kiernan, better known as "Bik," or "Captain Yucky Poo" to his mates (he earned the latter nickname through his prodigious environmental activities), had in recent years become a household name in Australia. More than a decade earlier Kiernan's love for Sydney Harbour had motivated him to organize the successful "Clean Up the Harbour" community campaign. It soon grew into "Clean Up Australia" and then the United Nations–backed "Clean Up the World" campaign.

"It started with 40,000 people cleaning up Sydney Harbour in 1989," Kiernan recalls. "It has now grown to 40 million people in 120 countries cleaning up the world. I'm proud of every one of them."

Kiernan's yacht, the classic Alan Payne–designed 36-footer *Canon Maris*, had a historic link with the Hobart race. Its original owner, Jack Earl—a man whom Kiernan regarded as a father figure and mentor—was one of the event's founders. That link was strengthened when Earl's grandson, Matthew Tomaszewski, joined the *Canon Maris* crew. Also aboard were Jonathan "Gibbo" Gibson, son of John "Gibbo" Gibson, who was aboard *Winston Churchill*, and Richard "Sightie" Hammond, perhaps the most experienced competitor in the race, who was navigating. And to top it all off, 1998 was *Canon Maris*'s fortieth anniversary.

Canon Maris, a tidy, low-sided little wooden yawl with clean white topsides, a teak deck, and an immaculately varnished cabin, was meticulously maintained and, according to Kiernan, "probably better than the day it was built." A lot of water had passed under its keel since it came into Kiernan's hands in 1970. "I've sailed her twice to the United States, done four Hobarts in her, plus a single-handed Trans Pacific and a single-handed Trans Tasman." If that wasn't enough, Kiernan had also completed a single-handed around-the-world race, and had crewed for Australia in the Admiral's Cup in England and Clipper Cup in Hawaii. He knew this would be a tough race.

"For some reason I just picked it. Regardless, you should always be ready for rough weather. With the boat being forty years old, we always take our race preparation very seriously, but this time we were even more prepared. At the last moment I had a new storm trysail made, and we were attending to all of the issues for a heavy race. I ordered a new life raft and had an EPIRB [Emergency Position-Indicating Radio Beacon for rescues at sea] fitted to that. All of our crew were provided with full sets of Musto HPX wet-weather gear with flotation vests and integrated safety harnesses. I wanted everyone to be dry and comfortable because on *Canon Maris* we live, eat, sleep, sail, and breathe the race. No one gets out of their sailing gear during the race. Everyone is ready to go on deck at all times. That way there's none of the frigging around with guys saying, 'who's got my seaboots and my safety harness?'"

The six *Canon Maris* crew were at Mosman Bay Marina at 9 A.M., resplendent in their red shirts, white shorts, and the traditional *Maris* beret, a tribute to artist and original owner Jack Earl. *Canon Maris, Winston Churchill,* and *Southerly* were set for a veteran's race among themselves. The wager was beers and rum and cokes, and the bets would be paid and collected at a Hobart waterfront hotel.

As *Canon Maris* headed out of the bay the crew enjoyed some light banter with the team preparing one of the hottest contenders for handicap honors—Syd Fischer's 50-footer, *Ragamuffin*. Fischer, now at the ripe old age of seventy-three, had, without question, been Australia's most successful ocean-racing yachtsman. He had won just about everything that mattered, including the Hobart race, the 600-mile Fastnet Race, the Admiral's Cup, and the Kenwood Cup. He led the Australian team to victory in the disastrous 1979 Fastnet Race. This was to be Fischer's thirtieth Sydney to Hobart.

A fleet of yachts, including his 1995 America's Cup race entrant and of course the mighty "Rags," was docked at the harborfront doorstep of Fischer's three-level dark-timber residence. The large room on the lower level was devoted to yacht-racing memorabilia and photographs covering Fischer's nearly forty years of offshore competition. Minutes before *Canon Maris* glided past, Fischer had assembled the crew—a powerful blend of experience and raw, young energy—in the "racing room" so sailing master Grant Simmer could brief them on race weather and tactics. For twenty-one-year-old crewmember Nathan Ellis, this was his initiation to the classic. Once the briefing was over, the crew moved outside to make the important final checks.

Immediately adjacent to the CYC, the Royal Australian Navy's headquarters at Garden Island was also bristling with prerace activity. The Navy's youth-training vessel, the 144-foot *Young Endeavour*, Britain's bicentennial gift to Australia in 1988, was preparing to go to sea. The classically proportioned brigantine would again be the radio-relay vessel. The previous week the CYC's chief radio operator Lew Carter and his team of technicians had installed the bank of radios needed to communicate with the fleet.

It was a symbolic Hobart race for Carter. He had completed sixteen races aboard yachts and had done an additional nine as radio operator, which took him to the magic number of twenty-five. Lew's two volunteer assistants, Michael and Audrey Brown, were also entrusted with a highly demanding job. They would provide strong support for Carter in what is an around-the-clock task. When the trio arrived at Garden Island on Boxing Day and were welcomed aboard by the ship's captain, Lieutenant Commander Neil Galletly, Carter had two concerns.

"I always thought it was going to be a rough year, just by looking at the weather patterns leading up to it, even over a couple of months. I was at the race briefing, and after listening to Ken Batt deliver his forecast I thought he was pretty skeptical about the whole thing. He didn't seem to be able to say what he thought we were going to get. I sensed he glossed over a few things without giving his true opinion. He seemed to have a bet each way."

Carter was also worried about the radios for the race.

"The radios are checked while the ship is at the dock, but I have said for a number of years I considered the procedure insufficient. The radios should be tested at sea, probably a fortnight prior to the race and preferably during some of the club's short ocean races. I think it would be a good idea to incorporate skeds [from *schedule*, a prescheduled news and weather update with fleet "roll call" and position reports] into those short ocean races to acclimatize ourselves and the yachties again with procedures. It is very difficult to test the radios on *Young Endeavour* at Garden Island. You don't get out properly because there are so many buildings and other areas of interference. I wasn't happy with the radio from the start, right from when we were in Garden Island. I didn't appear to be getting to some of the places I thought we should have been able to contact."

Back at the CYC, the atmosphere was electric. Driving to the club with John "Steamer" Stanley, young Michael "Beaver" Rynan's eyes were like golf balls, his mouth agape as he took in the excitement of the morning of his first Hobart race. The pair made their way to *Winston Churchill* and met up with the rest of the crew. Crisp new boldly striped shirts and shorts were issued and once everything had been readied, most of the crew paraded back along the dock in their new attire to enjoy a few drinks with mates before they put to sea.

Steamer spotted race meteorologist Ken Batt. He sat down with him and showed him some old photographs of *Winston Churchill* in the first Hobart race in 1945. "Ken had some relatives racing on the yacht that year, and I was trying to see if he could identify them." Naturally they also discussed the weather, and Batt confirmed what he had said at the briefing: there was a chance the fleet would be buffeted by winds up to 50 knots and that it was going to be southwest turning west. Steamer thought, "Hang on, this doesn't sound right," but Batt could offer nothing more due to the instability of the pattern.

Meanwhile, Ian Kiernan was easing *Canon Maris* into "the Pond" next to the outdoor bar. Kiernan's wife, Judy, was put ashore to join a spectator boat. The bar was buzzing and among the myriad faces, Kiernan recognized plenty of mates, including Stanley and Mickleborough. "We had to put up with the bloody ragging of Mickleborough and his bloody larrikin *Southerly* crew—'We'll be on the dock with a beer for you, and all that shit,'" recalls Kiernan. "Then I looked across and there was Steamer just sipping on a schooner. I gave him the finger and he knew what it meant: the race was on. He smiled, gave me the Hawaiian Salute—the thumb and the little finger—and continued drinking. Jim Lawler was nearby and I shouted out 'Hi' to him. He was looking just like a bloody prince of a man in his sailing hat. I exchanged calls of 'Good luck' with Gouldy and Richard Winning. They had brought *Winston Churchill*'s performance right up, and we knew they were going to be bloody hard to beat."

The *Canon Maris* crew pushed their yacht away from the dock, Kiernan slipped the engine into gear, eased the throttle forward, turned his charge away from the marina, and powered off toward the start line.

On the way out, Kiernan reminded the crew of what was expected. "Guys, I think we're going to have a heavy and wet-weather race," said Kiernan. "We've all got plenty of experience, but I want to remind you that the executive decisions are made by Dick Hammond and myself. We want your feedback all the time, but we don't want chatter in times of decision. Keep yourselves clipped on. Sail conservatively but quickly and enjoy the bloody race." Hammond confirmed the heavy-weather prognosis and outlined what he expected for the run down the coast that afternoon and when the blow might arrive that night.

Winston Churchill's crew had also decided it was time to move. They returned to the yacht, said good-bye to their support team, including Stephanie Winning and the children, then guided the historic boat into the harbor. Peter Joubert's *Kingurra* had gone out early, for what crewman Peter Meikle recalls was a very good reason.

"Peter always makes us put up the storm jib and the trysail before the start. He does it every year so the old-timers are reacquainted with the settings and any new guys know where it all goes—and learn how not to scratch the varnish. I remember distinctly sailing past a few race boats with lots of people wearing smart, matching shirts. They were all pointing at us, laughing and carrying on. The same blokes would probably be saying later on that what we did should be a compulsory prestart practice."

The team from North Queensland aboard Wayne Millar's yacht, *B-52*, departed the CYC marina and headed out onto the harbor grinning from ear to ear. The forecast northeasterly for the first half-day should allow them to produce their secret weapon—a blooper. The youngest sailors in the race would never have heard of a blooper. To them the word meant an embarrassing mistake, nothing more. A blooper was, in fact, a special offshore racing sail in vogue in the 1970s. It was a lightweight headsail attached to the bow and set outside the leech (trailing edge) of the mainsail when the yacht was sailing directly downwind under spinnaker. In the Hobart race it was deemed illegal for the Grand Prix division, the IMS (International Measurement System) yachts. But as the boys from Townsville discovered, it was quite legal in their division, the CHS (Channel Handicap System) section.

That youthful ignorance had prompted its resurrection. *B-52* crewman and Townsville solicitor John Byrne had discovered the blooper loophole in the CHS rule just before the Hobart. "I mentioned tallboys and bloopers to a group of young sailors, and they looked at me with blank stares," Byrne recalls. "They'd never heard of those sails. For some reason that sparked my interest. I knew the blooper was illegal under the IMS rule, but I wasn't sure about CHS. I checked the rules, then went to the committee in England that controls CHS racing. They agreed it would be legal."

Byrne told Millar of the breakthrough and the pair swiftly contacted North Sails in Sydney, stressing the need for total secrecy. North Sails management researched the project and found that their loft in South Africa still had designs for bloopers . The new sail was shipped to Sydney just before the start. Secret tests had showed that speed increased from 8 knots to 9.5—which could produce a gain of 18 valuable miles over their rivals if it was used effectively in the first twelve hours.

Don Mickleborough's sloop *Southerly*, known as "the Floating Hotel," was probably the least conspicuous yacht on the CYC dock. Built in 1939, she was one of the grand old ladies in the fleet. She boasted the oldest and most experienced crew, with an average age somewhere around 60 and a group total of more than a hundred Hobarts. Mickleborough had done thirty, while Tony Cable topped the list with one more. The sign swinging in the breeze on *Southerly's* mast revealed this team's attitude toward their younger rivals: OLD AGE AND TREACHERY WILL OVERCOME YOUTH AND SKILL.

Over the years, Mickleborough had become something of a traditionalist. The oldest yacht, he felt, should see "the youngsters"—that is, everyone else—off. Two hours before the start, when most other crews were clambering aboard their yachts as families and friends waved good-bye, the senior citizens from *Southerly* were still firmly ensconced in the bar enjoying perfectly poured beers. They left at 12:15 P.M., forty-five minutes before the start, when they were certain all others had departed. They walked leisurely down the dock to the yacht, laughing and appearing casual and carefree. The docklines were cast off and they motored the old girl out into the fray.

It seemed that just about anything that floated was out on the harbor that glorious Boxing Day morning; everything from large luxury vessels to ferries, yachts and powerboats, and even canoes, surf skis, and paddleboards carrying some of the more adventurous. Waterway authorities, water police, and volunteer groups patrolled the boundaries of the course in small boats keeping watch over the no-go zone. At this stage their job was relatively easy, but once the post-start stampede toward the harbor entrance began, they would be tested to their limits.

Sydney's harbor is one of the world's most beautiful. The modern and vibrant city sits superbly on its southern shore some seven miles from the Heads. The famous Opera House with its sail-like roof, and the gunmetal gray "coat hanger"—the Harbour Bridge—recline like a proud guard of honor at the entrance to Circular Quay, the bay that is the city center's maritime doorway. The harbor forms a magnificent natural amphitheater, and the surrounding hills are an appealing mix of bushy parkland and seaside suburbs dotted with a broad spectrum of homes. Ribbons of golden sand, backed by grass-covered picnic grounds, give the city folk, lovers of the outdoor life, excellent access to the water.

Thousands of moorings, marina berths, and private docks are filled with every conceivable type of craft, from multimillion dollar megayachts to the tiniest of "tinnies"—small aluminum dinghies. On Boxing Day the surrounding homes, hills, and headlands are packed with more than 300,000 people waiting eagerly to witness the spectacular start. On South Head, the rocky bastion marking one side of the port's entrance, the outside broadcast television unit from Network Ten was already on the air. Overhead, between fifteen and twenty media helicopters buzzed like dragonflies.

At the controls of one of them was Gary Ticehurst, chief pilot with the Australian Broadcasting Corporation (ABC) television network in Sydney and a man who had become somewhat of a race legend over the previous sixteen years. Flying helicopters was his first love, and his pet assignment each year was to shadow the Hobart fleet as the aerial camera platform supplying shots to the television news pool. His efforts had resulted in spectacular footage beamed around the world of the 1984 and 1993 events, two of the roughest races on record. In 1993 Ticehurst took part in a number of search operations that located upturned and badly damaged yachts. Each year he would spend up to two months planning the filming and communications strategy—how the signals would be sent back, what frequencies would be used, where he would locate the base to transmit all the signals, and how he would talk to the yachts. Before the start, preparations for the 1998 event had been running smoothly.

"I went out to the ABC and readied the helicopter. The frustration really started because the fuel pump at the ABC failed. We couldn't fuel the chopper and it was less than thirty minutes before we had to be in the air. There was no way the pump was going to be fixed by the time I was due to do the coverage. Eventually we went to Channel 9 and did the shuttle service over there all day. It was tiring but at least we got the chopper going." This was the first of a number of long and tiring days for Ticehurst.

While many yachts stayed near the starting line off Nielsen Park Beach—about three miles up-harbor from the Heads—some of the more serious contenders for line and handicap honors cruised to the harbor entrance. The aim was to let everyone on board get a feel for the conditions developing on the ocean, and to help settle any prerace jitters. They were greeted by a sparkling blue ocean with gently rolling swells from the northeast. Some of the more commercially inclined yachts sailed the 5 miles inside the harbor up to Manly, turned, set the spinnaker that was plastered with their sponsor's logo, and cruised back to the starting line.

Half an hour before the official 1 P.M. start, most of the 115 contenders had maneuvered themselves into the starting area. Large, circular Telstra decals on the bow, plus flags fluttering from the stern, identified them as race boats. The yachts left a lattice-like pattern of white wakes on the blue water as they crisscrossed the harbor with only mainsails set. It was the aquatic equivalent of thoroughbreds parading in the ring before the start of the Kentucky Derby. The massive maxis with their towering rigs were the most easily identifiable. Sail number US17 was *Sayonara*, C1 *Brindabella*, M10 was Grant Wharington's exciting new *Wild Thing*, and 9431 was *Marchioness*, whose crew looked as pleased as punch, for they knew the strengthening northeasterly breeze during the day could give them an edge on the downward run. They also knew that a southerly would hamper their progress—*Marchioness* was far from fast when sailing to windward.

One yacht that stood out was David Witt's *Nokia*, a ketch with a bright blue hull and the sponsor's name written proudly on the side. *Nokia*'s sail number, COK1, revealed that it was the first big boat racing internationally under the Cook Islands flag. Papa Tom stood on deck absorbing the excitement, his long, shiny gray hair flowing in the breeze.

The dark-hulled radio-relay vessel *Young Endeavour*, with its crew of twelve officers and eighteen trainees aged between eighteen and twenty-three, made a magnificent sight as it moved slowly down the harbor past the race yachts and spectator craft. It would wait for the race fleet outside the Heads. Lew Carter didn't take in the scenery; he was in the radio room, still frustrated by poor communications.

"I found it difficult to contact some of the yachts. We probably kidded ourselves [about the problem] at the time, thinking 'it's only because of where we are.' Then, when we got outside the Heads we still had problems. I noticed that the squelch button on the radio wasn't working at all. It acts as a sort of fine-tuner on the radio to give you your best possible signal. I tried to contact Penta Comstat, a land-based communications station located north of Sydney, but the signal that I was getting from them was nonexistent. I had to do something about it."

Carter started to weigh his options.

The northeaster would create an upwind leg from the "invisible" starting line (a line between the start boat on the east side of the harbor and a buoy to the west) to the Heads and beyond. This would in turn mean tighter maneuvering and skilled handling. Collisions were a distinct possibility. A downwind start with the harbor ablaze with bright color spinnakers would have been a visual bonus on such a beautiful summer day. It wasn't to be.

The smallest yachts, those around 30 feet (9 meters) in length, like Jim Dunstan's tiny 1981 race winner, *Zeus II*, had just six crewmembers aboard. The maxis, measuring some 78 feet (24 meters) long, had around twenty-six aboard—the equivalent of two rugby league teams.

At 12:50 P.M. the *boom!* from a cannon aboard the start boat and the raising of flags signaled the ten-minute countdown. Every thirty seconds the helmsmen would ask the crew how much time there was to the start gun. The helmsmen and tacticians were talking, fine-tuning their start strategy while the man on the bow and others amidships warned of any yachts that might be too close.

Boom! Another cannon shot signaled five minutes to go. Most crews were now beginning to line up their yachts, hustling for a good position. The lookout on the tip of the bow was sending hand signals back to the braintrust in the cockpit. Three fingers up, three boat lengths from the line; two fingers, two lengths; one finger, one length; closed fist, on the line and holding. The calls differed according to position, but one thing was for certain—no one wanted to cross the line early.

On the dot of 1 P.M., Australia's golden girl of swimming, Susie O'Neill, tugged the cord that fired the cannon starting the race. It was a clean start. But there was already drama. On the eastern shore the race's biggest boat, the 83-foot *Nokia*, had collided with *Sword of Orion* and Hugh Treharne's cruiser-racer, *Bright Morning Star*. *Sword of Orion* was damaged, with stanchions supporting the lifelines—the safety fence around the yacht's perimeter—torn out of the deck and a small crease in the aluminum mast. Treharne checked his boat and discovered the damage to *Bright Morning Star* was superficial. *Nokia's* only wounds were scarred topsides near the bow. Crews heatedly debated who was right and wrong and hoisted protest flags, bright red squares with a dovetailed trailing edge. But there was nothing more to do but get on with the racing and sort out the rest in the protest room in Hobart.

The incident didn't detract from the stunning spectacle of 115 yachts pushing their way toward the Sydney Heads in a strengthening sea breeze. The armada of spectator craft joined the charge, churning the narrow laneways reserved for them along the shore into a blur of whitewater. The race yachts tacked from one side of the harbor to the other, and after only minutes of racing the maxis, *Sayonara*, *Brindabella*, and *Wild Thing*, were at the head of the pack.

Less than fifteen minutes after the start, *Sayonara* showed the fleet the way around the first buoy off South Head. It continued in this authoritative manner, rounding the offshore mark ahead of the rest before turning south, setting her spinnaker aloft, and accelerating away in perfect downwind sailing conditions.

"Sayonara, Sydney."

Four
Sailing into a Brick Wall

A southerly buster is a summertime weather phenomenon that spreads its influence over much of the New South Wales coast. It is a bit like Nature turning on the air-conditioning to bring relief from the oppressive heat and humidity. Known originally as a burster, it has its origins in the early days of European settlement. For many decades inner-city Australians called it the "brickfielder" after the clouds of red clay dust it carried in from the St. Peters brickyard.

"It is a particularly viscous form of cool, southerly change—a shallow cold front that becomes trapped on the eastern side of the Great Dividing Range that runs down the Australian east coast," says Roger Badham. "It is locally enhanced by the strong temperature gradient across the front. The most violent southerly busters arrive in the Sydney region in the afternoon or evening, enhanced by the afternoon heating ahead of the change. They move up along the coast with clear or partly cloudy skies, sometimes with scattered thunderstorms.

"Southerly busters are most vigorous on the Illawarra and Central Coasts, particularly between Ulladulla and Newcastle. Immediately ahead of the buster the wind dies, then the southerly winds build very quickly (usually over ten to fifteen minutes) to 30 or 40 knots with occasional gusts up to 50 or 60 knots as it passes. However, the strong winds are generally short lived, easing to less than 30 knots within a few hours."

Sometimes a southerly buster is nothing more than a slight glitch in the Sydney to Hobart, a chilly whisper blowing only 20 or 30 knots and disappearing almost as quickly as it arrives. But occasionally they charge up the coast gusting up to 80 knots. They often follow strong northeasters, and the challenge for all racers is to predict just when they will hit. When the change does arrive, the yacht must quickly be converted from a downwind racing configuration into one that will cope with the approaching blast. The wind rapidly rotates through 180 degrees.

Sometimes the front's arrival can be quite daunting, heralded by a rolling, cigar-shaped, lead-colored cloud that stretches from horizon to horizon. Often there will be no visual warning in a clear sky, the only harbinger a sudden darkening of the ocean surface ahead as the wind whips the water. In just minutes a light breeze from astern can be replaced by more than 40 knots on the bow.

It's like sailing into a brick wall.

There is yet another unpredictable and challenging element for racers when a southerly buster blows—the fast-flowing southerly current that streams down the New South Wales coast, bringing warm tropical water from Queensland's Coral Sea. It can run like a river at three or more knots. Pit that massive current against a 40-knot gale from the opposite direction, and the ocean soon swells into liquid mountains.

The *Sayonara* team had impressed everyone with some slick work after their spinnaker blew apart just south of the Sydney Heads. In less than three minutes a new one was set. But in those conditions the American entry would have stiff competition. *Brindabella*, sporting a powerful new asymmetrical spinnaker, was pushing out to sea in search of the strongest current. She had drawn level with *Sayonara*; close behind, the syndicate-owned *Marchioness* was making its move.

Together with *Wild Thing*, the big trio headed the race at speeds approaching 20 knots. It was exciting, satisfying, but intense racing. Boat speed was paramount. Sails were continually trimmed while the helmsman worked the yacht down lingering blue swells in an effort to promote surfing. Long, white wakes streamed astern like vapor trails. There was constant talk about the weather, especially when the menacing gray-and-white clouds of a thunderstorm forecast for the evening could be seen building to the south. Belowdeck, navigators devoured the latest meteorological information from weather facsimile receivers.

Aboard *Young Endeavour,* radio operator Lew Carter and his assistants, Michael and Audrey Brown, were still hampered by communication problems. Just south of Sydney, Carter decided to contact the technician who'd installed the radio. His advice to Carter was to "continue with it for a while and see how you get on." That didn't sit too comfortably with the trio. Carter realized that the last opportunity to correct any problems would be off Wollongong, 45 miles south of Sydney. Again he contacted the technician.

"I wanted him to know that I wasn't happy at all," said Carter. "We thought we were going to get a hectic Hobart, and we needed everything to be spot on with the radios. The guy said that he had another radio at home. My problem was how the hell to get it on board. Fortunately for us, the police launch *Nemesis* was proceeding down the coast with the fleet as far as Eden. The obvious solution was to have the technician drive from Sydney to Wollongong with the new radio. He could be picked up by *Nemesis* there and carried out to us.

"There was quite a swell running—about 3 meters—and a strong wind blowing, but still the *Nemesis* crew did a marvelous job. The technician was worried about how he would get on and off *Young Endeavour* in those conditions, so I pulled a bit of a con job on him and told him all would be OK. I knew that once I had him on board I had no more worries. It wouldn't worry me if he couldn't get off, because we'd have our new radio and that was all we wanted. He could come all the way to Hobart with us as far as I was concerned. As it was, we did get him off and home. Four minutes after he left we had our first 'sked' with the fleet—loud and clear."

By 3 P.M., two hours after the start, Roger Badham had returned to his home south of Sydney. The moment he arrived he went straight to his office and hurriedly downloaded the latest weather prognosis from the international computer models.

He didn't like what he saw.

That afternoon he told a journalist, "I've just looked at all the latest charts and there's only one thing I can say. If I were on half those yachts out there this afternoon, I'd be taking my spinnaker down right now and turning back to Sydney. They're going to get hammered. There's a bomb about to go off in Bass Strait. A low is going to develop and intensify. They're going to get 50 knots, maybe more, and huge seas. This race is going to be worse than 1993."

The low-pressure system that formed over Bass Strait had its genesis in a sharp, cold, upper air trough that slowed, tilted, and deepened as it engaged warm, humid air pulled in from the northeast. Badham described it as "a textbook frontal low pressure development," quite common across the waters immediately south of Australia. The cold upper air mass showed up clearly on satellite images as it crossed the Great Australian Bight on the days immediately preceding December 26. Cut off from the upper air westerly flow when the system deepened to the surface during the early hours of Sunday, December 27, it was this "cold pool of air" that brought summer snow to the high country of Victoria and New South Wales that day.

The official race forecast issued from Sydney at 1450 hours (2:50 P.M.) on December 26 read as follows:

SYNOPTIC SITUATION: A HIGH NEAR NEW ZEALAND IS RIDGING ONTO THE CENTRAL NSW COAST. A LOW AT 995HPA NEAR LORD HOWE ISLAND IS SLOW MOVING. [Hectopascals, hPa, are equivalent to millibars, mb; thus, 995hPa is the same as 995 mb.] A COLD FRONT IS OVER CENTRAL VICTORIA.

WARNINGS: STORM WARNING IS CURRENT SOUTH FROM MERIMBULA.

GALE WARNING IS CURRENT SOUTH FROM BROKEN BAY.

WIND: NORTH TO NORTHEAST WIND 20/25 KNOTS AHEAD OF A W/SW CHANGE 25/35 KNOTS, WITH STRONGER GUSTS, EXPECTED NEAR JERVIS BAY AROUND MIDNIGHT–2 A.M. AND THEN NEAR SYDNEY AROUND 3 A.M.–5 A.M. SUNDAY. WIND MAY TEND BRIEFLY NORTHWEST 15/20 KNOTS PRIOR TO THE CHANGE.

WAVES: 1 TO 2 METERS, RISING TO 3 METERS OFFSHORE WITH W/SW CHANGE.

SWELL: 1 TO 2 METERS.

WEATHER: SCATTERED SHOWERS AND THUNDERSTORMS DEVELOPING TONIGHT AHEAD OF THE CHANGE, THEN CLEARING TOMORROW.

OUTLOOK FOR NEXT 48 HOURS: WINDS MODERATING NORTH OF JERVIS BAY SUNDAY NIGHT. GALE TO STORM FORCE W WINDS SOUTH OF JERVIS BAY EXPECTED TO MODERATE MONDAY EVENING.

The Bass Strait forecast issued from the Victorian Bureau of Meteorology office at 1646 hours read

EASTERN BASS STRAIT: NORTHEASTERLY WIND 20/30 KNOTS IN THE FAR EAST AT FIRST. A WEST/SOUTHWEST CHANGE AT 20/30 KNOTS EXTENDING THROUGHOUT THIS EVENING AND INCREASING TO 30/40 KNOTS TOMORROW MORNING AND TO 45/55 KNOTS DURING THE AFTERNOON. SEAS/SWELL 2 TO 4 METERS INCREASING 3 TO 5 METERS DURING THE MORNING AND 4 TO 6 METERS DURING THE AFTERNOON.

According to that forecast, there was going to be one hell of a battle in Bass Strait.

The crews hadn't yet heard the latest reports, but already the experienced sailors suspected something big was brewing. The northeasterly wind was strengthening all the time and was now well above the predicted velocity of around 25 knots. The sea breeze and favorable current remained so strong throughout the afternoon and evening that the entire fleet was ahead of the race-record pace set by the state-of-the-art German maxi, *Morning Glory*, two years earlier. Lew Carter, Michael Brown, and the *Young Endeavour* skipper, Lieutenant Commander Neil Galletly, noted that the fleet was flying. They were twice as far from Sydney as they were most years.

"We discussed with the skipper what we would do," recalls Carter. "We always talk tactics throughout the race because it's important for us to be in a position where we can be of assistance if needed, even though that's not our primary role. We try to keep ourselves about mid fleet, maybe with a leaning toward the back. We were up on the bridge and had a bit of a chat about the weather patterns and the current. We'd had a look at the chart and were talking about the problems that we might experience down the bottom, off the southeast corner of the mainland.

"The depth of the water drops dramatically as soon as you get beyond the 100 fathom line down there. We were thinking about the convergence of three to four knots of very warm current from the north against the waves from a southwesterly change. We decided if we were going to have any problems, it would be there."

They were right.

By midafternoon Gary Ticehurst had reconfigured the ABC helicopter so that it was ready to cover the race, and he and his two passengers, Scott Alle, a producer for the ABC, and cameraman Peter Sinclair, began their chase of the yachts down the coast.

"The plan was, as in most years, to lay over at Merimbula for the night," recalls Ticehurst. "We usually plan to arrive in Merimbula about half an hour before last light—it's 185 nautical miles south of Sydney. With such a strong following wind I was hoping we could cover the lead yachts and then come back in. On the way to them, and while flying over the smaller yachts, we were listening to the weather forecasts. They were predicting 40 to 50 knots. They said the change would come about midnight with local thunderstorms all the way down to the coast.

"Sure enough, they were spot on with the latter part. You could see the lightning. It was that typical, sultry gray afternoon and you could feel the change coming. One thing that was pretty impressive was the speed at which the entire fleet was traveling south. The forecast for 40 to 50 knots the next day didn't concern us. In fact it excited us. I thought, this is going to be a little bit tougher than just a southerly buster. This is going to last a day or two. We're going to get some action—great vision.

"When we arrived at Merimbula that evening, we literally had to poke our way around the thunderstorms to get to the airport. There were so many of them. It was pouring with rain, torrential rain. We were certain then that the fleet was going to cop it overnight—there'd be a few things going on. We wanted to be out over them at first light."

Throughout the afternoon and early evening the crews enjoyed exhilarating rides. Then, as darkness closed, there came the added spectacle of the huge thunderstorms Ticehurst had encountered, moving out from the land and across the course.

"What we saw was almost unbelievable," said John Messenger, sailing master of the maxi *Marchioness*. "The lightning was all over the place—horizontal and vertical. It was horrific. It lit up the night. It was incessant. The trouble was, we didn't know if the storm was going to bring the change or not. We were always on full alert. There was a bit of apprehension on board." *Marchioness* was at least level with and possibly ahead of *Sayonara* and *Brindabella*, which were farther out to sea. That situation changed in an instant.

"The wind was coming from around 035 degrees and blowing at around 20 knots. We had the spinnaker on and were really flying. We were surprised that the wind didn't drop when the thunderstorm got to us. Instead it held and began flicking between 035 and 350. We were forever chasing it, changing course all the time to keep the wind at the right angle over the stern. It was as though the wind couldn't make up its mind what to do. Suddenly one big wave got under our quarter and lifted the stern. We lost control and broached wildly. Now this is a big boat, but she stayed down on her side for what I guess was between three and four minutes."

Two burly blokes hung onto the wheel, keeping the rudder hard over in a desperate bid to get *Marchioness's* bow back toward course and give it a chance to come upright. A brief lull in the wind and the influence of another wave let the rudder bite the water—but all too quickly. With most of its twenty-two crewmembers clinging to a near-vertical deck, *Marchioness* bolted back upright, then took off downwind out of control at 20 knots. This time it speared off course the opposite way—to leeward. A classic flying gybe ensued.

The wind filled the mainsail from the opposite side, and the boom whistled across the yacht like a giant scythe. At the same time the spinnaker went aback. *Marchioness* was knocked flat once more, and the spinnaker filled with water instead of wind. Sheets and lines were tangled across the deck and under the hull.

John Messenger called for a cessation of racing. All sails were lowered and the spaghetti-like mess of sheets, wires, and lines was tidied up. It was thirty minutes before sails were hoisted and *Marchioness* rejoined the race.

With the northeasterly wind approaching 40 knots, Geoff Ross's *Yendys* (Sydney spelled backwards) was starting to do things a Beneteau 53 cruiser-racer had never done before: vibrating and humming and at times hitting 20 knots. By 10 P.M. the crew knew the time had come to take down the 1.5-ounce spinnaker. If they didn't, the rig might be ripped from the boat, especially if they broached and were knocked down. Just as the drop procedure started, *Yendys* went out of control, and the broach they'd sought to avoid was upon them.

"We were knocked well over," said Ross. "I was up to my thighs in water in the cockpit. The guy at the front of the boat for the drop, Peter Seary, wasn't clipped on and was sucked clean off the bow by the force of water. He was gone. What happened next was almost unbelievable. He shot down the side of the boat in the water and before you could even blink a huge wave picked him up, lifted him over the lifelines, and dumped him on the deck at the back of the cockpit. We were in a hell of a mess by then, and it would have taken a long while to turn back if we'd lost him."

By that time the spinnaker had all but taken itself down; it was blown to bits except for a small piece that fluttered like a flag from the halyard near the top of the mast. Seary went straight to the mast as though nothing had happened, clipped onto a halyard, and was hauled to the masthead to retrieve what was left.

Surprisingly, there had so far been no retirements. But this was soon to change. One of the race favorites, Ray Roberts's bright yellow 46-foot sloop *ABN Amro Challenge*, was the first to come to grief. It was spearing through the night when a sudden, sharp jolt hit first the keel and then the deep blade of the spade rudder. They had hit either a large sunfish or floating debris. The yacht careered out of control in an instant. The rudder had been ripped off and their race was run. It was a bitter disappointment for codesigner Iain Murray, who was aboard and hoping for a big win.

Around the same time another of the handicap honors contenders, Ron Jones's near new *Sledgehammer*, started limping back to port. The steering cables had chafed through.

Other crews, like that aboard Charles Curran's 60-footer, *Sydney*, were reveling in a great run down the coast. But *Sydney*'s race end was nigh. At 11:30 P.M., after averaging 18 knots for the previous ten hours, the crew heard a massive bang from the stern.

"We had the spinnaker up and were absolutely flying," said sailing master Dave Kellett. "While we searched for the cause of the first bang, there was another. We discovered that the lower rudder post bearing had shattered, and the rudder post was wobbling around. It didn't take much to realize that if we pushed on, the rudder post could break free and become a giant can opener. It would have opened up the hull."

They lowered the spinnaker, then the mainsail, then waited

patiently for the forecast southwesterly change. When it arrived they set a small headsail, turned the bow northward, and headed home.

Champion offshore yachtsman Roger Hickman, skipper of *Atara*, had completed twenty of the twenty-one Hobart races he had entered.

"The first night we had one of the most wonderful runs down-wind you could want," recalls Roger. "There was more lightning in the sky than I'd ever seen. At one stage I asked Peter Gardner, who's an extremely experienced sailor, if he wanted to have a drive. He said 'No, Hicko. It's your boat, so you play with it.' So play I did. I have to say that at the same time the situation was starting to concern me. I kept recalling what Ken Batt, the meteorologist, said not long before we left: 'You're going to have a lot on, Hicko.' He does a wonderful job representing the Bureau of Meteorology for the race, but unfortunately he's shackled by enormous bureaucracy. He and the other forecasters can't come out and make a punt on weather and give us a good guide. It always has to be so substantiated.

"What he said left me in no doubt that we were going to have plenty on once the change came. So we were already gearing up for 45 or 50 knots. We have a policy on *Atara*, and any other boat I race for that matter, that at 40 knots you get the mainsail down, roll it up on the boom, and then put the cover on it so that it can't catch water or blow away. That way you're as safe as houses. We just run with the headsail because you can get it down quickly if you have to and it doesn't go anywhere, like blow over the side. Our plan in a blow is to go to the storm trysail [a tiny, loose-footed triangular handkerchief of a sail that sets where the mainsail would otherwise have been] with a No. 4 headsail, whereas most boats go to the storm jib and then to the trysail."

Different styles of yachts employed different techniques going into that first night. The strengthening northeaster, which was registering more than 35 knots on some sections of the course, was surprising a growing number of experienced sailors. Even *Winston Churchill* was bowling along with a bone in her teeth—a big, white bow wave that was cut and curled away like shavings from a bar of soap before disappearing into the night. John Stanley was enjoying it.

"We set the spinnaker at a gentlemanly pace after turning south at Sydney, then proceeded down the coast, knowing all the time that we were going to be hit somewhere along the line that night. We were out to make the most of the northeaster while it was on and get down the track as fast as we could. The breeze got fresher and fresher to the point where we couldn't overload the old *Winston Churchill* too much. So we took the spinnaker off. It was probably blowing around 30 knots at that stage. We then poled out a No. 2 headsail until that too proved to be too much. We pulled that headsail off and gybed inshore when the wind started to back toward the north and northwest. It was around 35 to 40 knots then."

The *Kingurra* crew was also concerned with the way the weather was developing. "It was just beautiful sailing through the afternoon and early evening," said Peter Meikle. "We were doing 12 knots over the ground with between 2 and 3 knots of current assisting us. At that point we knew we were in for a little bit of a belting, but all the time things were beginning to not add up. We had no idea what we were in for, but we were uneasy: it just didn't seem quite right. It certainly seemed strange that the northeasterly was continuing to strengthen. I remember thinking when we got down to the 2.2-ounce spinnaker that things were a bit odd.

"The one good thing about it all was that on the first night out, as is always the case on *Kingurra* in a Hobart race, there was a roast coming up. We had this enormous hunk of beef in the oven with all the trimmings. The game for Peter was to see if he could get the roast out of the oven and served before the change came through. That was probably foremost in the minds of at least half the crew. The other half didn't plan on eating."

Up front, *Sayonara* and *Brindabella* were surfing down wave after wave and maintaining amazing average speeds. But the conditions were no longer concurring with the forecast. Larry Ellison sensed things were changing, and changing fast.

"We thought things were getting a little bit screwy when we

were hitting 42 knots of wind running away from Sydney. We were doing 24 to 26 knots under spinnaker."

The downwind roller-coaster ride continued well into the night. As midnight approached, many yachts had replaced their spinnakers with poled-out headsails, a snugger rig that was easier to control. The grand prix boats hung onto their "kites" until the wind began its abrupt change in direction toward the west, then southwest. Sometime between 1 A.M. and 3 A.M., the southwesterly hit the entire fleet with a vengeance.

"At 0230 hours the wind went to 350 degrees from 020 degrees, and the sea became difficult," recalls Roger Hickman. "We had hit speeds of 19 knots plus and had done 86 miles in four hours and ten minutes with between 2 and 3 knots of favorable current. I felt the fun was up. We downed the 0.9-ounce chute [spinnaker], then put up the jib-top and poled it out. We gybed and then settled down. All boats our size were either behind us or retired. *Ragamuffin* was out of sight and *Ausmaid* was a white light to seaward. The breeze swung quickly to the west, around 20 to 25 knots. With the No. 4 and two reefs we were in good shape."

"Mayday, mayday, mayday." The chilling call penetrated the airwaves at around 2:30 A.M., December 27. Crews on race yachts across the course scrambled to their radios. "This is *Challenge Again, Challenge Again, Challenge Again*. We have a man overboard!"

The incident had occurred when the 41-foot fiberglass production yacht went into a wild broach—a near capsize. The moment the man overboard shout went out the experienced crew did everything they could. Owner Lou Abrahams, a Sydney–Hobart race veteran out of Melbourne and one of Australia's best offshore sailors, had been hurled across the cabin from his seat at the navigation station during the broach. Though dazed, he clambered back to his seat, and his index finger went straight to activating the MOB (man-overboard) button on the GPS (Global Positioning System) unit. At least that would define the search area and increase the chance of recovering the man. Watch Captain Fraser Johnston, a similarly experienced ocean racing sailor and professional yacht delivery captain, was jolted from a light sleep.

"I'd just dozed off after finishing my watch," Johnston recalls. "We'd had little sleep that night because we'd been sailing so hard downwind. The next thing I knew the boat was broaching and I was pinned in the aft quarter berth. I heard 'Man Overboard' and thought, 'Oh, Christ, here we go.'"

As he struggled to free himself from the bunk and fight his way to the cockpit, his mind flashed back to the 1993 race. He had been aboard *Atara*, the yacht that extricated John Quinn from his five-hour, death-defying battle with the ocean in almost the same spot. Johnston knew that everything needed to go like clockwork if the man was to be recovered. They would probably get only one chance. "I ripped straight up on deck and asked in haste who it was. There was uncertainty. Someone shouted out, 'We think it's young Nick.'" All that mattered, though, was to get back to the person, whoever it was. Johnston could see that the helmsman, Col Anderson, was taking the necessary steps.

"All I saw was a blur go across the boat in front of me," recalls Anderson. "This body was hurled through the air, from the weather side through the gap between the deck and boom. With the yacht heeled over so far, he missed landing on the leeward rail and went straight into the tide. I pulled the boat up onto a reach so we could turn and go back to him on a simple reciprocal course when we were ready. Then I started the motor and called on the guys to make a quick check for lines over the side. We didn't want to foul the prop.

"Fraser was over the back trying to sort out the man-overboard buoy. It was a tangled mess with thin cord going everywhere. I shouted that there was only one thing to do—get all the bloody mess on board before we put the engine in gear, because even a little bit of shit cord is enough to wreck your prop. I remember seeing some of the crew coming on deck still half asleep, wondering what the hell was going on. All I could do was shout to them to get the mainsail and jib down."

Although the crew were trying desperately to get the main and headsail down, somehow the long cords connecting the components of the man-overboard system had tangled around the rudder while the yacht had been lying on its side. As he called for a knife, Johnston heard someone finally identify the man overboard. It was "Skippy"— Victorian policeman Garry Schipper—and he had a flashlight.

Johnston cut the man-overboard buoy free and let it down, then headed for the next most important thing: the engine control. He called on crew to prepare ropes to throw to Schipper when they got close to him. He checked once more for lines in the water, then engaged the gearshift lever. "It was terrific that Skippy still had the torch. But just as with the Quinn rescue, there was much excitement going on—the adrenaline was running. You must make sure you don't make a silly mistake under those circumstances."

One crewman, Richard Grimes, had kept his eyes glued to Schipper from the moment he hit the water. He pointed to him at all times so Anderson knew where to steer to get back to him. Schipper's life depended on it.

"We'd pulled down a headsail and stuffed it downstairs, so everyone below had been disturbed," recalls Gary Schipper. "They were all awake—which turned out to be a good thing. We'd changed from the reacher to the No. 4—no real drama—and were flogging along with probably 25 to 35 knots coming across the deck from the west. I was coming back to the cockpit from the bow. I had a safety harness on and it was attached to the jackstay. The problem was that there were sheets and stuff across the jackstay, so I couldn't get all the way back. I decided to unclip myself from the jackstay and then reattach on something closer to the cockpit. I wasn't concerned about doing that because the boat was sailing nicely—we hadn't broached at any stage.

"Wouldn't you know it, just as I unclipped we got hit by a rogue wave at the stern, under the boat. It knocked the stern to leeward, caused the boat to go into a broach, and laid her over on her side. I had been on my knees, braced against the cabin side. When we broached I overbalanced and wound up sliding across the cabintop on my stomach, straight over the safety rail and into the piss. I didn't even touch the rail. I was flying. I remember grabbing hold of a winch as I went, but it was slippery and I lost my grip. It's hard to stop my weight in full flight—147 kilos [323 pounds]. What I didn't realize at the time was that I had a waterproof flashlight in my hand and took it with me.

"I was fully rigged in foul-weather gear, thermal underwear, and seaboots, but the water was warm. It was small consolation. One of the crew thought quickly enough to grab another floating torch, turn it on, and hurl it into the water toward me. That would also help locate me when they could turn back.

"When I surfaced the boat was probably 10 or 15 meters from me and moving away, still at a reasonable pace. The first thing I could think of was that the weight of water in my boots and gear would be pulling me under. I knew I wasn't going to be able to swim for the boat. I thought, *Don't panic.* For an instant I remembered what John Quinn said after he'd spent five hours in the water in the 1993 race—he just tried not to panic.

"After about ten or fifteen seconds I realized I had the flashlight in my hand. I turned it on, and it worked. Hallelujah. I was able to shine the torch on the boat. They had stopped probably 250 meters from me. I knew they'd see me with the flashlight—but that wasn't my foremost concern at the time. I wanted to get out of my harness and other gear so I could tread water more easily. But it was bloody impossible to get my harness off, because everytime I stopped using my arms to tread water I started to sink. I just had to continue breast stroking.

"I eventually got one boot and a sock off. That was bloody difficult because, like so many others, I'd taped my boots on to keep the water out. It was a lot of effort for a small result. Everytime I tried to do something with the harness or my boots I started going under. The guys seemed to take forever getting back to me. Obviously they'd had their problems getting sails down and trying not to get any lines over the side and around the rudder or propeller. All I can say was that I was feeling very, very lonely. I was already exhausted. I was breathing heavy, probably because of the adrenaline rush. I was tiring, but I just kept treading water.

"When I saw the boat coming toward me I was still worried. I didn't know if they could still see me. I kept trying to shine the flashlight at them from above my head. The rest of the time it was just under the surface. Before long I realized they had me spotted. That was a relief. But when they made their run at me to pick me up I thought I was going to get the bloody bow right through my head. Fortunately it missed."

"It was pretty scary for Skippy," recalls Col Anderson, "but I had to get the boat really close to him. I had to be certain that the guys could grab him. It ended up that getting the yacht there was the easy bit. Getting him back aboard was hard."

Strong, eager hands grabbed whatever they could that was attached to Schipper and clung desperately to it. Their arms were now his lifelines. The crew were lying on their stomachs on the deck, leaning out over the side, and all the while the yacht was bucking and the waves were trying to tear him away. If he were ripped from their grasp he would almost certainly drown.

"A couple of the young guys grabbed me," Schipper recalled, wiping away tears. "Suddenly I saw them as my kids. They were clinging onto me; they didn't want to let me go. They were going to save me. They were terrific. They were all over me, leaning down over the side, hanging onto me, attaching bloody ropes everywhere so they wouldn't lose me."

The rough seas, Schipper's bulk, and problems with a special sling designed to lift crew back onto a yacht's deck made it a perilous and daunting task.

"The biggest problem for everyone was that I was so bloody exhausted I just couldn't help them. Everytime I got near to being in the sling I slipped out. Eventually they clipped a halyard onto my safety harness as well as the sling and finally winched me up to deck level. Then, while I was still suspended, they guided me across the cockpit and lowered me into the cabin, where I collapsed." Schipper had been retrieved little more than ten minutes after going over the side. Abrahams checked with him and the rest of the crew on how they felt about the race. Their decision was to continue.

"The crew was fantastic. Bloody professional. I was very, very fortunate. I had nine good guys backing me up in an extremely difficult situation."

Five
The Cauldron
Begins to Boil

On December 27, 1998, a meteorological bomb fell on the hapless Sydney–Hobart fleet. Many of the crews, and even some of the weather services, had no idea what was brewing in the northeast corner of Bass Strait. Weather faxes confirmed that the low, which for days vacillated over where it would unleash its brutal winds—south of Tasmania, west of Tasmania, or in Bass Strait—had now made up its mind. Weather forecasters in Sydney issued the following race forecast at 2:13 A.M.:

> WIND: W/SW WINDS 25/35 KNOTS, WITH STRONGER GUSTS. WINDS INCREASING TO THE SOUTH OF MERIMBULA OFFSHORE, REACHING 40/50 KNOTS THIS AFTERNOON AS LOW DEEPENS.

> WAVES: 2 TO 3 METERS, RISING TO 4 TO 5 METERS OFFSHORE IN THE SOUTH.

> SWELL: 1 TO 2 METERS, RISING TO 3 TO 4 METERS OFFSHORE SOUTH OF MERIMBULA.

From the time the fleet experienced the southwesterly change in the early hours of December 27 through to midmorning, sailing conditions deteriorated markedly. As forecast, the wind increased in strength to between 30 and 40 knots, and the waves grew in stature and number. The first twelve hours of racing had seen hard downwind running, then, after the change, the yachts were reaching across the wind. Little wonder that the two leaders, *Sayonara* and *Brindabella*, were soon well into Bass Strait and setting a race record pace. Some pundits speculated that if the speedy conditions prevailed, someone would break the magical two-day barrier, carving more than fourteen hours off the record.

At around nine o'clock in the morning, Roger Badham reported on the worsening weather to a media contact:

"The situation is starting to look very grim, especially for the boats that will enter Bass Strait later this afternoon and night. The 6 A.M. observations showed Wilsons Promontory with 71 knots of mean wind speed. The Promontory overreads some 25 to 33 percent in wind speed, but regardless, this was a very significant observation. Fifty to 60 knots seems certain."

Badham suggested the worst winds were probably in a thin, elongated band on the western flank of the low-pressure system that would drag over the fleet as the system moved east into the Tasman Sea later in the day. The strength of the west-southwesterly winds had forced most of the yachts east of the rhumb line, the 585-mile direct passage between Sydney and the first corner in the course, Tasman Island, at the entrance to Storm Bay. They were all benefiting from the south-flowing current.

Some navigators and tacticians had set a course well offshore believing it would prove fastest. Other crews found themselves 30 and 40 miles offshore due to the influence of the wind and waves. All these yachts now had their last remaining sanctuary before Bass Strait in Eden, almost directly upwind. Some crews were already discussing their options: to continue racing or to head for a safe haven on the New South Wales coast. Equipment failure made the decision for other vessels, like the maxi *Marchioness*. John Messenger had trouble slowing his yacht during the morning, even with a No. 4 headsail and three reefs. After losing the baby stay—which extends from halfway up the mast to the middle of the foredeck and controls the pumping action of the mast in rough weather—they considered fixing the fitting, but read the latest weather fax and decided the race was over for them. The crew tacked *Marchioness* and steered back toward Sydney.

Grant Wharington had seen a crack develop in the carbon fiber mast of his new yacht, *Wild Thing*, when it nose-dived. He advised race control at 6:30 A.M. that the maxi had retired and was heading for Eden. It was a disappointing result for the line honors favorite.

By midmorning Roger Badham was deeply concerned. Wilsons Promontory, in Bass Strait, less than 100 miles west of the rhumb line, had recorded a wind gust of 92 knots. It reaffirmed his belief that strong winds and terrible seas would strike the yachts off the southeast tip of Gabo Island, where the confluence of the currents would be at its worst. He again confirmed that the fiercest conditions would be between 3 P.M. that day and 3 A.M. the following morning, and predicted that more than half the fleet would be knocked out.

Badham later explained how the storm developed: "Intense low-pressure systems frequently develop across the waters around eastern Australia, and the Sydney–Hobart storm was right up there among the worst of them. This particular low-pressure system was a classic textbook development of a 'frontal' or 'secondary' low-pressure system. The original front and associated upper trough and vorticity center burst up from the Southern Ocean into the western region of the Great Australian Bight on December 23. On Christmas Eve and during Christmas Day the system began to intensify as it became strongly baroclinic—the associated jet stream winds becoming much stronger and wrapping around the whole vorticity center.

"Late on Christmas Day, telltale cirrus leaf-type clouds began to appear on the northeast side of the towering cumulus and thunderstorm clouds, indicating strong upper shear and guaranteeing surface convergence. A low-pressure system would develop in twenty-four to thirty hours, but where? Even at this time, the computer forecast models were uncertain of the exact location; it was still most likely to develop just off the Tasmanian coast, most probably between Flinders Island to the north and Maria Island to the south. At no point, until the low actually began to develop, did any of the models indicate that the low would 'spin up' within Bass Strait, west of the rhumb line.

"On Boxing Day, as the race started, the complex meteorology was unfolding. Only as the upper low and vorticity center entered western Bass Strait did it become apparent that the surface low was actually going to form in eastern Bass Strait and not off the Tasmanian coast. The surface low-pressure system deepened as air aloft was drawn away in the jet stream at a faster rate than the air could feed in at the earth's surface. The barometer readings over eastern Bass Strait were already low and still falling, but at Wilsons Promontory between 3 and 6 A.M. on the morning of December 27, the surface pressure fell 8.1hPa [8.1mb] in three hours. Good sailors know that such a severe pressure fall heralds Force 10—50 knots of wind speed.

"The morning of December 27 over southeast Australia was no normal summer morning. As the cold upper air spread across the highlands of Victoria and New South Wales, snow began to fall—good falls! The computer models gave forecasters exceptionally good guidance on every aspect of this weather system, except for the exact location of where the low was going to develop. Only in hindsight was it apparent that the U.S. MRF (Medium Range Forecast) global model picked the development many days ahead of time. As early as December 21, the MRF model output for December 27 indicated that a 986hPa low would develop immediately east of Flinders Island with southwest winds of 40 to 45 knots over the eastern Bass Strait. In fact, the MRF model consistently called for this development, whereas the other major models were far more uncertain in both the timing and position of the developing low pressure system. Such an intense and rapid development is unusual over Bass Strait during December, so it was logical for forecasters to expect the storm to develop further south.

"Forecasters, like anyone else, can be lulled into false thinking. For the two-week period leading up to Christmas, the ECMWF (European global model) had been the preferred model on nearly every day, but in the days leading up to the race, this model didn't offer consistent guidance with the low-pressure system. Both the GASP (Australia) and ECMWF models showed that the development would be weaker and would more likely be east or southeast of Tasmania—certainly not the intense system that actually developed over the eastern Bass Strait."

John Quinn, who had been rescued after five hours in a horribly turbulent and storm-ravaged ocean off the New South Wales coast in the 1993 race, now decided that he and his crew aboard *Polaris* would seek shelter and watch what developed before deciding to continue or retire. Quinn was a veteran of seventeen Sydney to Hobart races.

"We knew before the start that we were going to get a little bit of a blow. Initially we were talking about 30 to 45 knots, but as we went south the expectations went up to 45 to 55. We'd had a good run down the coast on the first day with a good set [current] behind us. The old *Polaris* was going like a bloody bullet, actually. We were being pushed out to sea, probably because the set had a bit of an easterly component. After the front came in we changed to two reefs in the main and a No. 4 jib. We were just slightly 'sprung' because I was sailing higher than course. I really wanted to be back on the rhumb line or just inside it by the time we got to Gabo.

"I suppose the wind was maxing out at a little above 30 knots at that stage. We ran the weather fax, which gave us a prognosis for 11 a.m. the next day, and we saw immediately it had changed a lot from the previous day's prognosis. It showed a low in the same position, but instead of being at 990hPa, it was down at 984hPa. I said to the guys, 'Oh shit, this is not good. This is another '93. There's going to be a lot of damage tonight.' The fax showed this bloody tight little eyeball, down at 984, just squashed between a high and the land. In reality it looked as if it was going to be a bit worse than '93. I added only one comment: 'We're going for shelter.' I passed the weather fax around, and nobody disagreed."

Quinn knew their best option was to tack and aim the yacht directly at the coast. A bay just south of Eden was the eventual target. The new course meant *Polaris* was sailing away from the low, toward presumably better conditions, after which they would continue on to Hobart. Quinn had been enjoying a race within a race with two sisterships, Tony Mowbray's *Solo Globe Challenger* and Peter Heanley's *Ruff N Tumble*, both from Lake Macquarie, north of Sydney. They were fiberglass Cole 43 designs, sweetly proportioned 43-foot (13.1 meter) yachts about twenty years old. Mowbray, a sailmaker from Newcastle, had once owned *Polaris*. In 1984 he sailed it nonstop around Australia with one other crewmember "just for the heck of it." It was a fifty-four-day voyage.

Mowbray had bought *Solo Globe Challenger* in Melbourne six months before the Hobart race but had no intention of competing. His goal was even grander: to set sail in October 1999 on a single-handed, nonstop odyssey around the world. He planned to follow the course taken by Australia's Kay Cottee in 1988 and to use the voyage to raise money for the local John Hunter Children's Hospital. While he was preparing the yacht, friends suggested he enter the Sydney to Hobart and offered to help with the substantial financial require-ments. It was an offer he couldn't refuse.

The rig was removed from the boat for five weeks and com-pletely rebuilt to the standard required for the circumnavigation. Its final engineering specifications far exceeded what the average Hobart race could dish up. Mowbray decided to combine experience and youth in the race crew. His mentor, Bobby Snape, who would make his twenty-third trip south, was his first choice for the team of eight.

"We weren't going out there with guns ablaze and trying to win," said Mowbray. "We were going to have a go, for sure, but really we were only just in there to make up the numbers. At the same time I spent a lot of time getting the boat ready because I'm not the sort of person who goes to sea undercooked."

After a great run down the coast that saw them ahead of their arch rivals, the *Solo Globe Challenger* crew were justly content. Early on Sunday morning, when the breeze started to clock around to the north and northwest, they gybed the yacht and headed back inshore to maximize their advantage. Mowbray noticed that the wind strength was fluctuating. Toward the end of the morning, they were southeast of Gabo Island, approximately 30 miles into Bass Straits and had done a respectable 210 miles in twenty-five hours.

Rob Kothe and the crew of *Sword of Orion* were closely moni-toring two concerns overnight and into the morning of December 27: the crease in their mast and the weather. Kothe found weather analy-sis and application as satisfying as reading a good book: the more he got into it the more he enjoyed it. He used the SatCom C unit and weather fax and kept close tabs on the reports on the radio channels. When the wind began to move toward the north, then northwest around midnight, the crew dumped the spinnaker and went to a poled-out No. 3 headsail. The best current was along the edge of the continental shelf, and by 2 or 3 A.M. they were still making good time. When the wind started to move toward the west, then southwest early in the morning, they went to a double-reefed mainsail.

At around three in the morning, crewmember Sam Hunt discovered a serious problem aboard *Sword of Orion*: bananas! Hunt had been rummaging through the galley for a snack when he found them.

"Superstition on the *Sword* says you don't have bananas aboard," said Kothe. "Sam decided they were the reason for our start-line 'bingle' with *Nokia*—so he made us eat all the bananas. Then he discovered a banana cake! That was just as bad as having bananas, so he made us eat all the banana cake because we didn't need any more bad luck. There we were, all sitting around stuffing ourselves with bananas, then banana cake. As it turned out, it would be the last solid meal we'd eat for a while. We were all fueled up."

As *Sword of Orion* sailed into a rugged gray dawn, Kothe was listening on the radio to the Bass Strait oil rigs reporting their weather conditions. When he started to hear 987hPa as a barometric pressure reading, he called Eden Coast Guard and asked them what was happening in their vicinity. As the winds increased in strength, the crew continued to reduce sail but still had no thoughts of retiring. The wind was then starting to top 40 knots. The fast-flowing east-coast current and wild waves coming in from the west were colliding. It was now clear that the yachts in the middle to back of the fleet would be the ones to feel the full force of the storm.

Averaging 15 knots since the start of the race, *Sayonara* and *Brindabella* were neck and neck and had entered Bass Strait before sunrise. Around dawn, ABC chopper pilot Gary Ticehurst and his television crew were airborne and heading away from Merimbula in search of the leaders. He was stunned when they found the fleet.

"I've never in sixteen years seen them so far south. We got to *Brindabella* first, and she was in 40 to 50 knots from the southwest.

The seas were already around 30 feet, with nasty breaking tops. I remember one shot Pete got while we were hovering alongside *Brindabella*. She came out of this wave and the front half dropped about 15 feet into the trough. The whole mast vibrated and the boat shook."

Brindabella had already lost communications. The crew had missed the morning sked and was anxious to have a message relayed back to *Young Endeavour* and to shore that they were progressing well. Ticehurst did the relay for them. He then turned east and found *Sayonara*, about 5 nautical miles abeam of *Brindabella*, fairing somewhat better due to more favorable weather conditions. Ticehurst was astonished to find such wild weather fluctuations in such a small area.

Sayonara's navigator, Mark Rudiger, was troubled: the digital barograph was dropping alarmingly and the satellite imagery showed they were right in the middle of the system. After scanning weather faxes and forecasts with Rudiger, Larry Ellison was convinced they were tackling a storm of hurricane proportions. He was right. A hurricane was forming right where *Sayonara* and the other big boats were sailing. Fortunately for them, they would be far enough south to miss the worst of the wind and seas. Those following, however, were headed straight for the cauldron.

Team Jaguar Infinity III, owned by Sydney's Martin James, had covered 220 miles in the first twenty hours of the race. The eighteen crewmembers were comfortable and increasingly confident they would achieve their goal of a top-five place across the line. The 65-foot sloop was George Snow's previous *Brindabella*. Built in 1989, it took line-honors in the 1991 Hobart. Since assuming ownership, James had gone to great lengths to improve the performance, including having a carbon fiber mast fitted for the 1997 race. When *Team Jaguar* was about two hundred miles down the course, that very expensive piece of equipment sheered at deck level and tumbled over the side.

This year, with the reliable old aluminum mast in place, the crew aboard *Team "Jag"* were hoping for better fortunes. The crew included Melissa McCabe, a student at Eden Marine Technology High School who had been chosen from a host of applicants by the race sponsor, Telstra, to sail as part of a sporting youth promotion scheme in rural regions. The CYC had organized offshore and inshore sailing training for her so she would be fully prepared.

In the early hours of December 27, the crew of *Team Jaguar* pushed into Bass Strait, thinking they were prepared for what lay ahead. The yacht was sailing comfortably around 10:30 A.M., traveling at around 13 knots with the sheets slightly eased and little heel. Principal helmsman Tim Messenger had the mainsail trimmer easing the mainsail to cope with gusts. The sleek green-and-white sloop rose over a 25-foot wave, crested it, and plunged into the trough. The shockload of the landing, though not severe, was enough to make the yacht shudder. Looking up at the mast, the trimmer saw a diagonal piece of stainless steel rigging (the D2) break with a loud bang. The rig began to fold like a broken wing.

The yacht had suffered considerable damage, leaving the crew with the onerous task of repairing what they could. The crew used hacksaws to cut away the rigging, but as the mast went over the port side it took with it several stanchions and lifelines, the VHF radio antenna, the HF backstay antenna, the GPS unit, the satellite communications unit, and dan buoys and life rings from the stern! After waiting ten minutes or so to ensure that the mast had indeed sunk and was well out of the way, Messenger returned to the helm and set a course between 350 degrees and due north so that the seas came at the yacht from the port aft quarter, 45 degrees off the stern, a comfortable angle.

They motored steadily for nearly two hours, fearing a mammoth wave would topple them. When it finally came, the yacht resembled a watermelon seed squeezed between two fingers. The wave caught the stern of *Team Jaguar*, and the yacht nose-dived almost half its length before it was tossed sideways. The mastless yacht rolled to more than 90 degrees. Two crewmembers, one sitting near the companionway stormboards and the other on the starboard side of the cockpit, were caught by the broken crest of the wave and hurled over the side. When the hull settled, the crew scrambled to grab the "swimmers'" safety harnesses and haul them back into the cockpit. Messenger thought the engine had simply stalled, but in fact one of the crew who had gone over the side had grabbed a fabric bag fitted in the cockpit where many of the sheets and lines had been stored. In the water, the ropes had burst out of the bag and ensnared the propeller, strangling the motor. It would take a diver in Eden an hour to remove the tangle.

The thirteen crew below deck, many by now chronically seasick, had been hurled about the cabin. Hundreds of gallons of water had been forced below: through a gap in the stormboards; via the hole left where the instrument panel had been in the cockpit; through the mast gate in the deck; and through various control line exits. Incredibly, the forward hatch had not imploded, despite fantastic pressure. The deck had compressed six inches, and the deck frame above the galley had fractured. The compression on the main cabin grab post sheared it at the deckhead.

The eighteen crewmembers had neither propulsion nor communications, they didn't know their position, and they were aboard a badly damaged yacht. They activated their remaining means of communicating with the outside world, the EPIRB. While some crewmembers began pumping and bailing, two others attempted to rig a whip antenna for the HF radio. Later they succeeded, contacting Race Control aboard *Young Endeavour* to advise them of the situation.

Locky Marshall, a professional fisherman out of Eden for some fifteen years, had witnessed plenty of rotten Sydney to Hobart weather. When the police car arrived at his home in the midafternoon of December 27, he sensed a request for assistance would follow. Local Sergeant Keith Tillman told him that a yacht, *Team Jaguar*, was in trouble in Bass Strait. Marshall and Tillman went directly to Marshall's office on Eden's commercial fishing dock.

Moira Elizabeth, the rugged 70-foot steel trawler that Marshall managed, was just heading for Gabo Island to shelter from the storm.

It was on a passage to Portland, on Victoria's Bass Strait coast, when the weather forced a retreat. Marshall called the skipper, Tom Biddy, on the radio and asked if he could go to the assistance of *Team Jaguar*. The severity of the storm and the yacht's distance from the trawler made Biddy hesitate, but the eighteen lives at stake prevailed.

Biddy turned the helm of *Moira Elizabeth* to starboard, and the big boat plowed the horrendous seas into Bass Strait, making a mere five knots. He plotted an approximate position for *Team Jaguar*, then tried to calculate the drift in those conditions. An intercept position was plotted and an ETA of 11 P.M. advised.

Team Jaguar's drift was far greater than even its crew could anticipate; at times up to 6 knots, it turned a "perfect intercept" into a dangerous downwind chase. Five hours after the initial ETA, *Moira Elizabeth*, its deck and searchlights ablaze, loomed high over a mountainous wave and finally cornered its quarry; another nine hours passed before the trawler was able to tow *Team Jaguar*, the majority of its crew still in shock, into Eden.

In the early afternoon of December 27, *Young Endeavour* was just south of Montague Island, around two hundred miles from Sydney and carrying little more than steadying sails. The officers' wardroom had, as in previous years, been converted into the communications center for Lew Carter and his fellow radio officers. A comfortable rectangular cabin, about 4 by 3 meters, it lies one deck down from the main deck and a few meters aft of the bridge.

The cream-colored sidewalls and bulkheads were crowded with memorabilia, primarily plaques and photographs, including a signed photo of Queen Elizabeth II and the Duke of Edinburgh. These and other photos told of *Young Endeavour*'s many voyages, visits, and visitors over the previous decade. Carter and Michael and Audrey Brown were seated on the dark, floral-patterned lounge in one corner of the cabin with the bank of radios—HF for long-range communications and VHF for the more local links—on a table immediately in front of them. They were preparing for the 1405 (2:05 P.M.) sked. Carter would broadcast to the yachts the special race weather forecast received from the Bureau of Meteorology in Sydney.

Three times a day, prior to each sked, the radio room receives a weather forecast specially compiled for the Sydney to Hobart. The staff breaks the forecast into sectors, depending on where the fleet is located. It may be from Sydney to Gabo Island, Gabo to Flinders Island on the other side of Bass Strait, or Flinders to Tasman Island. There is an additional report for Storm Bay and the Derwent River.

Carter and Michael Brown read the 12:09 P.M. weather report received from the Sydney Bureau:

WIND: W/SW 25/35 KNOTS, WITH STRONGER GUSTS, INCREASING TO 40/50 KNOTS OFFSHORE SOUTH OF MERIMBULA TODAY. WIND DECREASING TO 15/25 KNOTS NORTH OF MERIMBULA MONDAY AND 25/35 KNOTS SOUTH OF MERIMBULA DURING MONDAY.

WAVES: 2 TO 3 METERS, RISING TO 4 TO 5 METERS OFFSHORE IN THE SOUTH TODAY.

SWELL: 1 TO 2 METERS, RISING TO 3 METERS IN SOUTH.

A second race forecast was issued from Hobart at 1240 hours:

FORECAST FOR NEXT 24 HOURS—38S TO 40S: WEST TO SOUTHWEST WINDS 30 TO 40 KNOTS—LOCALLY 40 TO 50 KNOTS NEAR THE VICTORIAN COAST—EASING TO BE 25 TO 35 KNOTS BY EARLY MONDAY MORNING THEN 20 TO 25 KNOTS BY MIDDAY. 5 TO 6 METER SEAS SLOWLY ABATING. SOUTHWEST SWELL 3 METERS. SHOWERS. VISIBILITY FAIR TO GOOD.

At around the same time, 1210 hours, the Victorian Office issued the following forecast:

EASTERN BASS STRAIT: WEST/SOUTHWEST WINDS AT 45/55 KNOTS EASING TO 30/40 KNOTS OVERNIGHT AND TO 20/30 KNOTS TOMORROW. SEAS/SWELL 5 TO 7 METERS ABATING TO 3 TO 5 METERS OVERNIGHT AND TO 2 TO 4 TOMORROW.

In the minutes leading up to 2:05 P.M., all navigators aboard the ninety-plus yachts still at sea were tuning their radios into *Young Endeavour*. Many of the off-watch crews, prone in their narrow bunks, had their ears pricked, anxiously awaiting the forecast as well as news of what was happening elsewhere on the course. They also wanted to know how they were performing against their opponents. Some crew, though, were already too seasick to care. The yachts were now climbing swells some 30 to 40 feet high, and despite the helmsman's best intentions there was not always a soft landing on the other side. Often the yacht would spear into midair, all 10 or 20 tons of it, and plunge down into the trough that followed. It was like repeatedly launching a truck off a 30-foot ramp and awaiting the crash.

Many competitors didn't know that wind strengths and wave heights given in official forecasts were merely mean, or average, figures. For wind strengths, a plus-or-minus factor of 1.4 can be estimated; for wave heights the factor is 1.86. Thus, for example, a mean wind of 50 knots can be expected to bring gusts of up to 70 knots.

After broadcasting the weather forecast, Carter began to call all yachts in alphabetical order for their position on the race course. At that stage *Sword of Orion* was around seventy miles south of Gabo Island. Rob Kothe had wedged himself into the nav station. Every massive wave—some waves peaking at 40 feet—threatened to dislodge him from his seat and the resting crew from their bunks. On deck, the two on-watch crew were securely harnessed to strong points. They had been in "storm-mode" since early that morning and had thus far evaded seasickness. Kothe continued to gather information and plot the weather into the afternoon, checking the barometric pressure constantly.

By the time the sked had reached the letter F for position reports, Kothe was amazed that no one had talked about the weather. He knew that doing so would breach race radio procedures and might be seen as providing outside assistance to other yachts, but he also knew that the "thumbprint" of the swirling storm on the chart in front of him and what was going on outside should outweigh everything. His decision to say something and warn others came only moments later.

"They were calling yachts that were six or seven before us on the list when our wind speed instrument read 78 knots," he recalls. "The boat was now laying over fairly well on its side. I considered it a safety issue. So what I did was I gave my sked position and I said to Lew that during this sked we have had wind strengths regularly over 60 gusting to 78."

It was a statement that echoed in a frightening fashion around the fleet. For the first time, every crew, every navigator, and every skipper knew that this storm was developing horrific proportions. The news hit like a hammer and confirmed their worst fears. Most yachts were then between 30 and 100 miles from shore.

"It's important during the sked that we don't get any chatter on the air," said Carter. "We try to get through the position reports— otherwise you find that you block up the airwaves for way too long. But I consider that what Kothe did was wise. To alert myself and others of the pattern of wind that he was getting was commendable. On hearing that report, I asked if any other yachts were in the area and could confirm what *Sword of Orion* was saying. *Yendys*, owned by Geoff Ross, came in. It was a little bit north and east of *Sword* and confirmed the weather conditions. I spoke to *Sword* again, and they confirmed gusts of 80 knots, and that the seas had really built up. They were breaking over the boat, but they didn't show any concern at that stage.

"Considering the circumstances, and the fact that I was in charge of communications, I took it upon myself to broadcast to the fleet a suggestion to the skippers that they consider their situations. I suggested that, with night approaching, the seas building, and the knowledge that there were worse winds further down the track, they take a good look at their position. If there was any suggestion of motor trouble, rig trouble, or seasickness, my suggestion would have been to seek shelter. Not necessarily to retire, but to seek shelter for the evening until the weather improved and maybe continue on in the race after that. I repeated that a couple of times. At that stage quite a few yachts decided to either seek shelter or retire."

Fundamental Rule 4 of the Australian Yachting Federation's

Racing Rules of Sailing reads: A boat is solely responsible for deciding whether or not to start or to continue racing.

In his twenty-five years of being part of the race, nine as radio
officer, Lew Carter had never seen nor heard anything like it. And
for the first time he and the Browns needed to reassess their options.
They called the skipper down and discussed their own situation. They
decided not to proceed into Bass Strait but to monitor an area north
of Eden down to Gabo Island and 20 miles out to sea.

Little more than an hour after the sked, the storm had begun
to turn. The waves were now huge, some six stories high and many
near vertical. They were breaking as though pounding a coastal
beach. They weren't the usual rolling monsters, and they had no
pattern. The waves made a low, powerful roar, and the wind shrieked
through the rigging. Yachts with their smallest of sails set heeled
over at precarious angles as they were raked by the wind and pummeled by the seas.

Most yachts had only one storm sail set—either a storm jib or
trysail—to maintain steerage over the raging waves. Sometimes the
yacht had to slow in order to avoid being overwhelmed by a cascading
wall of broken white water. Even the maxis were being flogged mer-
cilessly. On board *Sayonara* Larry Ellison had never seen anything like
it. At one stage, caught on deck without a harness, he was lucky not to
be swept away. Helmsman Chris Dickson tried to deal with the worry
his life-threatening situation must have been causing his wife of less
than a week, Sue, who was waiting for him in Hobart.

America's Cup winning tactician and Hobart race veteran
Hugh Treharne was similarly stunned by the waves he was seeing:
endless 20-foot monsters with broken white water stretching to
the horizon. Almost every crew discussed whether to retire or continue. For most, retiring meant the same set of conditions on the
opposite tack. Those farther east faced an enormous upwind battle
back to safety. The options were to continue, turn back, hove-to
with a small storm sail set and the helm locked, or lie a-hull and
just drift under "bare poles," with no sails set.

Tough little *Canon Maris* was coping admirably with the conditions and was pushing well into Bass Strait by midafternoon. While the yacht was handling it under a No. 4 headsail and reefed mizzen and was in second position on handicap, Ian Kiernan was annoyed with himself. If conditions worsened, it might be safest to set a sea anchor and ride out the storm. A sea anchor is something sailors can use to slow a boat's progress. It takes the form of a drogue, in the old days a large canvas tube that looked like a windsock, that can be set just below the water surface behind the yacht. But modern race yachts don't carry such cumbersome equipment.

"I realized I'd forgotten some of the good things that I'd learned about seamanship with this yacht over the years," Kiernan recalls. "I used to carry an old car tire for a sea anchor and 50 to 60 fathoms of heavy polypropylene line. I have a special bridle that drops over the primary winches in the cockpit. The bridle trails out over the stern of the boat. You attach the polypropylene line and sea anchor or the car tire—even an anchor on a chain, if you want—to the bridle and just ride it out. It allows the boat to slow down and keep its transom to the approaching wave, and it lets the transom rise. By having it attached at the cockpit and not the stern, the hull can 'hinge' with the waves: the stern can rise as the crest approaches. Jack Earl taught me this. As things got worse in Bass Strait, Dick said, 'We've got to slow this boat down.' Without a sea anchor, the only way I could slow it down was to go to a spitfire jib, so that's what we did. I didn't want to go to a trysail because we would be over-canvassed to buggery. We would've had to take down the mizzen, and then we wouldn't have been balanced."

Life aboard an ocean racing yacht is cramped at the best of times, but in a vicious storm it's abominable. Seasickness incapacitates some crew: they become almost comatose and are unable to help themselves, let alone contribute to sailing the yacht and surviving. Stronger crewmembers often have to care for the incapacitated crew as well as for the boat. Life below deck is miserable. Consider having ten people inside a narrow and extremely small caravan; there is barely any headroom, and because there are insufficient bunks most people are prostrate on the floor atop wet sail bags. Everything is sodden, people are vomiting and moaning, and this cavern of horrors is buffeted, bashed, and belted by mountainous waves. That's when the sufferers agree that the joy of ocean racing is one of the world's best kept secrets.

Dave Haworth's experience aboard *Foxtel-Titan Ford* painted the grim picture with sobering clarity. For him the Hobart is an occupational hazard. He's a very talented television cameraman who happens to love sailing. Not surprisingly, he is one of the first to be called when it comes to racing aboard a Hobart yacht and shooting film for the news and race reports. The 1998 race was his fifth and roughest, but he recalls that even when they were in the thick of it they didn't consider turning back.

"Once the shit hit the fan—when we were hit by bombs—it became chaos. It's hell on board. For one, you can't stand up. The whole boat is subject to violent movement all the time. You're standing in the cabin one minute hanging on, and next thing you know you've been hurled into your bunk or headfirst into the stove. That's how a lot of people were injured—including Stan Zemanek and another guy and girl on our boat. You might be hanging on, but as far as I can see the only safe place is on the floor. You'll be hanging on—the boat will come up out of a wave and it will just drop, almost like a free fall. You're still standing where you were, but the whole boat has all of a sudden moved around you. Then, when it thumps into the bottom of the wave and stops, you are still moving. You catch up with it. You think you're in a safe spot, but there is no safe spot.

"Down below there's just people everywhere. It's a disaster scene, and it's disgusting. A lot of people are just dead to the world. They're in the bunks and they're just quiet. They don't move. Everything is wet. If it's not wet, it's damp. There's water sloshing around over the floorboards. In our case we had diesel fuel sloshing everywhere because one of the tanks had ruptured, which made the whole thing even more dangerous. It was like a skating rink. Everything was like ice, it was so slippery."

Those who were capable did what they could, when they could, to purge the bilge of its fetid cocktail. Dave Haworth paid a price.

"One of the guys, Tony, had been bucketing out the bilge for some time, so I thought I should do my bit and give him a hand," Haworth recalls. "He passed me a bucket that was bloody full, just four or five inches from the top. I started to pass it up from the cabin through the hatchway to Johnno, who was standing on deck so he could pour it out over the side. Just as I passed it up the boat fell out of a wave. Johnno didn't have hold of it properly, and the whole thing tipped back down all over me, from my head down. I had my bib-and-brace wet weather trousers on and the bib at the front was loose, so it acted like a funnel. I could just feel it go all the way down the back and front of my trousers, down through the legs. There was vomit, piss, diesel, salt water, and I'm thinking, 'This is pretty low. This is a low point in the race.' All I did then was go up into the cockpit and sit there wanting a couple of big green waves to wash over me. I didn't care that my thermals and other clothing were soaking wet. I couldn't live with myself. I just wanted to go into the rinse cycle."

By late afternoon crews were facing a new fear: darkness. The crew of *Sword of Orion*, like so many others, watched the barometer continue its descent. It was heading toward 982hPa. Weather faxes only confirmed what they already knew. The cauldron was well and truly boiling.

Part Two

Six Destined for Disaster

When Lew Carter began the 1405 sked on December 27, the off-watch crew aboard the South Australian yacht *VC Offshore Stand Aside* were listening intently. They wanted to report their position and let everyone know they were safe, and they needed the latest weather forecast. They also wanted to know how they were faring against other yachts from Adelaide. To keep radio airtime to a minimum, Carter called each yacht's name and waited for a response: the yacht would repeat its name, then give a latitude and longitude. Michael and Audrey Brown would each note the positions and cross-check them later.

"*VC Offshore Stand Aside*," called Carter.

There was no response.

"Nothing heard," he said before moving onto the next yacht. At the end of the sked he went back through the yachts that had failed to respond and called *Stand Aside* again.

Nothing.

Stand Aside had just become a casualty.

Sailed by Jim Hallion, the 41-foot fiberglass composite sloop was built in New Zealand. It was a Young 12 class—a plump, relatively lightweight design renowned for its downwind speed. Hallion, his brother Laurie, and a friend bought the yacht soon after it was launched in 1990 and had raced with some success in St. Vincent Gulf around Adelaide and across Spencer Gulf to Port Lincoln. The Sydney to Hobart was an inevitable goal, and 1998 was its debut.

In early December, *Stand Aside* left Adelaide for Sydney with a crew that included some of those who would be aboard for the Hobart and a couple of friends. Trevor Conyers, a Hobart race rookie but capable offshore sailor, was aboard for the delivery to Sydney. Conditions were reasonably smooth until the yacht reached Cape Jervis, and the crew decided to pull into Wirrinya for the night and head for the local pub, expecting to set off the following morning when the weather had cleared.

Although it didn't improve, they pushed on the next day and reached Kangaroo Island about lunchtime. They stopped on the island's eastern end to eat. Jim Hallion had caught a virus that refused to go away, and when they set sail again around eight that evening, his condition quickly worsened. The rotten weather soon took its toll on most of the crewmembers, and they decided to turn back to Wirrinya. Conyers sailed back almost single-handed. Considering Hallion's condition, that time was rapidly running out for the trip to Sydney, and that bad weather might further delay them, they decided to return to Adelaide and put the yacht on a truck.

One week before the start of the Sydney to Hobart *Stand Aside* was docked at the CYC, rigged and ready to race. The crew was in good spirits and confident. One of the crewmembers, forty-five-year-old father of three Mike Marshman, in his second Hobart, had taken up sailing only seven years earlier. Before his first in 1997 aboard Gary Shanks's *Doctel Rager*, he'd proudly announced, "I don't get sick and I don't get scared."

On the ride down the coast on December 26, *Stand Aside*'s crew were "whooping and hollering" as the yacht notched an average speed of around 18 knots on a tailor-made spinnaker run. With spinnaker and mainsail straining in the building sea breeze, *Stand Aside* was picked up by a sharp following sea and hurled down its face, surfing for hundreds of meters. It was exhilarating sailing. That evening, as they threaded between two spectacular thunderstorms, the crew regularly monitored their radio. Like so many competitors, they still weren't exactly sure what they were in for.

By the morning of December 27, they were "nicely placed." As the wind strengthened and the seas grew, they reduced their sail area correspondingly. *Stand Aside* handled the conditions surprisingly well, only occasionally spearing off the backs of waves. The twelve crewmembers were far from comfortable, but they were happy with the yacht's performance. They sailed under a storm jib until early afternoon, when the weather seemed to go from bad to horrific in just a few minutes. Gusts were strengthening—first 55 knots, then 60, and soon 70.

Stand Aside staggered under the storm jib and was getting flattened by gusts on the wave crests. They decided to lower the jib and run under bare poles until the weather improved. But there was no talk of retiring or returning to Eden. At 1 P.M. they were well into Bass Strait. They knew if they could reset sail soon and get the boat back to speed, they would be off the Tasmanian coast around midnight.

As on most other yachts in such atrocious weather, on *Stand Aside* a crewmember was posted on "wave watch," since the helmsman could not look upwind into the near horizontal rain and spray. The man on wave watch shouted information on how best to angle the boat for the approaching wave. The one thing none of the crew liked hearing on deck was "This one's going to break!"

As the weather continued to worsen, they faced two choices: ten to twelve hours back to Eden or about eight hours forward to the other side of Bass Strait. They decided to continue. With no sail set, *Stand Aside* was beginning to behave erratically. It was difficult steering up and over the monster waves, so the helmsman decided to "let her have her head," letting the yacht find its own way down the wave's face. He would use the helm only if or when possible.

Much of the time, *Stand Aside* was choosing a course more toward New Zealand than Tasmania. No one wanted to finish on the other side of the Tasman Sea and fly home, so they set a storm jib again. With the wind blowing more than 70 knots and the yacht tossed by mighty seas, resetting the sail took forty minutes. *Stand Aside* returned to a more desirable course as the 1405 sked approached. Rod Hunter and Andy Marriette were wedged into the tiny navigation area to starboard, near the bottom of the companionway, waiting for the position reports to commence.

The forecast from *Young Endeavour* certainly didn't correlate with what the *Stand Aside* crew was experiencing. Hunter and Marriette discussed the seeming chasm between forecast and fact and agreed that their position meant the yacht was right on the edge of the worst of the depression. They also agreed, based on the forecast, that things would get better sooner rather than later. They were aware that numerous yachts had retired and weren't surprised to hear *Sword of Orion* warn the fleet that it had experienced 78 knots of wind.

"*Young Endeavour* was about three quarters of the way through the sked when I heard one of the guys on deck shout with considerable alarm, 'A real bad wave, *watch out!*'" recalls Marriette. "The boat went up and up and then we started to roll, and roll rapidly. The noise was sickening—first it was water pouring in like a river through the companionway, then there were cracking and tearing sounds. The deck and cabintop were splitting open."

The cabin roof had imploded. The force of the water as the yacht rolled tore away a huge section around the companionway slide. It hinged down like a giant trapdoor and pinned both Hunter and Marriette in the nav station. To Marriette's amazement, when the yacht came back upright he found himself in the same position as when it all started—still holding the radio microphone. The two set about smashing their way out of the nav station to save themselves and whoever else might still be on board.

Bob Briggs rushed up from the cabin and started calling out names to make sure everybody was still on board. To his horror he saw John Culley swimming frantically toward what was now a wrecked yacht. Culley had been going on deck to attach his safety harness to a strong point when *Stand Aside* rolled.

Mike Marshman was one of the eight crewmembers on deck when the monster wave thundered out of nowhere. He turned in time to see it coming but knew they were powerless. It broke and with an almighty crunch threw him into the air. As quickly as it had rolled, the yacht righted itself, reefing him through the water by his harness and depositing him underneath the rigging, underwater. Instinctively, Marshman felt across his chest, searching for the clip of his safety harness. Then he remembered an early sailing lesson: never let go of your boat. He felt the rigging wound around his right arm loosen, so he kept trying to wind his arm around it. The loops became larger and quickly the end of the thin and flexible wire that was trapping him slipped free.

The crew on deck saw his head burst through the surface like a released balloon. As he was surfacing, Marshman realized that Simon Clarke was in the water alongside him. He too had been trapped underwater by the rigging less than a meter away. Marshman saw the boom in front of him folded in half, and he grabbed a stanchion with his right hand.

John Culley was in the water upwind of the yacht. A couple of big waves along with wildly flailing arms quickly delivered him back to *Stand Aside*. Crewmembers grabbed and dragged him aboard. The remainder of the on-deck crew had been left dangling over the side at the end of their orange lifeline tethers. They were hauled in one by one, lifted from the water, and dumped on deck.

Marshman had made no effort at all to get back on deck. He just continued to hang onto the broken base of the stanchion and wallow, all the time reminding himself he was alive. When Hayden Jones came across to help him up, Marshman noticed the blood pouring from one of his fingers. Although he'd lost about half of the top joint of the ring finger on his right hand, he felt no pain. Andy Marriette, a registered operating room nurse, discovered that others were wounded, as well: Clarke had damaged the cartilage in his ankle; Bob Briggs had a severe laceration on his forehead between his eyes; Trevor Conyers had a large gash across the back of his head. Marriette himself had a badly cut thumb.

Those still below deck were waist-deep in water. Bulkheads and much of the internal structure of the yacht had failed, and the sides of the hull were panting with each passing wave. There were pieces of cabin roof and deck floating around, and razor-sharp pieces of carbon fiber and fiberglass threatened to slice hands, fingers, and legs. The floorboards and food were floating, bunks had been ripped off the side of the hull, diesel fuel was spewing from the motor, the batteries were submerged, and clothing was bobbing around in the water.

There was little doubt *Stand Aside* was destined to sink, so the crew broke out the life rafts. The first six-man orange-and-black raft, which had been stowed below, was triggered, and much to everyone's relief it took only seconds to inflate and be attached at the stern by a rope tether. The second life raft, brand new, had been stowed on deck. In the water it wouldn't inflate, and the crew watched in disbelief as increasingly desperate efforts failed. Nothing worked. They tried to pull it back aboard to trigger the inflation mechanism manually.

Then, to the crew's horror, the painter line attached to the raft capsule snapped. They now faced a sinking yacht, one six-man life raft for twelve crewmembers, and mauling, relentless seas. The yacht itself was now their one real hope for survival, and keeping it afloat became crucial.

The crew brought massive bolt cutters on deck and within seconds used the giant jaws to snap through solid metal rigging as though it was a carrot. The mast was cut free and jettisoned, eliminating the chance of the broken sections of aluminum punching a gaping hole in the hull. Two crew below deck bucket-bailed continuously while two others worked manual pumps. Everything possible was thrown overboard: it was imperative the yacht be made as light as possible, and it was important to leave a debris trail so, should *Stand Aside* sink, rescue crews would have a distinct search area and a better chance of spotting survivors.

Grab bags holding essential stores for the life raft were put on deck. Someone found a handheld VHF radio, and Charles Alsop began to send out a continuous mayday call. Amid the confusion, a waterproof camera popped to the surface between Rod Hunter's legs in the cabin, and he took some of the most harrowing and graphic photographs imaginable.

Gary Ticehurst, at the controls of the Australian Broadcasting Corporation chopper covering the race, and his journalist and cameraman had completed the day's filming and were heading back to Mallacoota to refuel. It was late afternoon and Ticehurst was worried. He had been filming *Foxtel-Titan Ford* fighting 50-foot waves in 60 knots of wind and had been amazed to see *Helsal II* also grinding its way through the storm.

"We headed back to Mallacoota to refuel and let the journo jump on a small plane and fly back to Merimbula with his videotapes," Ticehurst recalls. "He was keen to get across Bass Strait to Flinders Island that night because the leading yachts were really sailing fast. I knew I had to convince him that we should stay where we were for the night. I was a little concerned about the winds we might encounter crossing the Strait, but more importantly my experience told me that most of the drama would be just off the coast where we were."

Five minutes later a police car raced across the tarmac toward them. The police asked Ticehurst if he could scramble his helicopter and head out to sea. AusSAR had received an EPIRB signal and mayday call. Assisted by a 60-knot tailwind, Ticehurst and his cameraman, Peter Sinclair, shot out of Mallacoota like a rocket at about 3 P.M., hitting 180 knots of ground speed. As the chopper neared the search area, they felt as if they were entering a small hurricane. The chopper was handling the conditions well and Ticehurst was reassured by the presence of a fixed-wing aircraft also searching from above. They both spotted *Stand Aside* at the same time, about 40 miles east of Mallacoota.

As Ticehurst hovered closer, he established VHF communications with the damaged yacht. He didn't have a winch aboard his chopper, so he radioed AusSAR to report *Stand Aside*'s condition and position and alert them that injured crewmembers were aboard. AusSAR responded to Ticehurst that a rescue helicopter was on its way.

It wasn't the first time Ticehurst had been frustrated that his chopper wasn't fully equipped for rescues. He had gone so far as to install a homemade ladder, but the present circumstances were well beyond his capabilities. While the ABC chopper hovered like a guardian angel over *Stand Aside*, waiting for the rescue team to arrive, Ticehurst and Sinclair offered words of encouragement to the beleaguered crew below.

The Northshore 38 fiberglass production yacht *Siena*, owned by Iain Moray, was 30 miles southeast of Gabo Island when the 1405 sked was broadcast. The crew were elated, having covered some 230 miles in twenty-five hours. They heard the forecast for winds of 45 to 55 knots, but they were already seeing 75 knots, so, along with the euphoria, there was a growing anxiety about what might be ahead. *Siena*'s navigator, fifty-year-old Tim Evans, was struggling to keep himself jammed into the nav station on the high (starboard) side as the yacht was pounded by wind and waves.

Suddenly a mayday burst through the airwaves. It was *Stand Aside*. Moray and his crew waited deliberately for a few seconds to see if anybody else responded. No one did. Evans grabbed his radio microphone and acknowledged *Stand Aside*. They calculated the yacht was ahead of them and, after making contact with the ABC helicopter, proceeded to the location to lend what assistance, if any, they could.

"We found them right on the button," said Moray. "Initially, because of the size of the waves, we couldn't spot them. But we did see the chopper, and that gave us our goal. In fact we didn't see the yacht until we were about a hundred meters away. We told the helicopter we were putting our engine on. Our plan was to stand by and help pick the guys off the yacht if the choppers couldn't get some or all of them. We just had the storm jib up, and for about the next hour we were just tacking up and down around the yacht. We still weren't clear whether the chopper could actually get to them. I was one of two guys on deck when this huge wave hit us and knocked us flat—with the mast in the water. Tim, who was still on the radio talking to the helicopter, didn't hear the call from the deck of 'Bad wave!' The noise of the storm was too great."

The force hurled Evans like a sack of potatoes across the cabin and into the stove in the galley. The pain was instant and excruciating;

the result, he later learned, of three broken ribs and a punctured lung. He regained his feet and composure and, despite great pain, returned immediately to his radio. On deck, Moray made sure the helmsman was still aboard, then checked below. Evans's injuries soon proved too serious, and he staggered to a bunk. He was given pain medication, but lifting him in a sling or harness was out of the question.

Siena decided to head for Eden, using engine and storm jib until seawater forced its way down the fuel tank vent and into the fuel, killing the engine. Twenty hours later, *Siena* made the best possible landfall: Bermagui. Evans was rushed to Moruya, where he was stabilized and prepared for surgery. Doctors discovered that pneumonia had already set in: without medical attention, he might not have survived another twenty-four hours.

Above the mayhem, Gary Ticehurst was having problems of his own. Because the cloud cover was so thick, darkness was descending more rapidly than usual, and the fuel gauge reminded him that the time to return to shore was fast approaching. But he didn't want to leave *Stand Aside* before the rescue chopper arrived.

The Helimed chopper team did a remarkable job reaching their target little more than an hour after being directed to the rescue. They arrived to find the broken yacht taking on water at an alarming rate. The *Stand Aside* crew kept bailing as the big chopper moved around them like a huge dragonfly. The sailors didn't realize that their apparent saviors overhead were discussing whether they should forsake the mission because it was too dangerous. After much deliberation the Helimed team decided to make a rescue attempt and reassess the situation after that. Forty-year-old Peter Davidson, father of two teenage children and a Helimed airwing crewmember for eight years, was to be the "live bait," the man lowered from the chopper to make the rescue.

The *Stand Aside* crew were instructed to put the first two men to be rescued—the worst injured—into the life raft and let it drift a distance away from the yacht on an extended line. That reduced Davidson's chance of being slammed into the side of the yacht. It also made it easier for the pilot, Peter Leigh, to concentrate on the raft and not the yacht. Davidson clipped onto the wire winch cable and began to descend. Gary Ticehurst watched from the controls of the ABC chopper, fearing for Davidson's safety but lauding his courage.

"It was unbelievably difficult for the chopper to hold station with the yacht coming up at him in the 50-foot seas," Ticehurst said. "There were two survivors in the life raft tethered to the yacht. The raft was flicking around all over the place, being washed over and rolled. The crewman on the wire had to be in position near the raft. It was a nightmare trying to get him there. He was being rolled and dragged across the ocean surface by the wire from the chopper, sometimes on top of the water, sometimes under. At times he was snatched out of the water because the trough was deeper than the cable was long. It took ten minutes for the first survivor to be taken out of the life raft. The energy Davidson had to apply was amazing. That guy is a real hero. He went and did another seven rescues. I think it took forty minutes to get the rest of them."

Davidson was a human tea bag. After several unsuccessful attempts to get him into the raft, the chopper crew winched him back up to the helicopter for a rethink. They decided to place him into the water as close as possible to the raft so he could swim to it. This maneuver worked, and once Davidson completed his first rescue, the Helimed crew had all the confidence they needed. It was a perilous mission for both the chopper crew and Davidson—the chopper pilot concentrated intently on the approaching waves because the cable on the winch was barely long enough. At times he would have to gain altitude rapidly to allow a rampaging wave to roll underneath. Mike Marshman and Simon Clarke, the two crewmembers with the most severe injuries, were sent to the chopper first. They were about 50 meters from the yacht in the life raft when an enormous wave rumbled in. As it curled at the top, the line securing them to the yacht went tight and flicked them through the top of the wave. They were shaken but survived. Davidson's effort continued until he had his full bag of fish: eight of the twelve *Stand Aside* crew in the chopper.

"There were two very bad moments for me," Davidson recalls. "One was when the chopper was buffeted by a wind gust. I'd just managed to get the harness around a guy when suddenly it felt as if we'd been caught in an explosion. One minute we were standing on our feet and the next second we were being picked up and hurled across the surface. We were both launched out of the raft, and as we hit the water one of the monster waves—a 50- or 60-footer—broke over the top of us. I didn't know what was going to happen. I thought I'd broken my back but then realized I could still feel my legs. The impact was incredible. I thought I'd lost the guy out of the harness, but he was still there. I managed to wrap my arms and legs around him and hang on." The next instant the chopper suddenly climbed, and Davidson and his man were launched from the water like a missile.

While the Helimed team was completing their part of the rescue, the SouthCare rescue helicopter out of Canberra took up a position over *Stand Aside*. The task of pilot Ray Stone, crewman Mark "Delfie" Delf, and paramedics Kristy McAlister and Michelle Blewitt, both helicopter rescue rookies, was to rescue the four crewmen remaining aboard. A few hours earlier the SouthCare chopper was on a return flight from Sydney to Canberra when it was dispatched to another emergency in the New South Wales country town of West Wyalong. Then the West Wyalong job was canceled. The four crew joked that they would probably get a rescue job with the Sydney to Hobart race. Ten minutes later they did: AusSAR told them they were needed in Mallacoota.

The chopper returned to the SouthCare base at Canberra airport to refuel and be equipped with special rescue gear. In the air and heading for Mallacoota, they were rerouted to Merimbula. They were to do a "hot refuel" without shutting down, then head 60 nautical miles off the coast to back up Helimed on the *Stand Aside* rescue.

Thirty-year-old McAlister grewt up on a sheep and wheat farm near Quandialla in western New South Wales and had joined the Ambulance Service in 1991. In 1994 she became a paramedic with

SouthCare and was selected as one of thirteen paramedics to work on the helicopter when it joined the ambulance.

McAlister had been airsick for the first time in her life on the way out to Merimbula. The worsening weather wasn't helping.

"I was feeling fine until we found the yacht and started doing tight circles waiting for *Helimed* to finish their winching. It was really turbulent, and next thing both Michelle and I were sick. I was also feeling scared. It was my turn to go down the wire. I was watching what Peter was doing and how much he was getting tossed about. Delfie was continually making little comments like, 'Oh, oh . . . oh, shit . . . oh, no!' Finally I said to him, 'Look, will you please stop it! I'm petrified already, and you're making it worse for me.' Delfie said, 'Oh, I'm sorry,' and he didn't say another word."

Once the Helimed chopper completed its rescue the SouthCare machine moved to hover 100 feet above the water just astern of *Stand Aside*. McAlister, wearing her wetsuit, put on her swimming fins before Delf handed her the winch cable. She clipped it onto her harness and moved to the open door. Almost instantly the immediacy of the situation cured her airsickness. While she was looking down, a large set of waves pummeled the life raft and one of the men went overboard. McAlister signaled she was going for him. In a classic initiation for someone making their first open ocean rescue, McAlister was pounded by a 50-foot breaking wave as soon as she hit the water. It pushed her under for fifteen seconds and rolled the life raft. Before she could catch her breath, another wave dumped her. When she surfaced again, she was miraculously only 10 meters away from the *Stand Aside* crewmember. She reached him, told him what the procedure was, and both were winched to safety.

Andy Marriette and Bevan Thompson were in the life raft when it rolled during McAlister's descent. Thompson drifted off but was picked up by McAlister. John Culley then jumped into the raft.

"I went down again, and by this stage there were two guys hanging onto the life raft," recalls McAlister. "I didn't realize it had capsized again. The waves were tossing the raft everywhere and the guys were getting thrown all over the place. I made my way over to one of the guys and had the strop half on him when the other guy started saying, 'No, don't take him, take me. I can't hang on any longer.' I could only say, 'Look, mate, I'm sorry, but I've already got this guy about ready to go. We're not going to leave you. You're just going to have to hang on.' What else could I do? The guy I was with then started saying, 'It's OK, you can take him.' I said, 'No, I'm taking you. You're it.'

"Just before we began to winch up, another set of waves hit us and the life raft tangled our winch cable. I didn't realize this until we started to be winched up and the life raft was coming with us, so we got plonked down into the water. As we hit the water, the winch cable got caught on the side of my neck and carved a welt into it. At that moment another set of waves came on. It was just sheer luck that the waves untangled the life raft from around the winch cable. As soon as I realized we were clear, I gave the thumbs-up and we were gone."

McAlister handed over the winch wire to Michelle Blewitt, a mother of two, who had spent the last few minutes being sick. By the time Blewitt got to the water, Marriette was distressed. She struggled with him to get the rescue strop over his safety harness and inflatable life jacket. It was soon apparent Marriette would have to float on his back so Blewitt could put his legs through the ring and move it up around his chest.

"As soon as they started the lift, I began saying to this wonderful woman, 'Will you hurry up and get us out of here? I hate heights, I'm the biggest chicken you could ever have on a rope,'" Marriette recalls. The pair were lifted about twenty feet above the water with the life raft tether wrapped around the winch cable. The chopper crew lowered them back into the water. As Blewitt tried to clear the rope, the life raft was caught by another savage gust of wind and flung into the air. The metal cylinders that supply the gas to inflate the raft, which hang on a strap, flipped up and smashed Blewitt on the side of her head, dazing her. After a few moments, Marriette suggested that they try again to untangle the rope. He was concerned because one crewmember, Charles, was still aboard the yacht, and the raft would be needed for his rescue.

"I said to the paramedic, 'I'll try to untie the rope, so we can keep the life raft and get it untangled.' She said 'No, no, no,' and ripped out her knife and sliced through the 10-mm Kevlar line as if it were butter," Marriette recalls. The life raft bolted like a wild horse freed from a tether. It immediately flipped up onto its edge and took off at around 80 knots, bouncing from wavetop to wavetop. Marriette couldn't believe what he'd just seen. He arrived at the welcoming door of the chopper "absolutely knackered." Blewitt went down again and did a quick and simple water rescue of Charles, who jumped into the water with his life jacket on, clutching a safety line attached to the yacht. If something went wrong, he could haul himself back aboard.

With all four *Stand Aside* crew safely on board, the door was closed on the SouthCare chopper and pilot Ray Stone turned toward Mallacoota. When the chopper landed, the locals were on hand with blankets for the survivors. They went straight to McAlister and Blewitt first.

"They thought that we were the ones who had been rescued," said McAlister. "Michelle and I were saying, 'No, no, not for us. Give them to the guys we just rescued.' I couldn't describe the looks on their faces. They were saying among themselves, 'Oh, my God, these girls are the ones who did the rescue.'" With the crew either hospitalized or released after a check-up by doctors, they each began to make plans to head home to their loved ones.

Mike Marshman, who had been trapped under the rigging when the yacht rolled, returned home a changed man. "I've been a pretty selfish bastard—just ask my wife. But all the emotions I faced out there really stunned me. All my values in life have changed. My relationship with my wife is ten times better. The house is fun again. I want to spend more time with my kids, and I'm actually enjoying my work again."

Andy Marriette didn't go straight home. He stayed one more night in Mallacoota to celebrate the fact that he was still alive. That night he was arrested and charged with drunk and disorderly conduct. His "motel room" for the night was a cell at Lakes Entrance police station.

Seven
AMSA

ts full title is the Australian Maritime Safety Authority, but AMSA's operations center is a long way from the sea: in Air Services Australia's rather drab building in the heart of the national capital, Canberra. AMSA regulates maritime operations in Australian waters, which includes the control and surveillance of coastal shipping. This all-encompassing group also includes the relatively new AusSAR—Australian Search and Rescue.

The rescues of round-the-world racers Tony Bullimore of Britain and Thierry Dubois and Raphael Dinelli of France in late 1996 and early 1997 convinced maritime authorities that Australia's search-and-rescue system was both inefficient and inadequate. All three were extracted from their wrecked yachts up to 1,000 nautical miles south of Australia in the largest exercise AMSA had ever undertaken. AMSA's seven national rescue headquarters across the continent were subsequently replaced by the centralized AusSAR.

AusSAR's Rescue Control Centre (RCC) occupies an open-plan room on the fourth floor of the Airservices Australia Building. It is alive twenty-four hours a day, with at least two officers on hand to monitor activities across a sizable chunk of the world. It seems incongruous to many visitors that such a small facility oversees such a vast jurisdiction. The AMSA umbrella covers the continent of Australia and beyond, in all 47 million square kilometers—one-ninth of the world's surface, extending from 75 degrees east to 163 degrees east and from the Indonesian archipelago south to the ice of Antarctica.

A bank of computers in the RCC incessantly digests information from three satellite tracking stations: Wellington in New Zealand, Bundaberg in Queensland, and Caves Beach near Albany in Western Australia. They are searching for signals from EPIRBs (Emergency Position-Indicating Radio Beacons), small devices that are activated either manually or automatically when a vessel, aircraft, or individual is in distress. AusSAR's EPIRB detection region, which is part of a worldwide safety net, extends even beyond its search-and-rescue domain, reaching into the South Pacific as far as Tahiti.

When a satellite detects an EPIRB signal, it delivers a latitude and longitude position, accurate to roughly 20 kilometers, back to AMSA. To pinpoint the position, SAR (search and rescue) authorities must send an aircraft into the area or wait for another satellite transit, which can take up to three hours. The information from the second satellite gives what is called a *merge*—a far more accurate beacon location.

EPIRBs that transmit on a frequency of 121.5 or 243 MHz (megahertz) do not indicate what the target might be. It could be anything from a vessel in midocean to a four-wheel-drive vehicle lost in the middle of the bush. The latest 406 MHz beacons, which are registered with SAR authorities at the time of purchase, emit both a position and an identification code. That code is cross-referenced to a database, which immediately reveals the nature of the target.

On the afternoon of December 27, Rupert Lamming was the Search Mission Coordinator in the RCC. There were four other officers working with him on what had been a quiet day, apart from an EPIRB activated after being lost accidentally from a ship in Bass Strait. The office was well versed on the Sydney to Hobart race, so much so that Sam Hughes, an AusSAR search-and-rescue coordinator, had been assigned to brief competitors on procedures before the race.

AMSA and the CYC had established this relationship after the rough 1993 race. With 371 yachts entered in the fiftieth anniversary race in 1994, both the club and AMSA wanted the best possible safety net in place. AMSA was always to have a representative at race headquarters, and Hughes was appointed liaison officer. An Air Force aircraft stationed at Richmond, west of Sydney, was assigned to race-related SAR should it be needed.

Rupert Lamming and his team were well aware that the intense low developing in Bass Strait was going to generate atrocious conditions, but the emergency strategic plan was in place, backed up by Naval vessels, the Air Force, and search-and-rescue aircraft. The yacht race was just one thing on their minds that afternoon. Between commercial ships, ocean liners, aircraft, and recreational vessels anywhere in their region, they had to be prepared for everything.

It began with a single blip on a computer screen in the RCC. An EPIRB had been activated at around 2:30 P.M. in the northeast corner of Bass Strait. It was the first drop in what would become a rainstorm for AusSAR. Mayday transmission relays started arriving from the coast. Then more EPIRBs appeared on the screens. Within minutes Lamming and his team knew something major was afoot. Their immediate questions were: How bad will the weather get? How many yachts are involved? What is the nature of the emergencies? How many more yachts will need assistance?

Lamming set about collating the beacon detections on the screens. The relevant charts were spread out on a large plotting table. The aviation group was working as fast as possible to find every available civilian fixed-wing aircraft and helicopter, recording their status and location on whiteboards on the wall. Extra staff were called in. AMSA public relations officer Brian Hill, who was on emergency call, was summoned to handle the inevitable deluge of media inquiries. Hill arrived at the office at 3:30 P.M. and, after a briefing from Lamming, called AMSA's public relations manager, David Gray, to warn him of what was ahead.

Gray waited for a while, all the time strongly suspecting a disaster was developing in Bass Strait. Before Hill's next call he said goodbye to his family, who had gathered for a post-Christmas celebration, and drove to the office. Arriving around 4:30 P.M., he was astounded by the sheer scale of the calamity. The seven people busy in the SAR room grew to more than twenty within an hour, and they were all needed. What had started as a trickle of beacons soon turned into a torrent as more and more yachts activated EPIRBs.

AusSAR's disaster plan ran to capacity and beyond, reaching levels never previously experienced. Navy Sea King and Sea Hawk helicopters out of Nowra and Air Force aircraft from Richmond in New South Wales and Edinburgh in South Australia would be needed. The Royal Australian Navy frigate HMAS *Newcastle*, which was on eight-hour emergency stand-by, would also need to be enlisted through a multistep official procedure that Lamming initiated with a call to Aus-SAR's Assistant Manager of Operations, Steve Francis.

"He explained the situation with the weather and detailed an increasing number of beacon alerts," said Francis. "He then requested permission to spin up the *Newcastle* because, in his judgment, things were going to get worse. I then went through the challenge process with him. It's not an interrogation, just a procedure. To spin up the *Newcastle* and send her out to sea is to spend a whole lot of money, so you'd better know why you're doing it. I agreed with Rupert and authorized the request."

Steve Hamilton had enjoyed the Christmas break with his wife, Susan, and their five-year-old daughter, Amber. It was the first time in four years that they had been able to use their South Coogee home at that time of year, and in particular they'd enjoyed lazing on the nearby beach. Even as he relaxed, however, Hamilton knew that the next telephone call might send him to sea in a matter of hours. He was the recently appointed commander of HMAS *Newcastle*, "Warship" *Newcastle* in navy parlance, the Navy vessel on emergency stand-by. In one more day the task would rotate to HMAS *Melbourne*.

Although the ship's complement was also on leave, at least half the crew had been instructed to remain close enough to the ship's berth at Sydney's Garden Island Naval base to depart within eight hours. They had been briefed on what circumstances might recall them to the ship. In particular, further riots and general unrest in Indonesia and around East Timor might require them to "evacuate nationals." Hamilton, known to his friends as "Twister," knew he wouldn't mind if the ship was called out. Although he had joined the Navy upon leaving school in 1973, HMAS *Newcastle* was his first command and a source of pride and excitement.

The phone call came just before 4 P.M. on December 27. The weather had turned nasty in Bass Strait, and there were problems with the Sydney to Hobart fleet. Could he reduce the ship preparation time from eight hours to four? Hamilton began recalling as many of the ship's crew as possible and told the crew of the ship's Sea Hawk helicopter that they would most likely be needed. Soon after, AusSAR confirmed that they wanted the helicopter immediately, but the decision to "spin up" the ship was put on hold until further notice.

The Sea Hawk was at HMAS *Albatross* in Nowra, where the flight crew had "put her to bed" on December 3 while the ship was on stand-by. Because the helicopter needed enough hours in reserve before its next scheduled service to carry out emergency work, the crew had flown it just long enough at midmonth to fulfill a three-week minimum flight frequency regulation.

On the television news that evening, Hamilton and his family saw film footage of the unfolding drama. At eight o'clock he put his daughter to bed. "Daddy might not be here when you wake up in the morning," he said as he kissed her goodnight.

"Oh, over Christmas?" Amber inquired.

"Yes, darling. I think we're going to be involved in the rescue of the men you saw on television."

"Oh, in that case it's all right, then. You can do that."

Just before 6 P.M., Lieutenant Commander Adrian Lister, flight commander of HMAS *Newcastle*'s $40 million Sea Hawk helicopter, alerted his crew that they were likely to be needed. Lister already had an interest in the Sydney to Hobart. He had taken his family to the Navy base HMAS Watson at South Head on Boxing Day to watch the start. Lister's copilot, twenty-eight-year-old Lieutenant Mick Curtis, and his wife, Melissa, were preparing a barbecue with friends at their Bondi Junction home when Lister called. Twenty minutes later, just as their friends arrived, Curtis was waving good-bye. His bag packed, he was on his way to meet Lister, whose wife would drive them to Nowra.

Their first task was to collect from the ship the special equipment they might need: immersion suits, wetsuits, and swimming fins for the diver. They would then pick up the chopper's sensor operator, Lieutenant Marc Pavillard, from Cronulla, and finally another crewman, Leading Seaman David Oxley, from farther south at Albion Park. U.S.-born Pavillard, his wife, Jodi, and two children, Kate and Alistair, had had a hectic Christmas with family from both sides crammed into their three-bedroom townhouse. After spending the day at the beach, Pavillard had "just cracked a beer" when the call came. He put the beer down, grabbed a small bag of clothes, and said good-bye to his family.

Chief Petty Officer Henry Wakeford was in charge of the Sea Hawk maintenance team aboard HMAS *Newcastle*. On Boxing Day he'd also seen the race start on television, with his parents-in-law at their home at Shoal Harbour, near Nowra. They were surprised a few hours later when they looked seaward from the house to see the first of the race yachts charging south under spinnaker.

Soon after, Wakeford received a call from Lister telling him he was wanted. The entire team had been called. In a remarkable effort, the Sea Hawk left Nowra for Merimbula just four hours after first notice.

AusSAR's effort was unprecedented. With an ever-increasing number of EPIRBs and mayday calls coming in, the logistics of coordinating the massive task were complex. Fixed-wing aircraft and helicopters descended on the airports at Merimbula and Mallacoota like bees to a hive. They refueled as fast as possible and were assigned to SAR targets. Mallacoota was chosen as the main airfield for SAR by virtue of its proximity to the search area, but it presented two problems: its small size constrains takeoffs and landings, and it was running out of fuel. Mission coordinators established their base at Merimbula, which provided better logistics and communications.

The speed of incoming emergency calls was daunting. Steve Francis and his team were continually changing priorities as yachts in more serious circumstances called for help. With so many aircraft flying out of Merimbula, a huge amount of fuel would be needed. AusSAR asked the New South Wales Southern Police Command for help. Within hours, the State Emergency Service and other community groups had dispatched fuel tankers from Canberra and Nowra along highways toward Merimbula.

AusSAR soon realized they needed a closer proximity to the unfolding events, and one of their officers, Arthur Heather, established a forward field base at Merimbula. That gave the RCC direct communication with search aircraft and allowed a better briefing process for SAR personnel. With the magnitude of the disaster still unknown and daylight running out, helicopters were the first priority. The AusSAR people knew that they were sending these chopper crews into an extremely dangerous situation.

"We were sending choppers 50, 70, and more miles offshore and when they were coming back they were bucking a hellish head wind," said Francis. "Some of them, I suspect, were probably coming back close to empty. We had to make sure when we tasked the helicopters that we weren't putting them into an absolutely ridiculous situation. Of course, once they got out there, it went tactical on their part, and there was nothing more we could do for them."

Dave Gray was thankful the emergency hadn't happened in too remote an area. Farther toward Tasmania would have spelled even greater disaster.

Eight

HMAS *Newcastle*

According to the Australian Constitution, a Naval ship cannot put to sea for a search-and-rescue mission before a due process of elimination is undertaken. The situation must be of sufficient severity to exceed the scope of every available resource, starting with the local police force and ending with whatever facilities the state can deliver. If it is deemed too treacherous for any of these authorities, then and only then are the armed forces called in.

After being alerted in the late afternoon that his ship, HMAS *Newcastle*, might be needed for race search-and-rescue operations, Commander Steve Hamilton began planning ways to halve the normal eight-hour preparation time for sailing. He suspected his ship would be called out on the night of December 27. Sure enough, at 11 P.M. the telephone rang at his home. It was time to go, but Maritime Headquarters didn't know with certainty what the ship's task would be.

The ship's car picked up the second officer, then Hamilton, then the executive officer, and during a quick brainstorm on the way to Garden Island they organized responsibilities so that by the time they arrived at the dock, each officer knew what his tasks were. In his cabin, Hamilton met with senior officers before going to the operations room to review search and rescue procedure. Lieutenant Mike Harris, the warfare officer and the navigator from HMAS *Melbourne*, was aboard in place of *Newcastle*'s usual navigator, who was on leave.

It wasn't easy to contact crewmembers at that hour. "It was hectic," said Hamilton. "We had a telephone tree going. People would be phoning five or six people, and they'd in turn ring another five or six. We were waiting for answers to come back, all the time reviewing the people we didn't have. We got the doctor who was on standby at HMAS *Penguin*. We rang St. Vincent's Hospital, which is nearby, and got some of the extra bits and pieces we decided we'd need. The fact was, we didn't know what to expect out there, so we were going for the worst-case scenario rather than the best."

At 3:30 A.M., with the ship's powerful turbines raring to go, the crew of HMAS *Newcastle* assembled on the flight deck at the stern. A head count revealed 74 of the usual complement of 200 to be present. Checks were made: how many engine room watch-keepers, radar operators, helicopter controllers? It was a bare-bones crew, but it was enough. They had the capacity to remain at sea for eight to ten days. At 4 A.M., in the steely silence of a Sydney morning, the dock lines were dropped and *Newcastle* edged toward the main channel that would take it out to the Sydney Heads and the open ocean. As the ship passed between the two towering cliffs at the harbor entrance, the crew got a taste of what was to come.

"The first indication that it really was rough came when we went through the Heads and turned south," recalls Hamilton. "We took a big roll—35 or 40 degrees. When you're a captain you sit there and you hang on, and you listen for *clunk, clunk, clunk,* which tells you something's not been secured. We passed that test."

The ship increased speed to 25 knots as the pursuit of the Hobart race fleet began. However, it was soon obvious the ship couldn't maintain such a speed in the horrible head seas. *Newcastle* was taking a pounding. Hamilton called for 19 knots, and as the lights of Sydney disappeared astern he went to the operations room to discuss with the crew their plan of action.

Soon after nine o'clock on the morning of December 27, just when the crew of *Brindabella* was battening down for a battle across Bass Strait against 50 knot winds, a twin-engine high-winged aircraft, an Aero Commander, swooped out of the sky and started circling the yacht. Experienced crew knew immediately who it was: Richard Bennett, the highly respected yachting photographer out of Hobart.

It was the start of what Bennett had hoped would be a big day for business. Forty-eight hours later he would set up shop on the edge of Constitution Dock in Hobart and sell to yacht owners and crews photos of their yachts during the race. He had done the same thing with considerable success for the previous 23 years. The big difference this year was the weather. While most of the "yachties" thought otherwise, Bennett saw it as "fantastic": rough conditions invariably meant spectacular shots.

The TasAir aircraft was piloted by Ralph Schwertner with John Townley as copilot. Bennett was wedged in the back against an open window so he could capture the widest possible angle. His daughter, Alice, also a photographer, sat alongside her father to assist him with the quick reloading of film. Bennett photographed *Brindabella*, then did the same with *Sayonara*, which was seven miles to the east. They decided to return to Merimbula and refuel so there would be time to cover the bulk of the fleet in the same region in the early afternoon. They had as yet no inkling from forecasts how bad the weather would become.

"We flew back out to the same location expecting to see the yachts in 45 to 50 knots," said Bennett. "We knew the barometer was amazingly low at the time, but we didn't expect what we saw. It was only when we went down low to look at the first yacht we spotted—*Bobsled*—that we realized how bad it was. I reckon there must have been 80 knots of bloody wind, not 40. In places the wind had blown the wave tops nearly flat and there were streams of spume coming off them. It was pouring down rain. You couldn't see where the sea ended and the bloody sky began. The air was full of salt. The scene with *Bobsled* was amazing: a pocket maxi just going sideways with a storm trysail up. Then we found *Aspect Computing* in among the big waves, the really *big* waves where the top 30 feet were just breaking off and rolling like breakers you see surfboarders riding in Hawaii. They were sailing remarkably well. When we got to *Midnight Rambler*, the wind was so hard it was blowing the surface off the water and into the air like smoke. It was an incredible sight."

It was not long before Schwertner knew that the pursuit of pictures was approaching the "silly stage." He had worked as Bennett's pilot for many years and was similarly enthusiastic about getting the best possible results, but this time, given the low visibility and intense buffeting from the wind, it was time to "pull the plug."

"We were all pretty depressed, even Ralph, because we felt we had been cheated out of getting some ultimate sailing shots," said Bennett.

As Schwertner began preparing the Aero Commander for its final approach into Merimbula airport, AusSAR in Canberra asked him to investigate an EPIRB that had been activated on the race course. After refueling, the plane was back in the air within minutes and heading for the yacht *VC Offshore Stand Aside*. Richard and Alice Bennett were still in the back of the plane, but this time they were search-and-rescue observers aboard the first fixed-wing aircraft to enter the disaster area.

Radio communications were already problematic, so the Aero Commander circled above *Stand Aside* at 1,500 feet to relay information to helicopters and AusSAR. While they listened intently to the radio, another mayday pierced the airwaves. It was *Bilstex Ninety-Seven*, Graham Gibson's 47-footer that had taken line honors in the harrowing 1993 race. Disabled with a steering failure, it was now on a collision course with a huge container ship that had emerged from the murk 400 meters away. The container ship was approaching from the east after having been forced to turn into the enormous waves. It too had limited maneuverability. The crew on the yacht fired off a collision flare while Schwertner tried to make radio contact with the ship. Seconds later the ship's crew advised that they had spotted the yacht. They altered course slightly, and *Bilstex Ninety-Seven* got a reprieve by a narrow margin.

For the next four hours, Bennett and his team remained as a communications post over the fleet, relaying to AusSAR in Canberra vital information on yachts in distress.

Nine

Winston Churchill,
Part I

After hovering as a sentinel for some time over *VC Offshore Stand Aside*, the ABC helicopter was running low on fuel and faced a battle with 65- to 70-knot headwinds to return to Mallacoota. Gary Ticehurst had continually monitored his tanks, calculating how much he would need on the return journey. As part of his preparation for a "worst-case scenario," he calculated how far it was to the coast should things go wrong. He could always land on a beach or headland somewhere if he had to, but that would put his machine out of action. It could take a day or more to get fuel to an isolated location, and there were plenty of them on the coast. He knew there was a limited supply of aviation fuel in drums on Gabo Island, so he telephoned them. No one answered.

With fuel for an hour and a quarter left, Ticehurst knew that in five minutes he must leave *Stand Aside*. Just as that five minutes expired, another spine-chilling mayday penetrated his headset.

"Mayday, mayday, mayday. Here is *Winston Churchill, Winston Churchill!*"

"*Winston Churchill, Winston Churchill,* ABC chopper, go ahead with your position. Over."

"We are twenty miles southeast of Twofold Bay. Over."

"Nature of your mayday. Over."

"Affirmative. We are getting the life rafts on deck. ABC chopper, we are holed. We are taking on water rapidly. We cannot get the motor started to start the pumps. Over."

Ticehurst reassured the nine *Winston Churchill* crewmembers that their mayday was covered and that he would relay the message to *Young Endeavour* and to shore. Ticehurst faced a dilemma. He couldn't initiate his own search even though the yacht was probably within 10 miles of the chopper—perhaps five to ten minutes away. All he could do was relay the mayday back to AusSAR and then make the slow return trip to Mallacoota to refuel.

The mayday and Ticehurst's communications with *Winston Churchill* were also heard aboard *Young Endeavour*. The instant he heard the call, the ship's captain, Lieutenant Commander Neil Galletly, ran the fifteen paces to Lew Carter and his team in the race communications center to explain the situation. For only a moment, Carter was stunned into silence. He felt sick to his stomach: he knew most of the blokes aboard *Winston Churchill* and had sailed with many of them over the years. Carter shook himself free of his thoughts. They were already dealing with emergency situations involving *Stand Aside* and another yacht, *Miintinta*, and they were about to be bombarded with more distress calls. Minutes earlier he had been up on deck, and he had been horrified by what he saw.

Galletly and Carter agreed that the gravity of the situation called for combining forces. Galletly would plot while Carter and his team monitored the radios. The plot for *Winston Churchill's* position had it about 11 miles from *Young Endeavour*. Because the *Churchill* crew was preparing to take to their life rafts, getting there was a definite priority. Yachts were struggling to stay afloat in those conditions. It would be living hell in a raft. Darkness was still about three hours away. *Young Endeavour* would proceed immediately to *Winston Churchill*. At that stage the *Young Endeavour* team didn't know that the *Churchill's* reported position was based on dead-reakoning (DR) assumptions, not a GPS fix.

Despite the conditions, an element of excitement was building among the Navy crew and youthful sailors aboard *Young Endeavour*.

The ship had executed an excellent rescue from an upturned yacht during the gale-ravaged 1993 race; they were hoping they could repeat that performance. Galletly was already developing a rescue plan. The scuba diver was briefed. It would be too dangerous to launch the ship's large, diesel-powered, rigid-bottom inflated boat. The best and safest procedure would be to inflate a life raft, hold the ship directly to windward of the person or object, and let the raft drift to them with the diver playing a pivotal role as a "direction control unit."

En route to *Winston Churchill*, they received a new report directing them to a different position. Despite feeling their original course was correct, they prepared to turn. The seas were on their starboard side, and, with only the stormsails up for stability, they would have to gybe to head north again. Turning dead downwind in 40- or 50-foot waves would be dangerous.

The captain alerted all watches that all hands were needed on deck for the gybe. Everyone donned foul-weather gear, life jackets, and safety harnesses. After some twenty minutes, just as they were completing the gybe, a monster wave rumbled in out of nowhere and picked up the massive vessel as if it were a toy. *Young Endeavour* heeled over dramatically—close to the point of capsize. Carter had all he could do to cling to a safety rail. Eventually, through good seamanship on Galletly's part and the pendulum effect of the ship's keel, the brigantine came upright. Chastened and shaken, *Young Endeavour*'s crew headed off to the new and considerably more distant location. Night was falling, the storm was worsening, and visibility was down to 100 meters.

A classic yacht of powerful proportions, *Winston Churchill* had been restored to perfection by its owner, Richard Winning. Winning had assembled an experienced and well-balanced crew that included Bruce Gould, John "Steamer" Stanley, and Jim Lawler. Gould's impressive credentials included thirty-two Sydney–Hobarts; Stanley had notched up sixteen. Like the other yachts still in the race, they were down to minimum sail by early afternoon on December 27. At that stage, clouds of spume were starting to burst from the tops of the waves as 50- to 55-knot winds whipped them into a frenzy. Occasionally the alarm on the wind instrument would activate, the signal that a gust had topped 60 knots.

Winning, Stanley, and Gould were pleased with the way the "old girl" was handling conditions. Each could, however, manage only thirty minutes at a time on the helm. It was impossible to continue much longer because the rain and spray, propelled by the savage winds, ripped at eyes and face. Gould was on the helm for half an hour in the early afternoon. They were down to a storm jib and doing about 5 knots, sailing at about 50 to 60 degrees to the face of the waves. They debated the next step but ruled out going to Eden. Steamer had some reservations about whether it would be safe to heave-to.

At around 3:30 P.M. Winning was on the helm with John Dean sitting nearby, seeking what shelter he could from the coach-house, a boxlike cabin near the stern. Stanley was in his bunk in the aft coach-house, while Gould was trying to sleep on the cabin sole of the main saloon—the most comfortable spot available despite the annoying leaks. *Winston Churchill* powered impressively through the big seas: 25 tons and 5 knots seemed a great combination. Stanley considered their options. Barepoling (taking down all sail) was one, but that would put the yacht completely at the mercy of the seas. *Winston Churchill* was a long-keel yacht designed to heave-to.

"A sea came out of nowhere," said Stanley. "I could feel it from where I was in the aft coach-house. It picked the boat up and then rolled it down its face—25 tons of boat—into the trough at a 45-degree angle. It was like hitting a brick wall when we got to the bottom." Stanley was pinned to the windward side of the coach-house, and the three windows were smashed. Hearing other crewmembers calling for help on deck, he rushed up to find Winning and Dean hanging in the backstay rigging and around the boom with their boots two feet off the deck. Stanley quickly untangled them and got them down.

John Gibson, with full gear on, including his harness, was rummaging in the main saloon looking for the trysail and tidying up some of the sails that had been taken below when the wave hit. Every now and then he'd been sticking his head up out of the companionway to observe the conditions. Although there was the odd bang, he didn't feel the situation was out of control, and he certainly wasn't aware the lee rail was under. He was moving along on the windward side of the saloon when suddenly the movement of the ship picked him up, twirled him upside down, and threw him seven or eight feet. The somersault gave him a nasty knock on the head. Covered in blood, he pulled himself from under the gear that had fallen from the lockers. He got up, saw that the other crewmembers were stirring, and then noticed that all the floorboards had been lifted and tossed. The boat was taking water from the bilge area, but the exact location was impossible to pinpoint. The companionway ladder had been dislodged, so he repositioned it and went up on deck.

Bruce Gould, also down below, had flown through the air, dislocating his thumb. "I told Mike Bannister, who was in the lower leeward berth, 'Here, grab hold of my thumb, will you, and pull it hard,' and that's exactly what he did. The thumb went immediately back in place. I then went straight to the deck. The boys were still dangling like puppets on a string. Steamer was trying to sort them out. There was no one on the helm, so I grabbed the wheel. I could feel straight away there was a lot of water in the boat. I stayed on the helm because the others knew the boat better than me. Steamer was going around trying to sort out the extent of the shit fight—on deck and below. He told Richard to try to start the motor so we could operate the bilge pumps."

Winning turned the ignition key, and the engine started. It ran for just five seconds and then spluttered to a halt. Gould had no doubt the yacht would sink and suggested they send a mayday. With the HF radio out of action because of water damage, Winning went to his only source of communication: the short-range VHF radio. It was vital to radio an accurate position, but the water that had wrecked the main radio had destroyed that chance. The monster wave had taken the yacht's charts and GPS unit with it. Winning could only guess where they were and give a dead-reckoning position.

Stanley went forward to go down the companionway into the main cabin. Six feet of the heavy timber bulwark amidships had completely shattered. A large section of the bulwarks, about six to eight feet near the leeward shrouds, had been carried away. The planking had been removed, and the ribs were exposed. When Stanley got below he discovered there was already 15 inches of water over the floor. Debris was everywhere. Immediately he told the rest of the crew to grab the life rafts and get on deck.

"We decided that we wouldn't put the life rafts in the water until the deck was awash," he recalls. "I had heard of people launching rafts too early and the boats going one way and the rafts going the other. Also, you should always step up into a life raft—not down." In the middle of all this, Stanley added dryly, "Well fellas, this looks like the end of our Hobart."

Bruce Gould told the guys to put on their life jackets and prepare to abandon ship. They took down the storm jib because all the rigging on the port side was slack. Gould wanted the headsail off: they had enough troubles already without the added hassle of the mast falling down. He pulled the boat away and sailed downwind. The sheets for the storm jib were flailing perilously around like lethal steel bars while Mike Bannister worked to lower it. Regardless of the danger, the crew did not panic and continued to work tirelessly and methodically. Dean and Lawler prepared the raft on the leeward deck. Someone asked if the EPIRB had been activated—yes. Gould steered the yacht dead downwind until the very end, some twenty minutes after impact.

"We were running in these huge seas with the wind over our quarter, getting lower and lower in the water," he recalls. "Next thing a massive wave, 40-feet plus, swamped us. It filled the boat. I said to Richard, 'Well, mate, this is it. You'd better tell the boys we're abandoning ship.'"

John Gibson followed Lawler into a raft and was one of the last to leave. "As the rafts were being launched, I was thinking to myself that I'd like to go in the same raft as Jimmy Lawler. That was because of my confidence in him, and that's exactly what I did. It happened that there was a spot available, anyway. I would have got into either raft, but I just consciously felt very comfortable out there because I regarded Jim as my mate. We were from the same club, and also John Stanley was in the same raft."

Winston Churchill was sinking quickly, but the line securing one raft was still attached. With a loud bang, the lanyard to the raft parted. Gould recalls being hit by another enormous wave before he left the helm. He ran forward and did a swan dive toward the open tent flap of the nearest raft, where the crew dragged him inside.

All nine crewmembers had managed to escape, and as they looked back from the relative security of the life rafts, the hull of the once mighty *Winston Churchill* sank gracefully below the surface.

Ten
Kingurra

The rapidly expanding team of coordinators at AusSAR, in the Australian Maritime Safety Authority headquarters in Canberra, had never seen anything quite like it. Their computer screens indicating the positions of EPIRBs were lit up like Christmas trees. The coordinators were focusing their attention on one particular zone: the northeastern corner of Bass Strait, between 20 and 80 miles offshore. The sheer scale of the search and rescue, the inability to prioritize targets, and the hellish conditions presented a mammoth challenge. Peter Joubert's robust sloop *Kingurra* was regarded as one yacht that could handle rough weather. In the last horrible Hobart—in 1993—not only had the boat and crew survived atrocious conditions over a tortuous eighteen-hour period, they had also rescued another crew from a sinking yacht before powering on to Hobart and completing the course.

Despite conditions that were considerably worse than anything seen in 1993, late in the afternoon of December 27 the strong, wood-and-epoxy laminated 43-footer was making good progress south under a spitfire jib set from the inner forestay. Like most of the other yachts in that locale—between 30 and 60 miles into Bass Strait—*Kingurra* was close to the center of the weather bomb. Winds were building to gusts of 60 to 70 knots, and the breaking seas were popping up like pyramids more than 60 feet high. In some cases, despite the size of the waves, a mere six or seven seconds was all it took for the yacht to travel the 60 feet down into the trough and then up to the next crest. Peter Joubert had been sailing for most of his seventy-four years but had never seen a tempest quite like this. He was trying to hold a course of 180 degrees but falling unpredictably down to 160 or 140 due to the ferocity of the storm. The waves were slightly on *Kingurra*'s aft quarter. Peter Meikle came on deck for his watch around 4 P.M. and was astonished at how bad things had gotten during his four hours below. Meikle suspected that what they were experiencing was only a taste of things to come. He had paid close attention to the skeds, in particular the report from *Sword of Orion* of 78-knot gusts.

Taking the helm, Meikle was impressed by how well *Kingurra* was coping. The wind instrument was consistently hitting the maximum 68-knot mark, and waves were breaking all around the yacht. This particular recipe of sea and storm was not exactly what Meikle had envisaged when he convinced his American mate John Campbell to come to Sydney for a third try at completing a Hobart race.

At thirty-three, Meikle had been ocean racing for almost twenty years. In that time he had started in eight Hobarts, four with Joubert. He met John Campbell in 1992 while preparing a yacht at the CYC for that year's Sydney to Hobart. Campbell, in Australia during a lengthy adventure trip around the world, wandered down to the dock a few days before the big race. Seeing Meikle on board, he asked, "Any chance of a spot on the boat?"

"Sorry, mate, we're full," was the response. "But, hey, if you haven't had any luck, come back tomorrow. You never know what might happen." By chance one of the crew fell ill, and Campbell got his ride. But the mainsail shredded off the New South Wales coast and they didn't go the distance.

Meikle offered Campbell a ride the following year on his family's race yacht, *Fast Forward*, and Campbell accepted. But the 1993 event was the most ferocious yet, and *Fast Forward* suffered rudder problems and was forced to retire. Meikle felt more or less obliged to get Campbell to Hobart, and a ride on *Kingurra* seemed like a sure bet. When a crew spot opened for the 1998 race, Meikle called Campbell and promised to refund his airfare if they didn't make Hobart.

On the afternoon of December 27, Campbell found himself sitting in the cockpit with Meikle, lashed by spray, wind, and rain. He was uncomfortable, chilled, soaked to the bone, and tethered by his safety harness, and seriously questioning his decision to sail.

"When I heard the warning from *Sword of Orion*, it was kind of like, *whoa!*" said Campbell. "But I never really sensed danger, because all I've ever known personally of this race is that it blows. Also, everyone had supreme confidence that the boat would handle anything, so I saw no need for panic. The rest of the crew were just kind of hunkering down because there wasn't much to do. I did the same. About every fifteen minutes or so we would get a great wave falling all over us and filling the cockpit almost to our knees. That reminded me that before we left Sydney I asked the guys how dry the cockpit was in rough weather, and they replied, 'Oh, no, you almost never get water here. Just a little bit of spray.'"

As though someone had flicked a switch, the wind velocity rapidly began to increase. "The wind went from your typical howling wind to screeching. It was very high pitched—like a police whistle. I sensed then and there that the conditions had stepped up a notch." Communication on board was near impossible due to the howling gales, and once more without warning, the seas rose dramatically to meet the gusts. Within minutes, Campbell would be in the water, drifting away from the boat and lapsing in and out of consciousness.

The experienced crew had prepared *Kingurra* well for the worsening conditions. They'd lashed the boom to the deck, since it was far too dangerous in those seas to lash it to the leeward rail, where passing water would certainly rip it from the yacht. They had secured it slightly to windward, clear of the life raft. This position made it uncomfortable for the crew perched on the steeply angled windward-side cockpit seat, but comfort was secondary to safety on board. John Campbell was just forward of the wheel and compass binnacle, Peter Meikle was forward of him with his cheek pressed against the windward side of the boom, and Damian Horrigan was at the front of the cockpit. Antony Snyders was on the helm. It was just before 7 P.M., and although it was still quite light, visibility was down to little more than half a mile due to the driving wind and rain.

The crew had two options: head for Hobart or for Eden. They decided to press on to the south, but it wouldn't have mattered which course they had chosen. The following harrowing seconds later blurred in the memories of those on board. Campbell was laboring to clear the cockpit drains when an enormous wave thundered in, swamping the yacht and rolling it over. Meikle found himself trapped beneath the cockpit in a tiny air pocket. After about five seconds, the boat rapidly righted itself and Meikle was left sitting alone in the bottom of the cockpit. He had no idea where the other three crewmembers were. The boom had torn the mainsheet winch from the deck.

Horrigan appeared from around the side of the cabin down near the leeward rail, having gone out through the lifelines and come back in again. Meikle then spotted two crewmembers hanging from the stern of the boat on their harnesses, one either side of the backstay. Snyders seemed to be suspended quite comfortably, although with a shattered knee, but Campbell was hanging under the stern of the boat with his strop around his neck. Meikle called for assistance, unaware of another significant emergency below deck. A large volume of water had flooded the cabin, and Peter Joubert was badly injured. Blood gushed from a gash in his head, and he was in severe shock.

Knowing he had to get his friend back aboard, Meikle straddled the pushpit and tried to lift Campbell by his harness strop. He could get Campbell's shoulders to the top of the lifeline, but not over the top. He lowered him down again, spun him around, and was then able to release the strop from his neck. At that point Meikle realized Campbell was unconscious. It didn't occur to him he might be dead.

Tony Vautin was dressed in a T-shirt and safety harness. He started to help lift Campbell, and that's when they got into trouble. Campbell was wearing his safety harness inside his foul weather jacket but over an interior liner, which was slippery for easy removal in an emergency. Campbell was soaking wet and heavy, and as they lifted him the jacket started coming off.

"To our horror—I will never forget the feeling—the jacket started to turn inside out and he just slipped out the bottom of it," recalls Meikle. "His right arm came out first, and I grabbed his hand and held onto him. He was totally unresponsive. Then his other arm slipped out. I desperately tried to hang onto his right hand, but he was getting washed around. He was facing me with his eyes closed, just making these gurgling sounds. It was as if he was aware that he was slipping out of his jacket. I won't forget the noises he made as he slipped out. Then another big wave came along, and I couldn't hold him any longer. He was torn from my grasp."

The life rings and man-overboard equipment had been knotted and rendered nearly useless by the capsize. Meikle shouted "Man overboard!," called for someone to write down the yacht's position, and took a bearing on Campbell's approximate whereabouts. The storm jib had been torn by the force of the water and was flapping around, but it still provided enough windage to move the yacht quickly away from Campbell. They hurled a life ring into the water and attempted to engage the motor, which had been powering the bilge pumps, but as they were trying, the engine took a large slurp of water and died. To the horror of those on deck, Campbell drifted away face down. They could only head the yacht into the wind as much as possible to slow its progress while the remnants of the jib were lowered to the deck.

The crewmember charged with the vital task of keeping Campbell in sight, Antony Snyders, saw Campbell's new seaboots float to the surface as he crested a wave, followed shortly by his foul weather pants. Peter Joubert, who had been injured when a crewman crashed across the cabin from a top bunk onto him during the roll, had staggered to the nav station and grabbed the high-frequency radio microphone. He pressed the red button indicating the desired channel and called Lew Carter at Telstra Race Control on board *Young Endeavour*.

"This is *Kingurra*. Mayday, mayday, mayday. We have a man overboard and we'd like a helicopter."

"Who's gone overboard? What's his name?" Carter asked.

"John Campbell."

"What's he wearing? Has he got a life jacket?"

"Negative. He's in blue thermal underwear."

"Have you activated your EPIRB?"

"Not yet." Joubert then collapsed. He had a ruptured spleen and numerous broken ribs.

Activated while Campbell drifted farther and farther away, the EPIRB was kept on since no one knew whether or not *Kingurra* was sinking. The trysail was thrown up on deck but not set. At that point Campbell was about 100 meters away but only visible when both he and the yacht crested waves simultaneously. *Kingurra* was turned to about 80 degrees, then gybed around, all the while keeping Campbell in sight. Minutes later, crewman Alistair Knox popped his head up from the cabin and announced that a ship was being redirected and a chopper was on its way. Now it was a waiting game.

Gary Ticehurst had made numerous futile attempts to establish radio contact with *Winston Churchill* while flying his chopper back to Mallacoota for fuel, and he was concerned. The mayday call he had monitored from the yacht kept replaying in his mind. At Mallacoota there was another concern. With so many search-and-rescue choppers and fixed-wings needing fuel, the airport's limited reserves were drying up. Ticehurst and a Police Air Wing chopper just arrived from Melbourne would have to share what fuel remained. Police Air Wing had refueled and Ticehurst was almost done when the local police approached with news of the *Kingurra* situation. One of the toughest yachts in the fleet had been hammered. Ticehurst feared for John Campbell. Police Air Wing soon scrambled and lifted off, bound for *Kingurra*, and Ticehurst and Sinclair followed five minutes later. Police Air Wing raced away from Mallacoota as though flung from a catapult, roaring toward the stricken yacht with a tailwind of at least 70 knots, and was in the thick of it within ten minutes. It was early evening, with no more than an hour and a half of daylight left.

Aboard *Kingurra*, giant waves were making it increasingly difficult to keep Campbell in sight. The crew could see him only about two seconds in every thirty, even though he was only around two hundred meters away. Two miracles were beginning to unfold, however. Two choppers—one fitted with rescue equipment—were rapidly approaching the area, and the hands of fate seemed to be supporting Campbell.

"My first memory is of coming out of an unconscious state and seeing the boat in the distance," said Campbell. "I was completely disoriented. It seemed like the yacht was about half a mile away. I had no idea where I was, how I got there, or why I was in the water. Then the realization that this was not a dream washed over me. I was in real trouble. A couple of things were going on in my mind, one of which was that I wasn't really sure of my level of consciousness. The guys said they saw me within about ten seconds of being lost, face down and apparently unconscious but then acknowledging the boat and waving madly toward them. I have no memory of that. Obviously, I was conscious sooner than I remember."

Campbell hoped as soon as the yacht saw him they would sail across and pick him up, and he tried swimming toward it, stopping every so often to wave his arms. He had no idea how he had managed to shed all his foul weather gear, but he remembered taking off his oversize seaboots. He was certain the yacht was his only hope. Being upwind of *Kingurra* and wanting to keep the yacht in sight, he was facing away from the waves and couldn't see them coming. The biggest waves repeatedly picked him up, sent him tumbling down their faces, and submerged him.

After a while he could see the yacht far less frequently. He thought he'd been in the churning ocean for ten minutes; it was actually thirty. Campbell thought he heard the sound of a chopper above the roar of the wild weather. He noticed a flare being lit on *Kingurra*'s deck, and when he looked up to the heavens there was a helicopter hovering close by.

"Next thing, they cruised away," Campbell recalls. "My heart sank. For the first time I thought I was nearing the end of my endurance, that I might have just another ten minutes of energy left."

Soon after four on the afternoon of December 27, the Victoria Police Air Wing departed Melbourne's Essendon airport in response to an AusSAR request to join the Sydney to Hobart search and rescue operation. Senior Constable Darryl Jones was the pilot, Senior Constable Barry Barclay the winch operator, and Senior Constable David Key the rescue crewman. Jones guided the chopper into Mallacoota to refuel ahead of Ticehurst, and once they'd scrambled and were back in the air, AusSAR advised them of the coordinates for *Kingurra* and the search area for Campbell.

The 84-knot tailwinds pushing the twin-engine, French-made Dauphin chopper were the strongest Darryl Jones had encountered in twelve years of flying with the Police Air Wing. It boosted their speed across the ground to an amazing 205 knots. As they neared the coordinates, rain showers and continuous sea spray met them, along with a cloud base ranging from 600 to 2,000 feet. They were 65 nautical miles southeast of Mallacoota. Wave height, wind, rain, low cloud, and a horribly confused ocean made it nearly impossible for the crew of Police Air Wing to locate *Kingurra* and positively establish a search area. Jones commenced an expanding circle search pattern, turning first to the north. Just as the turn began, Barclay spotted a red flare slightly ahead and to the left.

Jones accelerated toward it, and within seconds Barclay called out that they were about to overfly the yacht. Jones slowed as much as possible, trying not to lose visual contact. Barclay made radio contact, and they were told that Campbell was approximately 300 meters west of the yacht. They were about 300 meters upwind of *Kingurra* when Barclay spotted an orange life ring that he thought contained the crewman. It was empty. While looking at the ring, Key saw a man waving his arms about 400 meters away and 600 meters upwind of the vessel.

They immediately prepared the winch and reviewed the plan they'd discussed en route to the search area. Jones took up a 100-foot hover over Campbell and Barclay commenced winching Key down to him. Key saw the victim floundering in the water, going under a number of times as they closed in.

"I was trying to tread water using one arm while waving frantically with the other," recalls Campbell. "I was screaming 'Hey, I'm over here!' Then I thought to myself, that's a bit stupid. They can't hear you. Just keep waving. They hovered over me, and then I saw the guy coming down the wire. I tried to swim toward where he was aimed. The pilot did a phenomenal job by putting who I now know was David in the water very close to me. I swam hard for maybe 15 or 20 meters toward the harness he was holding out. It was a beautiful target."

Darryl Jones held his extremely tricky 100-foot hover above Campbell without a single reference point. Barclay, who was relaying Campbell's movements over the intercom, confirmed that he would have to pay out a large amount of winch cable to ensure Key's safety in such a large swell. Jones then looked ahead toward the gray horizon and was horrified by what he saw: a mountain of water emerging from the murk straight for the chopper. He shouted to Barclay that he was initiating an immediate climb to avoid being hit by the wave.

"Go ahead!" Barclay shouted back as Jones hauled his machine another 50 feet into the air. The chopper's radio altimeter, which displays height above the ground or water, confirmed that the crest of the wave passed just 10 feet underneath. Key, who was in the water, was confronted by the same monster.

"I hit the water, then when I managed to break the surface, I was in a trough and saw a solid vertical wall in front of me. It was a 90-foot wave. I was sucked up the front of it, then the buoyancy of my wetsuit took over and I was tumbled back down its face. I was driven under the water for ten or fifteen seconds before coming out at the back section of the wave. I was completely disorientated and had swallowed a large amount of seawater. I felt like a rag doll. I was hit by another wave and driven under the water once more.

"Then, as I came to the surface, I was looking straight at Campbell. He was just a few meters away. He had a blank look about him and was ashen-faced. We started to swim toward each other. I grabbed him as we were hit by another wall of water, and I held on to him as hard as I could while we were both pushed under. He was a dead weight; he had no buoyancy vest on and no strength left. When we resurfaced, I placed the rescue harness over his head, then put his arms through the strap. He wasn't able to assist me."

Then the pair were hit by yet another big wave. Key realized the winch cable to the chopper was wrapped around his leg. If the chopper moved or the wire tightened, he might as well have his leg in a guillotine. He quickly wriggled his leg free, then signaled to Barclay that they were ready to be pulled out of the water and winched to the helicopter. The rescue should then have been complete, but it wasn't. As they approached the chopper, the winch froze, leaving them stranded outside the door. When he saw that Campbell was exhausted, Barclay placed him in a bear hug and dragged him into the helicopter. Key then made his own way inside.

Campbell had sustained a broken nose and jaw, facial cuts and lacerations, and was suffering from severe hypothermia. Key and Barclay lay on each side of him to transfer body heat and try to stop shock from setting in.

Back in Mallacoota, Campbell was transferred by air ambulance to a hospital for treatment. His parents were roused from sleep at 2 A.M. by CYC General Manager Bruce Rowley. They looked at each other, stunned. This was the second time one of their sons had defied the clutches of death. A few years earlier John Campbell's brother, Clarke, had survived a climbing accident in the United States in which some of the party had perished.

Eleven

Midnight Special

an Griffiths had one and a half Sydney to Hobarts to his credit prior to 1998. The "half" effort was the brutal 1993 event. Griffiths's yacht *Devil Woman* was 50 miles east of Eden and punching its way into Bass Strait with 45 knots of wind on the nose when it came to an untimely demise. Then, too, the collision between the south-flowing current and a solid wind from the south had proven treacherous. *Devil Woman* had been behaving well despite the deteriorating conditions, and although giving the crew an uncomfortable ride, it was plowing on without any real dramas— until it went over a particularly short, sharp sea.

The yacht's bow launched into midair, and when it pounded into the trough on the other side, the crew felt two "bumps" instead of one. They suspected that the keel might have come loose. The helmsman pushed the helm hard over and the yacht responded immediately, heading up into the eye of the wind with sails flapping. The sails were lowered in haste while the bow remained pointing into the oncoming seas to relieve the pressure on the yacht.

A quick assessment revealed that the keel had done more than loosen. It had fallen off. All the high-tensile bolts attaching it to the hull had broken. To everyone's amazement, *Devil Woman* did not capsize, but certainly would have if the helmsman had not reacted as he did. The apprehensive crew donned life jackets and assembled in the cockpit for what became a long, slow passage back to Eden under power.

Ian Griffiths lives in the pretty coastal port of Mooloolaba, north of Brisbane. An offshore racing enthusiast without a yacht, he soon grew restless, so he formed a syndicate with four mates from Mooloolaba Yacht Club to purchase another yacht. Their choice was *Midnight Special*, a light-displacement 40-footer built by the fiberglass–foam core sandwich technique. It weighed only 5.2 tons. The syndicate was a cross-section of the local community: Griffiths, a lawyer, was joined by skin specialist David Leslie, earth-moving contractor Peter Carter, flower farmer Bill Butler, and bus company proprietor Peter Baynes. Their mutual goal of having fun united them.

After *Midnight Special* had campaigned along the east coast—Sydney to Mooloolaba, Brisbane to Gladstone, and Race Week at Hamilton Island—the big one, the Hobart race, loomed on the agenda. The nine crewmembers were all locals. At forty-nine, sailmaker Neil Dickson was the youngest in the team. He was an experienced offshore racer and had recently returned from a magical, four-year, 33,000-mile cruise with his wife, sailing their yacht to nearly every beautiful island in the Pacific.

Through sheer bad luck rather than lack of ability, Dickson had finished only one of his six Sydney to Hobart attempts. On two occasions he didn't even clear Sydney Harbour because of a mast breakage and equipment failure. This time, though, he was confident "a solid bunch of guys and a good yacht" would see him to Hobart.

Midnight Special was no specialist when it came to hard downwind sailing—its hull shape wasn't ideal for running under spinnaker—so the crew were pleased to be twentieth in the fleet as they began the tough slog across Bass Strait. Their tactic had been to hug the coast before the leap into the strait. The forecast for fresh westerly winds made them confident that this move would bring dividends.

At around half past two in the afternoon of December 27, the wind-reading instrument at the masthead was blown off in a gust that registered 56 knots. At about the same time, *Sword of Orion*, only a few miles ahead of *Midnight Special,* radioed a warning of extreme weather. About an hour later, race control aboard *Young Endeavour* read the race disclaimer, reminding all crews of the skipper's responsibility to decide to continue racing or not. *Midnight Special* had not yet hit the worst of the weather and was still sailing strongly under a storm jib, averaging between 7 and 9 knots.

With the waves growing taller minute by minute, the wind shrieking, and the spume and rain pelting horizontally at the on-deck crew, conditions were miserable. Although the waves were starting to break severely at times, while it was daylight the helmsman had no trouble threading his way around the worst bits and finding a safe passage over the crests. There was no talk of retiring. It wasn't until an hour or so later that they were tempted to turn back. The yacht then leading the race on handicap, Bruce Taylor's new *Chutzpah*, became a retiree and was followed soon after by Lou Abrahams and several other highly experienced sailors. With *Midnight Special* about 40 miles from Gabo Island and 120 miles from Flinders, they decided to head toward shore and seek temporary shelter behind Gabo Island or even Eden.

Seconds after the decision was made, the yacht took two exceptionally heavy hits from huge waves. The second knockdown, far worse than the first, hurled Griffiths from the chart table, where he had been plotting their position, across the boat and into the galley; the trip fractured his leg. He was put in his bunk and sedated by Dave Leslie, the crew's doctor. The yacht turned and set a northerly course. The wind seemed to be coming from the same angle to the bow on the new course, but the waves were more difficult to read and almost impossible to surmount.

At times the force of a wave would send *Midnight Special* surfing down the face at "ridiculous speeds" of up to 20 knots. The crew's concerns regarding sailing into the night—like going into a fight blindfolded—were justified as darkness closed in. Yet another monstrous breaking wave knocked the yacht down again, bringing it to the verge of rolling. There were two crewmembers on deck, and the others were resting below as best they could. Neil Dickson was lying on the cabin floor and remembers flying through the air and cracking his head on either a cabin window or a grab rail. The impact knocked him out for a couple of hours.

The near roll-over was sufficiently violent to rip cabin doors from their hinges and send floorboards flying like scythes through the cabin. The interior of the yacht was a shambles. *Midnight Special* was being hurled every which way, and the crew knew they could do nothing to improve their lot. The storm jib allowed only minimal control over the yacht's direction. Bill Butler recalls going down the face of a wave sideways, but the yacht struggled on.

Later, while one of seven crew below deck, Butler became aware of a massive crunch followed by a rush of water into the cabin. "All I heard was the crunch of the wave smashing into the boat, and then a deluge of water came through the cabintop as we rolled. The top was actually breaking open. It sounded like—and felt like—we'd been hit by a ship. The wave pushed in the windows and split the cabin along the port side where the cabin meets the deck. That side had been the windward side when we were upright," recalls Butler. *Midnight Special*'s rig had been ripped out, and there was a huge hole in the cabintop.

"The first thing we did was rush to get everyone a life jacket," Butler said. "The water was knee-deep, so I immediately used a bucket to bail out through the companionway into the cockpit. We didn't know the extent of the damage, but we knew we had a bloody lot of water in the boat that we had to get rid of. Some flares were sent to the crew in the cockpit and set off, and the EPIRB was activated. The whole thing was amazing. I didn't think we would get bombed like that, but we did."

Peter Carter had been on deck with Trevor McDonagh and was on the helm during the roll. Sensing the yacht about to go over, he fought hard to regain control. It was no use—the wave had already won. Engulfed by white water, Carter clung resolutely to the aluminum tiller, his only security apart from his safety harness. As the yacht inverted, the tiller broke off in his hands. When *Midnight*

Special came upright, Carter was back-slammed onto the deck, in agony. Crewmembers rushed to his aid and moved him below as gently as they could, laying him on the floor. He would find out later that he had broken two vertebrae.

After bailing and pumping for some time, the crew seemed to have the water under control and could properly assess the damage. There were holes in the deck the size of a human head, one split on the port side that went up over the cabin to about the center of the yacht, and another long split running along the side of the cabin at the deck.

The shock of the roll-over had been enough to jolt Dickson from his semiconscious daze, and he raced up on deck and started stuffing sleeping bags, sails, and then spinnakers into the yawning holes. "Baynesy and I then went and got rid of the rig," Dickson recalls. "We undid the rigging and tossed it over the side. We cut all the halyards and ended up with the whole rig hanging off the bow by the forestay. That wasn't fun, sitting on the bow cutting through it with a hacksaw. All the rails had gone, so I was only attached by the harness. I had cut only about halfway through the forestay when the yacht lifted on a big wave and it snapped. It went off like a bomb."

The continuous roar of breaking waves sending two-meter-deep walls of foam cascading down their faces like an avalanche was harrowing. The crew could hear 50-foot-high waves breaking upwind of them, and all they could do was hope they were not in their path.

The injury toll was alarming. Carter was incapacitated with his injured back; Griffiths had added two damaged ribs to his fractured leg; Roger Barnett was chronically seasick; Dickson was still suffering from concussion; and Butler had a broken nose. Almost every other crewman had either rib damage or broken fingers from being hurled around the cabin. If that wasn't enough, they were all soaked, freezing, thirsty, and hungry. The catering had "fallen in a heap" when the weather turned sour, and the lack of food and fluids affected everyone.

Although the crew was initially reluctant to set off the EPIRB, a quick tally of equipment damage and crew injuries soon confirmed it as the best course. The radios were no longer working, they had no instruments, they had lost the hand-held GPS, and all the charts had spewed out of the chart table and into the bilge. In addition, Peter Carter's injuries were more serious than anyone had first thought, and Neil Dickson was lapsing in and out of consciousness.

With its gel batteries, the yacht had sufficient power to start the motor. Using the batteries also meant that the crew didn't have to endure their night of fear in total darkness, since some of the cabin lights still worked. They strapped the broken tiller to both main sheet winches so they could hold the rudder straight. With the motor running slowly and providing headway, they were able to hold the yacht up into the waves. One crewmember was on deck for much of the night, watching for aircraft and ready to set off flares.

At around three in the morning an Air Force Orion flew over *Midnight Special*. The crew fired off flares, and the aircraft circled to signal they'd spotted the yacht. Around daybreak another fixed-wing aircraft roared out of the skies and acknowledged the yacht, and less than half an hour later, the first of the helicopters arrived. This should have signaled the end of the ordeal for the *Midnight Special* crew. In fact it was far from over.

Unable to communicate directly with the yacht, the crew of the SouthCare helicopter circled low overhead, signaling by hand to indicate how they planned to carry out the rescue. David Leslie, Bill Butler, and Trevor McDonagh were on deck at the time, and the motor had been stopped.

"The helicopter came down, and the guy at the door beckoned to one of us to get in the water," Butler recalls. "David, being a doctor and knowing the injuries we had on board, decided it was best that he go and tell the chopper crew of the situation. He jumped into the water—you have to remember it was still blowing and really rough—and drifted about 150 meters away from the boat. They dropped the flare beside him to gauge the wind direction and then got him up. The next thing I knew, our whole world exploded. A massive wave we hadn't seen coming picked up the boat and rolled it upside down. We were flung around like rag dolls."

It happened so quickly, the first thing Butler knew he was under the boat without any air, still tethered in his harness. The harness was stretched to its limit because he'd been flung over the top of the boom, which had been on the deck. He was trapped but didn't panic, assessing his predicament as calmly as he could. *Midnight Special* had been upside down for about a minute when another mammoth wave pounded the keel, righting the yacht. Butler was pinned between the lifelines and the boom, blood running from a cut to his head. He'd smashed his thumb and broken some ribs but was thankful to see daylight and breathe again. One of the crew who had been trapped belowdecks heard Butler's shouts for help and rushed up to cut him free with a knife.

Sixty-year-old Trevor McDonagh had been sitting in the cockpit and operating the manual bilge pump when the yacht rolled. Like Butler, he had his safety harness tethered to a strong point at half length— he'd looped it through the strong point and back to his harness—because it reduced the risk of being thrown by the violent motion of the yacht. He was watching the helicopter when the big wave hit and was taken completely unaware. He too ended up underwater, under the boat, without air. He was facing the stern and could see light coming in under the hull. Fresh air wasn't far away, but he couldn't get to it. He tried to free himself from his harness but there was too much tension on the tether, and before he could even try anything else the yacht had flipped back upright. Like Butler and so many other crewmembers, McDonagh's ribs had taken a beating.

Midnight Special suffered further structural damage in the second roll-over, and water surged in as the yacht settled. The six crew trapped inside the upturned hull could sense the water level creeping up their bodies. They didn't know if, or when, it would stop rising.

Neil Dickson was one of those below. "We heard a crash and then we were rolling around and tumbling in heaps of water again," he recalls. "Then it stopped and we all popped up, standing in near darkness on what had been the cabin ceiling. I was closest to the companionway. Some light was filtering through, and I figured we had to get out. There were two guys on deck, obviously tied on deck, and probably trapped. It was no good the rest of us being trapped in the hull. The yacht was making no move to come upright. She had a lot of water in her—waist deep—and seemed to be just sitting there. She didn't seem to want to move. I didn't stop to think about whether or not we were going to sink. I decided I was going to get out. The companionway hatch slide was gone, and the bottom storm board was in place. The top board wasn't in, and I guessed the gap was enough for me to get through, so I dived for that. I swam until I was about halfway through the hole and got stuck. I couldn't go any farther, forward or back. I had apparently tangled myself in Bill Butler's safety harness. I got angry with myself then. 'Shit, this is how it happens. This is the way it goes, hey? I'm going to drown. That was a pretty stupid move. I've left a perfectly good piece of air inside the boat and put myself under here.' I was still fighting pretty hard to get through the gap. I was trying to get out into the cockpit. I remember thinking to myself that even if I got through the companionway I wasn't going to be able to get out from under the boat because of all the stuff there. I didn't have time to think about it for long because next thing the boat went 'plop,' back up on its feet again. I ended up lying with my back on the cockpit floor and my legs still inside the cabin. I could see Bill tangled up and pinned by the boom. He was outside the lifelines."

Gary Ticehurst and cameraman Peter Sinclair were already shell-shocked from the destruction they had witnessed over the race course when they heard that *Midnight Special*, which was close by, was being abandoned. Ticehurst plotted the position and headed the ABC helicopter toward that point. "I kept saying to myself, how many people are we going to lose in this race? That was the trauma. When we got to *Midnight Special*, we saw some fantastic rescue work by the South-Care helicopter from Canberra. It was still blowing around 50 knots. Each time the paramedic went into the water he had to fight the winch wire catching his legs, arms, and throat. He was also being smashed by the waves. I said to Peter, 'Somebody's going to die in the water just being rescued. This is crazy.' But they had to try to do it. It was the only way these people could be rescued."

When *Midnight Special* came upright, it was closer to sinking than not. The water was just below galley bench height. With the cabin agape, it would take only one more big wave over the top to submerge it. The life raft was in the cockpit and ready to go, so the next priority was to get people off as quickly as possible.

After recovering five crewmembers, including Carter and Griffiths, the SouthCare helicopter turned and flew away, much to the amazement and consternation of the four crew remaining on deck. They guessed the chopper was running out of fuel and they were right. They turned the EPIRB back on again and gathered at the stern with the life raft between their legs. About half an hour after the first chopper left, another arrived. It was the Victorian Police Air Wing. The chopper had joined the search soon after 5 A.M. Senior Constable Darryl Jones, Senior Constable Barry Barclay, and Senior Constable David Key were first directed to search for *B-52* but were redirected en route to *Midnight Special.*

Their rescue technique was a little different from that adopted by SouthCare. Rather than a crewmember jumping into the water and the yacht drifting away before the paramedic moved in, the plan was to position David Key in the water about 10 meters astern of the yacht, and only then have a crewman jump in. They would then swim toward each other and hook up for the lift. It appeared to be a quick and efficient method, and in fact the entire operation was going smoothly. After each crewman stepped off the yacht it was little more than 30 seconds before he was secured in the rescue strop and lifted from the water.

After three rescues, Key was exhausted and vomiting seawater. He'd been hammered by 50-foot waves each time he went down the wire. He took a brief respite while the chopper circled the yacht, then collected the last crewman. "As we were being lifted back to the helicopter, I watched the yacht sink," said Key.

Peter Carter's back injuries kept him in a spinal bed for two weeks, and shock impacted heavily on the other crewmembers. Six weeks after the rescue, Bill Butler still felt significant emotional trauma. "My doctor says it's shock. If I knew what it was, and I could fix it, I would. I'm not performing like I should be. I'm finding it very difficult to concentrate. I'm certainly more forgetful than I used to be."

The nine crewmembers got together for a reunion four weeks after the rescue. Upon hearing that the SouthCare helicopter had carried out part of the rescue and that some female paramedics were on board, a friend asked Neil Dickson whether he had had "one of those nice, pretty young girls" come down and rescue him.

"No," Dickson replied, "but a 6-foot, 4-inch, 15-stone policeman looked bloody good to me."

It was a lovely summer day for the start on Sydney Harbour on December 26, 1998. Hundreds of thousands of spectators followed the excitement either from boats or from vantage points along the harbor shores.

The classic yacht *Winston Churchill* sets off on her fateful passage. This yacht was one of nine entrants in the first Sydney to Hobart race in 1945.

All the yachts, even those well away from the center of the storm, were launching off waves and crashing into the troughs that followed. Although this photo was taken before the height of the storm, *Brindabella* has already lowered its mainsail, lashed the main boom, and put up a storm trysail instead.

Going sideways as quickly as it moved forward, the pocket maxi *Bobsled* is trapped by the worst of the storm. The ferocious wind was blowing the seas flat, yet every so often a rogue wave would rear more than 60 feet high.

© Richard Bennett

Nowhere to hide. *Aspect Computing*, crewed by disabled sailors, probably provided the race's most remarkable result. They survived the storm and won their division.

So little sail is still almost too much. *Secret Men's Business* flies a tiny headsail, hoping to retain enough maneuverability to dodge the worst breaking seas.

Stand Aside lies at the mercy of the seas while its life raft trails behind. Forty feet long, the yacht is dwarfed by the seas.

Winning form. The eventual race winner, the yacht that won on handicap, was *Midnight Rambler.* Even when the storm was at its worst, crewmembers perched on the windward side to help keep it upright.

Trapped by 80-knot winds and mauling seas that at times were more than 80 feet high, the 12 crew of *VC Offshore Stand Aside* await rescue. This wave nearly rolled the yacht yet again.

© Peter Sinclair

Fear and exhaustion are etched on the faces of two crewmembers aboard *Stand Aside* while they await rescue below decks. The photograph, taken by a fellow crewmember, shows the cabintop ripped apart when the yacht was rolled by a mountainous wave.

With their yacht dismasted, the crew of *Team Jaguar* began to motor back toward the coast. Soon after, the yacht nose-dived down a wave and was buried for almost half its length before nearly rolling over. "Team Jag" was eventually towed into Eden.

The crew of *Stand Aside* await rescue. Two crewmembers were placed in the life raft at a time, then allowed to drift away from the yacht with a line attached so chopper paramedics could reach them in relative safety.

Salvation for the crew of *Stand Aside* as their waterlogged yacht lies low in the water.

In a search-and-rescue effort unprecedented in Australia, paramedics winched 55 sailors to safety.

The storm plays Russian roulette with *Aspect Computing*. If the yacht had been only a few meters ahead, it would have been hammered by this breaking wave.

Heeling dramatically in high wind even under trysail, *Bobsled* is blown sideways, its keel and rudder stalled and, for the moment, useless.

The race's first major casualty, *Stand Aside* (left circle) is abandoned and the helicopter carrying its crew (right circle) heads for the coast. The wave in the foreground is 80+ feet high. It broke over the yacht, sending it surfing down its face at more than 20 knots. *Stand Aside* is believed to have sunk soon after.

Floral wreaths floated at a memorial service held dockside in Hobart.

Mike Bannister
Winston Churchill

John Dean
Winston Churchill

Jim Lawler
Winston Churchill

Glyn Charles
Sword of Orion

Phil Skeggs
Business Post Naiad

Bruce Guy
Business Post Naiad

The six sailors who perished.

Twelve
Sword of Orion

Despite being a relative newcomer to off-shore sailing, Rob Kothe had extensive competitive gliding experience that held him in good stead when it came to reading and reacting to adverse weather conditions. He understood the synergy between the two activities and loved the sense of freedom and adventure they offered.

"It's the same sport. You spend a lot of time looking at the sky and understanding meteorology. In a sailplane you work the breezes over the mountains, while in ocean racing you work the sea breezes off the coast. Both sports are also similar in that they are noncontact—well, most of the time at least."

Family and business commitments kept him out of sailing for some time after he moved to Sydney from the bush in 1980, but in 1993 he began taking part in twilight regattas on Sydney Harbour aboard his sister's yacht. He was soon hooked, and after a few experiences on charter yachts, he bought his first offshore racing yacht, a 40-footer named *Witchcraft II*, in 1997. He took it to Hamilton Island Race Week and, although squarely trounced, he learned a great deal. The next outing was the 1997 Sydney to Hobart, in which *Witchcraft II* fared far better, finishing a healthy divisional second to *Yendys*. Kothe had promised his crew that if he did well in that race he would "step up"—find a better boat and get serious about ocean racing. He honored that promise.

At five o'clock on the morning after the bulk of the fleet had arrived in Hobart in 1997, Kothe began his search for a new yacht. He carefully inspected *Quest*, *Brighton Star*, and others, standing for up to half an hour on each vessel to get a feel for it. He returned to Sydney, and after consulting with a yacht broker decided that the Melbourne-based 43-footer *Brighton Star*, owned by David Gotze, was the one. He bought the yacht and had it registered in its original name, *Sword of Orion*.

First launched in 1993, *Sword of Orion* was a sleek, state-of-the-art yacht designed by the American Reichel/Pugh group. Like many offshore racers of this era, it incorporated a long open cockpit for maximum crew efficiency. The most outstanding feature in the cockpit was the large tubular aluminum steering wheel with a mass of spokes that stretched almost from one side of the cockpit to the other. It was a thoroughly modern and cleverly designed yacht, and Rob Kothe knew it would be competitive.

The 1998 Hayman Island Big Boat Series and Hamilton Island Race Week, both in Queensland's tropical Whitsunday Islands region, were the first targets. On the way up to Queensland, the boat broke its rudder, which ruled out winning the Hayman Island event. But after repairs Kothe and his crew were in tip-top form again and had a resounding win at Hamilton. Darren "Dags" Senogles had joined the yacht as "full-time yachtmaster" prior to the series. Kothe admired Senogles for "treating a boat like it's his own." Following the Whitsunday campaign, preparations began for the 1998 Sydney to Hobart.

Having warned the rest of the fleet about the horrendous conditions they were experiencing during the afternoon of December 27, Kothe and the *Sword of Orion* crew began monitoring their own position more closely. Listening to the radio, Kothe heard a report of 982 on the barometer from Wilsons Promontory. He was concerned that a number of yachts hadn't responded to the skeds—*Brindabella* hadn't reported her position, *Ausmaid* had been missing for two skeds, and *Team Jaguar* had not reported at all. The sailing conditions were extraordinary, and the wind was erratic, gusting from 60 knots at the bottom of a wave to 90 at the top. It would also drop without warning to a relatively meager 50 knots, leaving the crew scratching their heads and thinking they were out of the worst of it. *Sword of Orion's* report at the height of the storm told everything:

"Average winds during the storm 65 knots at 250 degrees magnetic. Strongest wind 92 knots at 250 degrees magnetic. Average wave height 12 meters. Biggest wave we encountered 20 meters coming from 240–250. Current of about 3 knots running north."

The last point meant that this region of Bass Strait, where the storm had exploded, had become a massive whirlpool. The strong current that had been racing down the south coast of New South Wales had taken a giant lick into the Strait. *Sword of Orion* was down to a storm jib by this stage and didn't need or want any sort of trysail. Adam Brown, one of the strongest young men in the crew, had valiantly steered for five hours during the day before relinquishing the job to Steve Kulmar. Kothe described Brown's effort as nothing short of heroic. Shortly after Kulmar took the helm, Glyn Charles went on deck to discuss their situation. Charles remarked dourly that people die in these sorts of conditions.

The pair talked of retiring, but Kulmar pointed out that 8 or 10 miles ahead it might be blowing only 50 knots or less and would be manageable. But they could only speculate what was ahead of them, and when the barometer flew across the cabin and smashed, they lost the ability to judge how low the local pressure was. Kulmar suggested Charles take the wheel while he talked the situation over with Kothe. Kulmar and Kothe decided to retire, so they called the *Young Endeavour*, and Lew Carter immediately rebroadcast the message to the rest of the fleet.

"We'd worked out a course that had nothing to do with going toward Eden," recalls Kothe. "It was more about steering around 320 degrees. We wanted to make sure for safety's sake that we were presenting the yacht to the waves at the right angle, and that meant keeping the seas somewhere between 60 and 65 degrees off the port bow. But the wave direction was varying, with rogue waves coming from about 30 degrees farther south, so that's when you tended to get beam on to them."

Glyn Charles was still at the helm when they decided to turn back. Darren Senogles and other crew were also on deck. Because of the irregular, threatening shape of the waves, they agreed it would be fastest and safest to gybe the yacht instead of tacking to the new course. They planned the maneuver carefully, right down to having the engine running and engaged to ensure the yacht maintained momentum through the 180-degree turn. It worked brilliantly.

"We then got things tidy on deck before some of the guys went below," Senogles recalls. "At that stage we had the boom lashed to the deck on the port side of the cockpit because that had been the leeward side when we were heading to Hobart. It was on the wrong side for the new course because it was to windward and blocked the view of the waves coming at you. Glyn continued to steer while three of us worked the boom to the other side. The other guys went downstairs while I lashed the boom to the deck. It was just Glyn and me on deck. It was still daylight—probably around 3:30 in the afternoon. We started chatting. Glyn was a little disappointed with himself because he had been a bit seasick. He was saying—it was more like shouting so I could hear him over the noise of the wind and sea—how he felt he'd let the crew down. My reaction to that straight away was, 'No, you haven't, mate. If you're not well, you can't be doing your job properly, so why do it? Let someone do it who is well.'

"He accepted that, and then we got talking about his foul-weather gear. He had brand-new gear and he was soaked. He said, 'I don't like where I am here in nature's test lab . . . and worse still, this shit's not working.' He wasn't enjoying it at all. Fortunately it wasn't cold, but the waves were bloody big."

Twenty minutes after announcing retirement and turning back toward Sydney, *Sword of Orion* and its hapless crew were pounded viciously.

"All I can remember was a big roar and then an incredible bang when the wave hit the side of the boat. It was like being slammed in a car accident," recalls Senogles. "The boat began to roll. I remember being amazed at seeing the mast on the surface of the water, yet it was angled down below horizontal. We were way past 90 degrees. The yacht was on its side sliding down the face of the wave, with the deck being pushed through the water. It seemed we were underwater—yet still in midair. It was a weird sensation. I don't know what was happening to Glyn at that stage. We crashed into the bottom of the wave and all hell broke loose. It just continued to roll the boat over. It didn't happen fast, but the force was unbelievable. I was pinned against the deck and unable to move."

The yacht was upside down for four or five seconds, during which time Senogles was tempted to unclip his safety harness, but a moment later and with an equally powerful force, the yacht righted itself. Had he managed to free himself he almost certainly would have drowned. He immediately began looking for Charles. It wasn't until he noticed the bright orange webbing strap of Charles's safety harness, still fastened to the yacht at one end, snaking over the side, that Senogles realized Charles was overboard. Senogles's concern turned to sickening fear when he grabbed the strap and yanked it. It came straight to him, weightless, with nothing attached.

"I looked back in the water where I thought we'd just come from and there he was—about 30 meters away. I knew it was impossible to get anything to him because you couldn't throw anything, life rings or ropes, upwind in those conditions. It would just blow back in your face." Senogles screamed at the top of his lungs, "Man overboard, man overboard!"

Below deck, crewmembers were injured and the yacht itself was a wreck, with gaping holes in the deck. The mast was destroyed—it had wrapped itself around the boat—and the entire starboard side was damaged, every ring frame broken. Distress flares were rushed to the cockpit and some fired off. Kothe had been strapped in at the nav station one second, then crashing from the top of the boat across to the other side the next. Sails had tumbled on top of him, and he was tangled in the restraining strap. Kulmar had been strapped into the upper forward bunk and was lucky to escape serious injury.

The crew instinctively split into two groups: some worked on the man-overboard situation on deck while others assessed the extent of the damage. Senogles was at the stern calling out to Charles.

"I screamed at Glyn to swim. I know he heard me, but he did all of six strokes and that was it. I guess he didn't realize he was badly hurt, but when he moved his arms to swim you could see it on his face. I can only guess he had broken legs and ribs. He was in pain. After just a few strokes he realized that he couldn't swim anymore."

Senogles started shouting to those below for a rope he could tie around himself while he tried to swim to Charles. There were only seconds before another wave would surely wash *Sword of Orion* an impossible distance away. The man-overboard buoy had been deployed and a heaving line thrown into the water, but both actions were as effective as blowing smoke into a fan. The wind was gusting at 80 knots and Charles was directly upwind. Everything was blowing back at the crew.

It was total chaos below deck. The only suitable length of line was the anchor warp. It needed to be unshackled from the anchor but no one could find the toolbox, which had broken free from its stowage point and disappeared. The search revealed another frightening problem. The base of the mast had been torn away from its step and was now angled into the toilet compartment. As the waves continued to rock the yacht violently, the mast was hinging at the deck. The bottom of the aluminum section was only centimeters from spearing through the hull. It would take only one more bad wave.

On deck Senogles began to remove some of his clothing but then realized that it was far too time-consuming. He elected to swim wearing much of his heavy clothing and foul-weather gear. "As I got some rope tied to me, another huge wave came through. It was so big it surfed the boat probably 100 to 150 meters farther away from Glyn. Suddenly it was hopeless. I probably would never have gotten to him, but at that stage I was still thinking about it. Then someone grabbed me and stopped me from going."

Steve Kulmar knew the yacht was rapidly moving away from Charles, and he also knew Senogles would have run out of rope before he reached Charles. In all probability there would have been two men overboard and drifting away from the yacht. Kulmar was overcome with grief. He was the one who had invited Charles, his friend, to join the crew, and he now faced the most horrific situation of his life.

"You could see him and then you couldn't," said Senogles. "He was just bobbing on the surface, trying to keep his head above the waves. Then he just went face down and disappeared. He seemed to be gone less than five minutes after we rolled. Even if I had been able to get him back to the yacht, I dare say he probably would have struggled to survive what I believe were terrible injuries."

The boom had been ripped away from its attachment on the deck, and had most probably taken Charles with it. The broken and buckled spokes in what had been a substantial aluminum steering wheel were further evidence of the force of the impact. The starboard-side deck at the gunwale had opened up from the stern to the aft end of the cabin, almost half the length of the yacht. Part of the deck and cabintop had caved in. The boat was cracked in half at deck level at the mast. The well for the steering wheel had split open like a melon.

Below deck the structural damage was equally extensive. The cockpit had been compressed six inches into the hull, and the companionway hatch had imploded, allowing a great deal of water into the cabin. Senogles realized they needed to get some form of sea anchor out and keep the boat head to wind, then cut the rig away before it damaged the hull further. He took charge of running the deck and clearing the mess while Carl Watson attended to the problems below. The EPIRB was sent up on deck, lashed into the cockpit, and activated. While Senogles believed the yacht was relatively safe, water was still pouring in. It was highly unlikely that this fractured hulk, which only minutes earlier had been one of the sleekest and most sophisticated ocean racing yachts in Australia, could take much more.

"We were calling 'mayday, mayday' on our VHF radio from the moment Glyn was overboard," said Kothe. "We had no HF radio because it had been under water. The GPS was still functioning, so we knew our position. The condition of the boat was another major concern. We knew we were taking water, but we didn't know where it was coming from. The old 'frightened men with buckets' approach was our quickest route to staying afloat. Actually, we could only find one bucket, so one guy was using a drawer as a bailer."

The ring frames that strengthened the hull, plus the bulkheads, were now little more than splintered pieces of carbon fiber, and the composite structure forming the shell was delaminating. The first priority was to bolster the hull and the deck to ensure they didn't separate or collapse further. The spare spinnaker pole was cut up and buttressed between the floor and the deck to stop the deck collapsing into the boat, and braces and supports were hammered into the most vulnerable hull areas to build strength.

The mast had wrapped itself around the hull and appeared to be broken in at least five places. There were sheets and lines everywhere, tangled around the hull and drifting in the water. Even if they had been able to start the engine, lines and rigging would have immediately fouled the propeller. The jagged and buckled mast section had to be jettisoned—the waterlogged yacht could be submerged at any moment. Help was probably hours, possibly even half a day, away. Crewmembers fired flares in a desperate bid to attract attention from any yacht, any vessel, that might be nearby.

The big bolt-cutters that are supposed to sever rigging in such situations were frustratingly difficult to operate in the sodden and slippery conditions. Hacksaws seemed more effective, and there was a constant call for new and sharper blades to cut rigging and the mast sections. While some crewmembers, all wearing life jackets and safety harnesses, sliced away at the mast and rigging, others turned to bilge pumps that could be operated from deck. Tired arms found new energy and pumped vigorously. An hour after the disaster, a blur blasted out of the horrible gray murk and rocketed by overhead. It was a search-and-rescue aircraft, attracted by either the constant signal sent out by the EPIRB or the nonstop mayday calls on the radio. The yacht and aircraft established radio contact, but it instantly became obvious that the range of the VHF was extremely limited, possibly only a few kilometers.

Kulmar had plotted the drift of the yacht since Charles was lost overboard: 3.5 knots at 070 degrees. The location of the rollover and the fact that Charles was missing was transmitted to the aircraft. The pilot acknowledged the information and the aircraft disappeared as quickly as it had arrived, leaving the crew uncertain as to what would happen next, though they hoped to hear and see a rescue helicopter before dark. A search for Charles would be started.

Nearly two hours after the roll, a crewmember saw something. He squinted, sheltered his eyes. He looked harder through the spray and spume and driving rain. He couldn't believe what he was seeing: another yacht, around 150 meters away.

"Get the flares, get the flares!" The first package was torn open and the flare fired—upwind, as required for the best effect. It rocketed off overhead and to leeward at somewhere near 80 knots. The yacht, now clearly visible, continued on its course. The second red flare was fired, then the third, fourth, and fifth. No reaction. For five minutes the battered crew watched in vain as the yacht, sometimes in full view and at other times hidden by the mountainous swells, continued under stormsails on a southerly course. The *Sword of Orion* crew could only surmise that either their flares went unseen or that the yacht was, like themselves, very much in survival mode. They hoped that if the yacht saw them but couldn't assist it would relay *Sword of Orion*'s position by radio to search-and-rescue authorities.

This lack of response from a fellow racing yacht, the loss of Charles, the concern over rescue, the constant threat of being overwhelmed by another rogue wave, and the approaching darkness was overloading the emotions of everyone on board. Lying in his bunk, Kothe knew the excruciating pain coming from his knee meant that it was broken or at least badly twisted. A crude splint had been attached using blue webbing sail ties, but it offered little relief. He called an emergency bunk-side crew meeting both to organize a plan of action and to bolster flagging spirits. They had to keep bailing, but they were all exhausted and desperately needed nourishment to maintain their energy. They ignited the stove and, with all cooking utensils and most provisions lost overboard, boiled water in an empty can for coffee. They searched for either of the two medical kits and found one under the engine box cover in the engine compartment. How it got there was anyone's guess.

Through sheer guts, skill, and determination, the crew stabilized the yacht, and an anxious wait began. Only two crewmembers remained on deck; the others rested and continued bailing when necessary. Those lying down were strapped into their bunks to prevent further injury. The approach of darkness was far from welcome, and it cloaked the predatory seas in a terrifying shroud; a thunderous roar was the only indication of the storm surrounding the stricken yacht.

Having made the difficult decision that a night rescue of the crew of the badly damaged 41-footer *B-52* was far too dangerous, the crew of the Navy Sea King helicopter *Shark 05* turned their attentions to *Sword of Orion*. They were aware that the yacht had lost a man overboard and was in danger of sinking. *Shark 05* headed south to a position about a hundred miles from Merimbula. The crew, constantly assessing weather conditions and endurance, knew they would have to fly through some very rough stuff before they returned to shore. The big gray bird lumbered through the stormy night sky at around 200 feet, crabbing at up to 35 degrees at times to counter the leeway generated by the fierce westerly winds.

The chopper found the savaged sloop with relative ease and established communications immediately. The first unpleasant task was to confirm that a man had indeed been lost overboard. Charles's name was relayed to "Wacka" Payne, who in turn communicated details back to AusSAR. It was then 10:45 P.M., and the chopper's fuel supply was running low. They had been flying for three hours and would be traveling through totally unpredictable conditions on the 100-mile return passage. Once they had determined *Sword of Orion* had been stabilized and was out of immediate danger, they decided to return to Merimbula. *Shark 20* would be assigned in their stead.

The decision to turn for home was justified a few minutes later when the weather turned particularly nasty, but *Shark 05* powered on and was soon away from the worst clutches of the cyclone. The lights of Merimbula appeared on the horizon. When it landed, between five and ten minutes of fuel remained in the tanks.

Although he had 7,500 hours on his helicopter flight card, Lieutenant Commander Tanzi Lea, pilot of the Navy Sea King *Shark 20*, had never experienced flying conditions like those he encountered that night over Bass Strait.

"When we launched out of Merimbula the weather was OK," Lea recalls. "Minutes later we were in it. We hit a turbulent wind sheer section that was the start of the bad weather. We went from seeing the stars one minute to a cloud base of about 400 or 500 feet. The sea was getting angry and building the further we went in. We couldn't see much because it was pouring down rain, as well. We were deployed to the *Sword of Orion*'s position, a position that saw horrible weather. The tops of the seas were being ripped off by the winds, so there was white water all around. Luckily, we had some brave guys in a light fixed-wing up there somewhere, and they were able to relay messages for us. I thought they were marvelous. With visibility so poor and nothing on radar, we decided on an expanding spiral search pattern to keep it simple. The distance between the spirals could only be as far as you could see with the searchlight on. In fact, you have to overlap. If you can only see 400 yards, then the distance between the spiral is probably 600 yards so you have that bit of an overlap toward the outer edge.

"And you can't go too fast, because you want to be able to see things in the water. We were flying at 60 knots air speed, which meant sometimes I was probably getting 10 knots ground speed upwind, so I sped up a little bit, then as soon as I would turn downwind I'd have to pull back. There was one humorous bit during the search. We kept coming across the same yacht while we spiraled. They saw us so often they wound up asking us if *we* were OK. We turned and within five or ten minutes we spotted some lights. It was *Sword of Orion*. They'd drifted about 10 to 12 miles from their previous position. It turned out they could hear us all the time on Channel 16, but we couldn't hear them."

The yacht appeared to be wallowing, and Lea couldn't see anyone on deck. *Sword of Orion*'s condition left the chopper crew in no doubt the sailors would require immediate evacuation. Lea didn't know a lot about ocean racing yachts, but he knew this one was definitely in danger of sinking. The *Shark 20* crew had to contend with the wind, rain squalls that could obliterate visibility in an instant, massively powerful and unpredictable seas, and a target that wouldn't stay still. Also, salt spray and spume—which helicopter jet engines definitely don't like—were whipping into the air from the peaks of the waves and lashing their machine.

Lea flew upwind from the yacht and threw out a smoke flare, but the smoke drifted away quickly. They then tried passing a line down. The Hi-line carries a weak link designed to break should it become entangled on an object during a rescue. The link means that the helicopter isn't irrevocably attached to a target if the chopper must pull away quickly. The 90-foot Hi-line passed from *Shark 20* to *Sword of Orion* parted within a couple of minutes of its retrieval by the yacht crew.

They decided to pass a 200-foot Hi-line without a weak link down to the yacht, with the understanding it would not be attached but simply held by hand. Once a crewmember had hold of the line, the end in the chopper would be attached to the winch hook. Then the crewmember on board *Sword of Orion* could pull down the harness and cable and be pulled to safety.

Once the rescue plan was established and the Hi-line lowered, Darren Senogles jumped into the water and started to pull the harness down from the chopper. The helicopter was downwind, toward the back of the boat on the port quarter. The boat began drifting away, and the harness landed about 20 meters from Senogles. Then the Hi-line detached itself from the harness.

"I guess I was down about a meter when I decided the best thing to do was unclip from the weight of the line," recalls Senogles. "I was straight up and down in the water and the life jacket by that stage had gone up around my ears. I tried to relax. That actually made the life jacket more buoyant, and it allowed me to put an arm in the air so they could see me better. The searchlight they had on me hardly ever lost me, even in those seas.

"I remember seeing an orange light in the water, and I thought it was another boat because I knew there was a ship close. But in fact the chopper crew had dropped a flare in the water to act as a guide for the pilot: he would look at that while the guys in the back of the chopper tried to get the rope or sling to the target. It was a bit like standing in the middle of a highway and having a Mack truck screaming head-on at you, then at the last minute veering away and dropping a rope."

Senogles managed to secure the harness and was lifted some 10 meters from the water, but only momentarily. On the way up he was hammered by an enormous wave. The retrieval rate on the helicopter winch, 500 feet per minute, was too slow to get him over the wave and into clear air for the lift. The chopper crew, always alert, saw the wave approach and feared the mass of white water on its crest could injure Senogles. They dunked him back into the water and pulled him through the bulk of the wave before lifting him out.

Once in the chopper, Senogles was given a headset so he could talk with Tanzi Lea and eventually the rescue coordinators at AMSA in Canberra. They needed to know about Glyn Charles, the condition of the yacht, and the names of those injured.

Despite the appalling conditions, the first two recoveries went almost according to the book. Steve Kulmar was the third man to be rescued. He had injured his shoulder and was severely weakened. He tried in vain to make it up unassisted, but when it became clear his injuries were making this impossible, crewman Dixie Lee immediately went down to help.

"When I swam out to this ring, I found it was hard to get into the harness because of the life jacket I had on," recalls Kulmar. "It was a bulky, old-fashioned life jacket, bloody useless. The first time I tried to get into the ring I had one arm through when he thought I was waving to him that I was ready to be pulled up. I got about five feet out of the water and dropped out of it. I'd lost the rope, as well. So I had to swim around in this terrible ocean for about ten minutes while they tried to get the rope back to me and keep a spotlight on me. They lost me out of the spotlight once, which wasn't a good feeling. The boat by this time was maybe 200 meters away. So I was absolutely at the mercy of the chopper.

"The same thing happened the second time: I got halfway into the harness and he lifted me off again. So I fell back into the water. The third time he sent a frogman down, and I think he then realized how bloody hard it was to get in the harness with the life jacket. When I finally got into that harness, I didn't have an ounce of energy left because I'd been swimming around in the ocean for 20 minutes. As I was lifted from the water, I remember looking up and seeing this brilliant white light above me. I didn't know if I was alive or dead. That was the defining moment. I knew that if I were alive then I would never do another Sydney to Hobart. My wife, my children, family, and friends meant too much to me—nothing else."

With three of nine crewmembers rescued in an hour, Tanzi Lea had to head *Shark 20* to shore. Fuel was running low and with a 100-mile slog back to Merimbula, Lea wanted to keep enough in reserve if another emergency developed. The conditions were extremely dangerous for any craft, at sea or in the air. Lea had heard that another rescue chopper was leaving Merimbula to go to *Sword of Orion*'s aid, but that was small consolation for the frustration of having to leave six men on a crippled yacht.

"We were monitoring all our instruments, and it soon became evident that the engines had salted up reasonably badly," recalls Lea. "The engine temperatures were going up. The salt spray had been coming at us so hard while we were doing the rescue it even got past a protection device on the front of the engine. It was a situation that could be dangerous if, for any reason, I had to apply power quickly. The salting restricts the air flow you need instantly for extra power." While not a serious emergency, Lea nonetheless took precautions and conservatively piloted the chopper back to Merimbula.

The wives, families, and friends of those on board *Sword of Orion* were overcome with shock when they learned that someone had been lost and the yacht was in danger of sinking. Their fears and anxieties were exacerbated by the sketchy information available. Libby Kulmar sensed the weather must have been pretty tough late in the day because the position reports that usually flowed from the club at regular intervals were slow in coming that evening. She knew that earlier in the day *Sword of Orion* was placed seventh in the fleet.

After going to the movies with her two daughters, her sister Pam, and Pam's children, Libby returned home for what she hoped would be a good night's sleep. She was still tired after all the Christmas activities. She put Madeline to bed and then took Pip to her bed upstairs. She tuned into the late news and was horrified by what she heard. "It's now common knowledge that there's a man overboard from *Sword of Orion*," read the reporter.

"The phone was ringing within a minute," recalls Libby. "My closest friend said, 'Do you want me to come over?' and I said, 'No, it's OK. I'm fine.' I was desperately trying to get in touch with anyone—the race press center, AMSA, anyone—who knew what was happening."

Finally, at 3:30 A.M., the phone rang again. It was Steve.

"Darling, I've only got about 30 seconds on this phone. I just wanted to tell you I'm safe. I love you. I'll call you again as soon as I can." Kulmar was phoning from Merimbula airport not long after he had arrived. He looked forward to a shower at the airport and was handed new clothes donated by a local surf shop. Stripping off his soaked T-shirt, he sensed something hanging around his neck. It was the plastic pink piglet "good luck charm" his daughter Madeline had put there the morning of the race and told him not to remove.

The Sea Hawk *Tiger 70* launched out of Merimbula at 2:47 A.M. on December 28 with veteran flight commander Lieutenant Commander Adrian Lister at the controls. In the seat alongside him was copilot Lieutenant Michael Curtis, and in the back Lieutenant Marc Pavillard and Leading Seaman David Oxley pondered the severity of the storm. Fifteen minutes later, 40 miles off the coast, circumstances began to degenerate, and the gray chopper was hurled headlong into the tempest.

"The conditions were atrocious: the worst I've ever flown in," said Curtis, an airman of four years. "The weather concerned me, but at the same time it was good experience, because, being a young pilot,

I had a trusted guy next to me. It was really good to be under [Lister's] command. I didn't have to make the decisions. That was his job. We certainly knew what we were heading for. We were listening to the Sea Kings talking about 50-foot waves and wind up to 80 knots."

They had heard how the crew of Sea King *Shark 20* had carried out their rescues, and they discussed the techniques that would prove most effective. They had no direct signal from the yacht, an EPIRB for example, to give them a target, so once they arrived in the area, they turned on the searchlight. The chopper's powerful light amply illuminated the enormous seas, and the crew was astounded that a successful rescue mission had already been performed in such conditions. It was an hour before sunrise when the remaining *Sword of Orion* crew first heard, then saw, the Sea Hawk emerge from a thick bank of cloud.

The chopper came in and remained at a high station, circling the yacht every 15 minutes, confirming the yacht's position and the prevailing weather. The Sea Hawk crew asked those aboard *Sword of Orion* if they wanted immediate rescue, but the sailors replied that they'd prefer to wait until daylight. The wind was still gusting at up to 80 knots, and a rescue attempt in pitch darkness would have been hazardous, if not downright foolhardy.

"When the guys decided to wait until first light, everybody was happy," recalls Pavillard. "The only problem was our fuel. I thought we would have 30 to 40 minutes to rescue all six remaining crew. It had taken the Sea King guys around an hour and a half to get three. We carry 3,800 pounds of fuel and burn roughly 1,000 pounds per hour. So while we were waiting we pulled back the engines and did it nice and slow. We waited about an hour until just before first light to make our first rescue approach. We'd already decided that Dave Oxley wouldn't go into the water unless it was absolutely necessary. We lowered the Hi-line and got it to the yacht first try. We dragged it across the yacht as it trailed out behind us at about a 60-degree angle."

As the Sea Hawk descended to the lowest possible altitude for the rescue, Lister lost sight of the yacht. Pavillard talked to Lister continuously to guide the chopper toward its target. With the side door open, Pavillard leaned out and kept eye contact on the yacht—"left on line, right on line, 10 yards, 5 yards, 4, 3, 2, 1, standby, steady." As well as monitoring the approaching waves to make sure the chopper wasn't too low, Curtis concentrated on all engine instruments to be certain everything was functioning perfectly.

The jet engines were working overtime as the chopper continually went between lift, descent, and hover. Engine failure at such a low altitude in that weather would be catastrophic. The pilot would have to try and fly out of trouble by dipping the helicopter's nose and gaining airspeed. If they were in the middle of a winch, the call from the pilot would invariably be to cut the wire and drop the man back into the water. Each crewman on the chopper had access to a button to activate the wire cutter.

The rescue process was going rapidly and smoothly. Each time the Hi-line reached the yacht, a crewmember would attach himself to it, jump overboard, wait for the yacht to drift away, and at the same time pull the rescue strop toward him. But again the bulky life jackets, which kept the sailors afloat, made it nearly impossible for them to get the rescue strop around their bodies properly. Pavillard was working the winch, making sure there was enough slack in the cable to allow the man in the water to maintain hold on the strop.

"The seas were falling so quickly I was basically just winching out, winching in, winching out to keep just enough slack in it but also have the control needed to stop them going too far away," he recalls. "At one stage it all got out of whack. A big wave came through and the guy slipped away from me. He fell down the back of one wave and the wire went taut. He got washed away from us at an angle that caught the cable on the right front wheel, metal to metal, which isn't good. When we winched him in we could feel a problem with the wire, but we just had to keep going with lifting the other guys."

Rob Kothe was this fourth "guy" having difficulties. When he went up on deck he could see why the helicopter was having trouble holding station: the yacht was bobbing up and down violently. Kothe was helped across the cockpit to the starboard quarter, and he jumped into the water only to realize he was on the leeward side. As the yacht swung around, Kothe went under, hitting his head on the hull. Underwater, he saw to his horror that the line to the chopper was looped around *Sword of Orion*'s carbon fiber rudder. Despite his injuries and his buoyant life jacket, he managed to dive down and untangle the line. On board the Sea Hawk, the crew saw Kothe go under and feared he had been knocked unconscious. Thankfully he surfaced after a few anxious seconds and was winched to safety.

"The very last guy to leave, Carl Watson, was really buggered when he got in the water," recalls Pavillard. "He got hit by some big waves. Time was ticking away and he couldn't get the strop on properly. He just had it underneath one arm. It was jammed somehow in his life jacket. He started to go down for the count, and it wasn't looking good for him. In the end we made the call." Half in and half out of the strop and suffering from severe exhaustion, Watson was finally lifted away from the damaged yacht.

With six sailors safe in the chopper the door was closed and the Sea Hawk headed for Merimbula. Adrian Lister was extremely tired but satisfied. It had been very close. Like Tanzi Lea and the *Shark 20*, the Sea Hawk made it back with little fuel in the tanks but plenty of sea salt around the engines. Once on the ground, Pavillard reported the chafe on the winch wire to the maintenance crew. They began pulling wire off the winch drum until they found the damage: three broken strands. One of the maintenance men gave the wire a sharp tug. The wire broke.

Thirteen

B-52

Wayne Millar is a giant of a man—about 6 feet, 6 inches (195 cm) tall and powerfully built—and a likable, no-nonsense bloke who wears a permanent grin. He loves a challenge, both in his profession as a coal mine maintenance contractor and in his sport of ocean racing. Millar's home is in Townsville in tropical, far north Queensland, and he is one of a growing number of offshore sailors from that area making a name for themselves.

His yacht *B-52*, a 41-foot sistership to Lou Abrahams's *Challenge Again* and former Hobart race winner *Raptor*, was crewed mostly by locals, including lanky Townsville lawyer and yachting administrator John "JB" Byrne. Having raced against many of the better boats from the south in the August 1998 Hayman Island and Hamilton Island regattas, Millar and the Townsville team decided to go to Sydney for both the Telstra Cup and Hobart race in December. The crew expanded to include Ray LaFontaine from Melbourne and Sydney's Don "The Admiral" Buckley.

After some lively competition in the Telstra Cup, they were primed and ready for the Sydney to Hobart. They had pulled out their secret sail, the blooper, on a couple of occasions and certainly turned some heads. They hoped the blooper would give them an edge in the early stages of the Hobart, but that wasn't to be. The wind wasn't coming from directly behind, the angle they needed to use the sail effectively. Still, they enjoyed their wild ride down the New South Wales coast on that first day and into the evening.

Byrne believes they were one of the few crews fully versed on the developing weather, and he's confident the bureau did its job properly. He felt the available information indicated clearly what they might be in for, and it was up to each crew to interpret the data and act accordingly. The *B-52* team had paid particular attention to forecasting as part of their race preparation. They knew that strategic positioning for any change in wind direction over such a long course could make the difference between winning and losing. Millar had employed the services of Roger Badham and also pulled in weather reports from every relevant coastal station and even some of the oil rigs in Bass Strait.

They sensed before they left Sydney that they were in for a hiding, and this inkling was bolstered during the first night and verified early the next day. As the morning unfolded, wind updates came in from the coastal stations in Victoria and the rigs out at sea. They were confident they knew from which direction the wind would blow and how strong it would be.

Will Oxley, *B-52*'s navigator, came on deck around midmorning with the news that the wind was gusting to 70 knots at Wilsons Promontory and that there were some "decent" seas at the oil rigs. As the morning progressed the crew peeled down the sails—from the No. 4 to the storm jib and the trysail—and then tried single-sail options as the wind continued to strengthen. The waves were on or a bit forward of the beam, and they soon found that the trysail kept trying to round them up into the waves, while the storm jib kept pulling the head away, rendering the yacht much easier to control.

They were reasonably pleased with the way things were going. The 2:05 P.M. sked put them in eleventh place for line honors. Despite their guarded confidence, however, they paid close attention to the news. They heard the reports of stricken or retiring yachts, the reminder to all owners about "responsibility," the transmission from Lou Abrahams that he was pulling out or at least seeking temporary shelter in Eden, and the report from Rob Ainsworth's *Loki* of a 180-degree knockdown.

The *B-52* crew agreed to continue south with caution, and in doing so keep the wind and waves at the most comfortable angle. They still felt in control and had no intention of endangering the yacht or themselves. For a time they took in the storm jib and steered under bare poles, but that only reduced their speed to 5 or 6 knots while removing the steerage needed to get over the worst of the waves. It was blowing 60 or 70 knots, and the seas were around 10 to 12 meters. With the storm jib back up they tore along at a manageable 10 or 11 knots. They decided to split each watch in half, with two crew on deck and the other two down below, dressed and ready if needed. When darkness fell, around 9:30 P.M., they planned to pull the storm jib down and bob around for the night. It would be light again around 3 A.M., so they would only be losing around six hours.

But by 4:30 P.M. the weather was steadily worsening. Like so many other yachts in the race, *B-52* was battling massive, unpredictable seas. Just when the crew thought they had worked out the wave pattern, an uncharacteristic new set would roll in to flummox them. Millar completed his watch and handed over the helm to Mark Vickers and Russell Kingston. Buckley had been on deck with him. Before they changed over, it was customary for the new team to sit on deck for a bit, have a chat with the retiring crewmembers, and generally acclimatize themselves to the wave and weather conditions. Vickers had been paying keen attention to the reports from the oil rigs and wasn't overly surprised at the situation that greeted him on deck. He began steering and quickly settled in, slowing the boat to let big breakers immediately in front of them go through, then speeding up to get away from others.

"About twenty minutes after I started steering, a couple of waves—well they were a bit more than waves, they were white-capped mountains—came through ahead, so I slowed the boat down to miss them," he recalls. "The scene was amazing; there was a whole heap of white water charging across our path. Clouds of spume were being ripped off the top of it. I got the boat back up to speed quickly, glanced up over my right shoulder, and immediately shouted, 'Russell, hang on. This one's going to hurt!' It was 10 feet away, 4 or 5 meters higher than any other wave and with a steep face. It was a huge, curling wave, like you would see on a surf beach. The next thing I knew the boat was upside down.

"The wave hit the mast and rig first, then dumped on us. I thought I'd gone overboard. I knew I'd gone through the spokes of the steering wheel, and it felt as though I was being dragged along beside the boat; it was that clothes-dryer effect of being tumbled by a wave. Then it stopped, and I realized that my eyes were open but I couldn't see. I knew then I was under the upturned boat. I knew I was attached, but I couldn't move, so I traced my way back along the harness to the wheel, which was only about eight inches away."

Vickers couldn't believe what he was feeling. His harness tether was wrapped *twice* around a spoke in the wheel, meaning that his body had been forced through the large gaps between the spokes *four times!* Astonished that the yacht had not self-righted, he calmly put his hand to the metal safety harness plate on his chest and unclipped. He then pushed himself down as deep as he could and swam out to one side. As he popped to the surface, gasping for air, he was greeted by the sight of Kingston clinging to the edge of the upturned hull near the stern. Kingston too had had a lucky escape. His first attempt to swim out from under the yacht failed, so he stuck his head back up in the cockpit well and found a small pocket of air. He took a deep breath and went under again. That time he was successful. Both men were on the downwind side of the upturned hull.

Vickers worried that they might be entangled in the mess of rigging and dragged under the stern, but before he could do anything about it a rogue wave lifted him and carried him a good 20 meters from the yacht. He was wearing his full foul-weather gear without a life jacket, and the weight and restrictive nature of the gear forced him to dog-paddle back to the yacht. As he was swimming he watched the hull begin to sink stern first and was certain it was going to right itself. He had the foresight to check the areas around the keel and rudder for damage. When he reached the boat he banged on the hull twice, but there was no response.

"I swam around to the stern of the boat and grabbed the back-stay. Then I just hung on and hoped the thing would come upright. Russell was somewhere up near the bow. We had both worked out that when, or possibly if, the yacht came upright, being near the ends would be safest. That way you wouldn't be hurled around as much."

Just before the yacht—named after a bomber—was bombed by the mammoth wave, the crew below deck could do little more than lie in their bunks. Moving around presented a serious hazard to health, akin to standing up on an extreme roller coaster. Sleep was nearly impossible. Around John Byrne, who was in the leeward aft quarter berth, the conversation rarely veered from the weather and how best to preserve the boat.

When the wave with *B-52*'s name on it did arrive, nothing out of the ordinary in the boat's motion could be felt at first in the cabin. The yacht might merely have been hit by a particularly strong gust and be-gun rounding up into the wind. But in another instant this round-up was accompanied by a thunderous crashing noise. Byrne had time to think the mast was breaking and that their race would surely be run. The next thing he knew, the boat was upside down and he had been pinned against the side of the hull by his hinged bunk. Sails and other gear had fallen onto the bunk, making it impossible to lift. The only way out would be to slither forward and climb out over the galley—or rather, *under* the galley and onto what had been the cabin roof.

"I waited there for a couple of seconds, thinking, it's going to come straight back up, but when I saw water pouring in I thought, this is a bit inconvenient to have to get out of here but, shit, we could sink. I bolted out of my bunk and found the other guys already there, sort of standing around taking stock of each other."

Millar was already arranging for the life raft to be readied and the EPIRB activated. There were eight crewmembers trapped inside. Byrne distinctly remembers the eerie, emerald-green light filtering into the cabin and the deathly quiet despite the chaos outside. They were disoriented; debris was floating all around, right was now left, and top was bottom.

"Even simple things like the engine became confusing because it was upside down," recalls Byrne. "And I couldn't work out what had happened with the stove. I thought the round metho tank from the stove was the engine filter, but then I realized the engine was now actually above my head. Fortunately fuel and oil didn't pour out of the engine and also, the fact that we had gel batteries meant that we didn't have battery acid going everywhere."

Before the race Millar and Oxley had watched a video on how British yachtsman Tony Bullimore survived inside his upturned yacht in the Southern Ocean. This was fast becoming a reality for them because their yacht showed no signs of righting. Millar moved into the bow area to check on the forward hatch; it would be their only way out if the yacht sank by the stern. "It's amazing what you do in situations like that," recalls John Byrne. "Ray LaFontaine grabbed the microphone on the radio and said, 'What about a mayday?' Will turned to him and said something like, 'I'll attend to that when it's appropriate.' Ray held the microphone to his mouth and let out this textbook perfect mayday. We all just looked at him bemused, as if asking, 'Who are you calling, Flipper the dolphin? Mate, we're upside down!'" Then, without warning, the ghostly silence was broken by an almighty *whoosh!* and all hell broke loose in the cabin yet again. *B-52* was back upright. It had been inverted for an estimated four minutes.

As the yacht settled, Byrne looked down and noticed a pair of seaboots protruding just above the water surface in the cabin. He recognized them immediately, grabbed them, and pulled as hard as he could. Lindy Axe came to the surface coughing and spluttering. She had been trapped underwater, under the stove, when it crashed back into place. She had a nasty-looking gash on her head.

The two men outside hung on as best they could when *B-52* self-righted. At the bow, Kingston grabbed the remnants of the storm jib and its sheets and, using the lifting momentum of one of the massive waves, managed to get himself onto the foredeck. Vickers grabbed a stanchion and clung for dear life. Because the cabin had been pushed out of shape, the crew trapped inside were slow getting on deck. It wasn't until LaFontaine literally smashed his way out through the stormboards that anyone could emerge to see if Vickers and Kingston were still there.

Kingston spotted LaFontaine followed closely by Steve Anderson as they emerged on deck. After ascertaining how much water was in the cabin, he went straight to the bilge pump and started pumping. He then began removing the twisted and tangled rig. Millar and his vanguard began assessing the situation below deck. They were unsure of the structural condition of the yacht and whether or not they should abandon ship. The crew split in half, one group on deck helping jettison the rig and the other below, trying to save the boat. With two men manning the pumps and others bucketing the water out, it wasn't long before the level began going down. That could only mean that the yacht, though badly damaged, was not leaking badly.

"Because [sailing] the boat is very much a team effort, everybody is encouraged to have their input," recalls Byrne. "The input from some people was that we should get off because we didn't want to risk sinking and being trapped. But as things settled down and experience came to the fore, attitudes changed. The thought was that maybe we should put the rafts on deck and inflate them and have them ready to go. That way we wouldn't have to wait while they inflated if we had to get into them in a hurry. While all that was being discussed, and with the water level continuing to go down, everyone became more certain the boat was going to stay afloat. The comment then was that we didn't need to inflate the rafts but we should keep them on deck and tied on. If they were inflated they were going to restrict movement too much and blow around everywhere. Then Lindy, who runs the bow, grabbed some gear bags and put into them things that we might need in a life raft: bottled water, warm clothes, flare container."

The EPIRB was located once more, and a debate began as to whether or not it should be activated.

"Well, we've got no radios because they've been flooded; we don't know if the engine's going to work; we've got no mast; we don't know what the structural integrity of the yacht is; and we're halfway across Bass Strait in 50 knots of wind and bloody big seas," said Oxley, the navigator. "Yep, this is severe and imminent danger. Yes, we should set it off."

The EPIRB was activated.

The crew on deck assigned to getting rid of the rig were thankful for the solid prerace preparation. Special effort had gone into ensuring that the pins in the rigging screws, or turnbuckles, could be easily removed in an emergency, and consequently the mast was consigned to the ocean in a very short time. Before long a fixed-wing aircraft, working off *B-52*'s EPIRB signal, appeared overhead. The plane "waggled its wings" in acknowledgment to their flares, then disappeared as quickly as it had arrived.

At about the same time, some crewmembers on deck thought they saw another sailboat in the distance, but it was difficult to tell because the waves were higher than most yachts' rigs. The sightings were intermittent and ephemeral. Nevertheless, flares were fired in the hope that something might be there. Nothing more happened. Millar and two other crewmembers then tried to start the engine. They turned the flywheel over to make sure the oil hadn't risen above the pistons when the yacht was upside down. They tested the electrics, then sprayed the terminals to displace any residual water. Just as the engine turned over, the crew on deck heard another noise. A massive gray Navy Sea King helicopter, emblazoned with numbers, its lights flashing, came charging toward them out of the storm clouds.

The Navy choppers, with their night search-and-rescue capability, were an invaluable asset for AusSAR's operation on the night of December 27. The Sea King *Shark 05* had gone from twelve-hour stand-by at HMAS *Albatross* at Nowra to airborne and fully operational in just two hours. When the machine launched out of the Nowra base at 7:45 P.M., Lieutenant Alan Moore was the aircraft captain; the second pilot was Lieutenant Commander George Sydney (then commanding officer of Sea King's HS817 Squadron);

Lieutenant Philip "Wacka" Payne was observer; and Petty Officer Kerwyn Ballico was the aircrewman. The chopper was carrying its maximum 5,000 pounds of fuel. It burned 1,000 pounds an hour, and regulations required it to land with 500 pounds in reserve. Its nominal flight limit was four and a half hours.

The initial task was to assist *Business Post Naiad*, but AusSAR redirected them to *B-52* with orders to assess the situation, make contact, and ask the crew to turn off the EPIRB if they were out of immediate danger. East of Merimbula the Sea King hit heavy rain, extremely strong winds (60-plus knots) and a low cloud base.

"The aircraft was washing around everywhere; we were being buffeted all over the sky," said Payne. "Because the winds were so strong we were drifting left at around 35 degrees, so to stay on course we were crabbing our way south. After a brief search we found them. We established ourselves in a hover—or more accurately, attempted to establish ourselves in a hover—and put some lights on them. The yacht was dismasted, but we were pleased to see so many crew mustered on deck. Just looking at the conditions I knew immediately there was no physical way we could get them off the yacht. It was way too dangerous. I knew the limitations of the aircraft and of the personnel.

"They had no communications at all, so we tried to get a line to them—a Hi-line with a monkey's fist at the end. We had written a note and put it into the monkey's fist, but the line got swamped and the note couldn't be read. Then we created a waterproof one, and as we lowered that the line parted. It was extremely difficult to get the line to them, remember it was also dark and raining. While we were hovering, we saw our altitude go at one stage from 80 feet to 10—that's how big the waves were. Obviously we had danger of our own."

Eventually a waterproof note was lowered to the crew, who responded that they were in distress but not in immediate danger. The conditions were so bad and the yacht in such a precarious position that a rescue would have been extremely tricky. It was decided that sending a man down would be overly hazardous, and even getting crewmembers into a life raft could prove disastrous. Given that the yacht appeared relatively stabilized, the difficult decision was made to leave *B-52* for the moment. *Shark 05* had received a call stating that *Sword of Orion* was taking water and had injured people on board. That was their next destination.

While the Sea King thrashed about overhead in the stormy night sky, the crew on board *B-52* had planned to put Lindy Axe into a harness and send her up to the chopper, if possible. She could describe their situation to the chopper crew and report that the motor might eventually be fully operational. Also, Axe could be flown to shore and receive medical treatment for her head wound. They knew that lifting her off the yacht was extremely dangerous but felt it would be suicidal to put her in the water for pickup.

But there would be no rescue for the time being. They were on their own. "Watching the helicopter fly off was like arriving at a cab stand late at night and seeing the last taxi leave," said Byrne.

After several attempts the motor started, and they decided the safest destination was Eden. That course put the waves at about 45 degrees to the bow. Occasionally *B-52*, which had already suffered considerable structural damage to the cabin, would be almost submerged under the weight of white water that continually pounded it. With windows cracked, the companionway cover gone, and fissures in the deck, water poured freely below each time a wave hit.

"It was then around 2 A.M.," recalls Byrne. "People were sleeping from exhaustion. They were lying on the cabin floor in wet weather gear with water leaking in through the roof, pouring on top of them. I'd been lucky enough to get a fair bit of rest during the day, so I figured it was time I stepped up to the plate and did some steering. We decided to leave the EPIRB on, because we knew that AusSAR in Canberra could track it and might see that we were making some progress against the wind and toward land.

"When you were on deck you would have to stand up every few minutes and have a good look around. There were other racing yachts out there, and the last thing you needed was a collision. At one stage I looked behind us and saw red and green masthead navigation lights just at the right angle to be a yacht. They appeared to be only a quarter mile behind us. At that moment the lights did about 200 knots straight over the top of us, then banked and flew off into the night."

Although *B-52* had been stabilized, the cracks in the deck were getting bigger, and all on board were acutely aware that another freak wave could easily roll them again. The yacht had been so badly damaged in the first roll-over that it twisted with every wave, and each time it twisted the cracks expanded. Then a window popped out and fell into the cabin. It was obvious that if a big wave dumped on them, the deck could cave in. *B-52* would be swamped and more than likely sink.

Oxley took the wooden locker covers from the bunk moldings and fashioned crude stormboards. He put them on the cabin side where the broken windows were located, then lashed them together across the inside of the cabin using webbing sail ties. That, along with sleeping bags stuffed in some of the cracks, helped stem the water flow. While they continued to make progress toward the coast, the *B-52* crew were unaware of the grave fears held for their safety. Their EPIRB was still activated, and the authorities believed they were still in serious trouble. Not until the ABC helicopter located them and reported that they were heading for Eden were those fears allayed.

At 8 A.M. they sighted the coast. In many ways it was a huge relief—a sign of sanctuary and safety. But, Byrne explained, it was also a tease. "I actually wished that that part of the coast was really, really flat. It was so mountainous we seemed to take forever to get there. After what we'd been through we wanted to see land and be there in the same minute. It took another five hours to get to Eden. As we got closer to shore we started to feel pretty good about ourselves and what we'd survived. Everybody started to peel their wet weather gear off. That made a nice old smell in the cockpit. When we got into mobile phone range we called AusSAR and advised them that we were going to turn off the EPIRB. Straight after that, once we realized we were within phone range, there were eight people on deck calling family and friends at the same time. It was a ridiculous sight."

The damage to *B-52* was so extensive that insurance assessors later declared it a total loss. Experienced sailors who saw the ruined yacht were awed that it had managed to limp back to shore at all, let alone in such horrendous conditions.

Fourteen

Miintinta

For most Australians, a "weekender" is a cozy little cottage tucked away somewhere beyond town. Dr. Brian Emerson and his wife Pamela's weekender was the 42-foot yacht *Miintinta*, which is Polynesian for "turtle." The yacht had many advantages over the average weekender, such as 360-degree water views—and, if the Emersons didn't like their surroundings at any particular time, they could move their "cottage."

Miintinta was more than that for the Emersons, however: it was their retirement project. At sixty, Dr. Emerson was looking forward to retirement. A former university lecturer, he currently provided expert opinion in engineering for court litigation. He and his wife had long harbored dreams of leaving the "big smoke" and devoting their days to sailing leisurely from port to port.

In 1998 Emerson decided to race his boat to Hobart. He knew it could be a tough course, but he also knew the yacht had the pedigree to cope with just about anything. It was designed by Ron Swanson, a legend in yacht design in the 1960s and 1970s. *Miintinta*, a Swanson 42 double-ender built in 1976, had since cruised to the United States and back and done two Hobarts, in 1976 and 1977. Swanson created the design as a go-anywhere world cruising yacht. It was constructed primarily of solid fiberglass and weighed in at over 12 tons.

Emerson had owned the yacht for little more than a year. The

1998 event was the third Hobart for a highly experienced yachtsman who'd sailed everything from small boats to ocean racers for more than thirty years. To ensure that the yacht was race-ready, he installed new pumps, checked the rigging and electrics thoroughly, and purchased some new sails. He chose five crew to join him: Lisa McKenzie, Uli Thiel, Bill Vukoder, Peter Volkes, and Robin Gordon. Thiel, a master mariner, navigator, and radio operator, had sailed around the world. She had been at sea for thirteen years as a professional and was part of that exclusive band of sailors to round the notorious Cape Horn.

Emerson and his crew's main objective was to finish the 1998 event unscathed, but they also fancied being the first cruising division yacht from the CYC over the line. *Miintinta* was definitely a cruising yacht, and from the start sailed more like a tortoise than anything else. Emerson's calculations had them second-to-last out of Sydney Harbour. But once outside, and with the big multicolored spinnaker set, they began to gain ground. In fact, as the wind strengthened, *Miintinta* was running faster than it ever had before.

As they neared Eden on December 27, Emerson was pleased with the yacht's placement: twenty-first of thirty-eight in its division. And *Miintinta* reveled in the rough going. The only problem was that McKenzie, an experienced harbor sailor, was not enjoying the rugged ride. Seasickness had hounded her from soon after the start, and things were getting rougher. When they heard the radio call from *Sword of Orion* during the 1405 sked, mental alarm bells started ringing. Those bells got louder for everyone as distress calls and announcements of decisions to retire crackled over the airwaves through the afternoon.

Emerson had decided some hours earlier to prepare the yacht for the worst possible weather. The mainsail was lowered completely and secured, and the storm jib and the trysail set. Emerson decided it was too dangerous to press on across Bass Strait. They would tack and head for the coast near Eden, where they would shelter.

"I didn't expect a cyclonic bomb, and I didn't expect waves of those proportions," Emerson said. "As we started to head toward shore around 5 o'clock, there was mayhem over the radio. Distress calls were coming from everywhere. We pushed on toward the coast for a while, and then I decided that with conditions deteriorating so much we would start the diesel and power toward shore. Using power meant we would be out of the race, but it also meant to me that we were probably safer. Soon we were dropping off backless waves, waves of ridiculous proportions. They were 10 meters at least, and some were probably bigger than that. Twice we crashed off monumental waves. The yacht shuddered when it landed.

"We had the trysail set, but still we didn't seem to have enough power. Sometimes, when the worst waves hit us, we did complete, 180-degree turns. One minute you would be heading on 270 degrees toward the coast, and the next minute you're heading on the reciprocal back out to sea. I reckon we got to within 20 miles of Eden when the damn diesel carked it. It just stopped—I don't know why. Steam was coming out of the engine compartment and filling the cabin. It was like a car radiator had blown. I went straight to the engine, and as soon as I got the rear compartment cover off I shouted, 'God, there's a lot of water in here!' It was stinking hot, so I couldn't do much except check all the hoses."

It was the amount of water in the yacht and not the failed engine that concerned Emerson. First he thought a skin fitting, a through-hull fitting, might have ruptured. He rummaged through the yacht checking every one: all secure. Crewmembers manned buckets and pumps, but buckets broke and pumps either clogged or busted. Emerson couldn't believe that a new, heavy-duty pump he installed for the race had fallen apart. Cut-down plastic milk containers became bailers, and only one pump remained functional.

Emerson continued looking for the source of the leak. The water came in fast at times and then, a few minutes later, would come in more slowly. He surmised that the greatest volume of water entered the hull when the starboard side of the yacht took a pounding. He concluded that the hull was badly fractured, probably in an area behind a fixed settee berth near the mast. When the yacht heeled over with the wind, and waves were on the starboard side, the weight of the keel opened the crack. It was possible that the hull had fractured at the point where a steel frame was built to take the loads of the mast. Because of the way the yacht was constructed, however, he couldn't get into the area to confirm this theory.

At the wheel, Thiel was having difficulty holding the yacht on course. *Miintinta* kept being blown back out to sea. Sometime between 11 P.M. and midnight, Emerson radioed Eden Coastal Patrol to report that, although their bilge pumps had failed and they were taking on a substantial amount of water, they were still in control. He refrained from calling a mayday and instead requested a tow. Emerson followed the Coastal Patrol's directions to fire flares. Aboard *Southerly*, Don Mickleborough sighted the flares, and the yacht's approximate position was confirmed with the coast station. Coastal Patrol then advised Emerson that the container ship *Union Roetigen* had been diverted to stand by *Miintinta*.

The crew were glad to see the big ship appear and were even happier when they were told the trawler *Josephine Jean* was heading toward them, as well. Believing that other yachts were probably in more dire circumstances, Emerson radioed in that *Miintinta* was stable and would not require immediate assistance.

Just 45 minutes later he was back on the radio. "We're now taking too much water. We can't control it. Can you stand by us again?" To the crew's delight, *Union Roetigen* soon returned to keep watch. About an hour after that, the *Miintinta* crew saw the trawler crest a wave. Their tow had arrived, but time was running out for the now badly breached hull.

Lockie Marshall and Eden police sergeant Keith Tillman were still in Marshall's office late that night coordinating *Team Jaguar's* rescue by the trawler *Moira Elizabeth*. The two-way radio in the office was almost jammed as search-and-rescue operations for so many of the Hobart race yachts continued. The pair heard the request from *Miintinta* for a tow. Both knew that if any vessel were to leave Eden in answer to the call, it would have to be one of Marshall's trawlers. Most were tied up at the dock, secured by double ropes and anchors to cope with the surge the storm sent into the small harbor.

The few trawlers working that time of the year usually reaped sizable financial rewards. It was the summer high season, and prices were up to triple the norm. Marshall had one trawler out that night, the 70-foot wooden-hulled *Josephine Jean*, but rough weather had forced it close to the coast.

When the call came in, Marshall assessed the situation and realized that with the yacht sinking the quickest response would come by diverting *Josephine Jean*. Marshall also knew that if anyone could cope with the weather, it was the trawler's skipper, Ollie Hreinisson. A native of Iceland and an extremely good seaman, Hreinisson had worked the big North Sea trawlers before coming to Australia.

"We could tell from the way the *Miintinta* crew were talking on the radio that they were physically and mentally exhausted. They seemed to be losing their ability to rationalize the situation, and that led us to think the position they had given to the Coastal Patrol was wrong," said Marshall. "I calculated that they weren't out quite as far as they thought they were. I proved that to them when the ship went to stand by them. We then knew exactly where they were. We plotted that and worked out it would take between two and three hours to get there."

Just over two hours later, the crew on *Josephine Jean* had *Miintinta* in their sights. Maneuvering the lumbering trawler over and around massive breaking seas in the dark and getting it close enough to *Miintinta* so that a towline could be thrown took great courage and skill. Hreinisson made it look easy.

"It was brilliant seamanship on his part," recalls Emerson. "He circled us about three times with his big searchlight on us and then he moved in. It was the most amazing situation. One minute the trawler was 50 feet above us and the next thing it was 50 feet below us."

After considerable effort, Emerson and Gordon secured and lashed the towline to the bollard on the foredeck, but not before *Miintinta* stuck its bow into one big wave and a three-meter wall of water picked Emerson up and hurled him over the side. His safety harness saved him. The next wave washed him back over the lifelines and onto the deck. He recalls that his main worry was losing his seaboots.

Emerson knew that they would have to continue bailing to keep the yacht afloat, but he was confident they would be able to save it. Volkes, a man in his fifties, ate and drank while he bailed.

"He cut off this blooming great slab of salami and then, while chewing on it, he drank a beer and kept bailing," recalls Emerson. "It was all too much for McKenzie. Her seasickness went from bad to horrible."

The crew didn't know *Josephine Jean* was making less than one knot headway back toward the coast. It was going to be exhausting to keep the yacht afloat during the time it would take to reach Eden. An hour into the tow, the last of the bilge pumps broke and both crews were faced with the possibility that the yacht might still be lost. As *Miintinta* became heavier with rising water, the load on the metal bollard at the bow increased dramatically until it simply disintegrated, taking the tow line with it. Hreinisson managed to get the towline back to the yacht, but even then, Emerson knew that his yacht was destined to sink.

At 3 A.M. Emerson radioed Coastal Patrol in Eden to report that the only alternative for the crew was to abandon the yacht. "For God's sake, don't fool around. If you have to get off, then *get off*," responded the radio operator. Emerson spoke with Hreinisson, who suggested the crew jump onto the trawler, but the state of the seas and the thrashing propeller blades ruled that out. The crew scrambled into the life raft, which had been tossed into the ocean and inflated at the stern of the yacht, and Emerson was about to follow. The umbilical cord between the raft and the yacht broke as a big wave washed through. Emerson threw a line from the yacht, and crew in the raft grabbed it. They struggled to hang on, though the line cut into their hands.

There was only one thing to do: leap. Emerson did, crashing on top of those in the raft. They watched as *Josephine Jean* began a long, slow loop back to the raft, *Miintinta* wallowing along behind, half-submerged. It took 45 minutes to close the distance. Large lights illuminated its decks, making the trawler easy to see. After circling into position directly downwind of the raft, Hreinisson again showed his skill by edging the trawler close. He recalls that the moment the big boat was within reach, the *Miintinta* crew scrambled up the side "like drowned rats."

The first light of day was appearing when the six exhausted sailors, still soaked and in their foul-weather gear, collapsed on the aft deck of the trawler. Soon after, they heard Hreinisson shout, "The tow's broken off!" As *Josephine Jean* continued on its slow passage toward Eden, the crew watched their yacht, then very low in the water, listing to one side. They lost sight of it on the eastern horizon before it went under.

When they reached Eden later that day, Emerson went straight to Marshall to thank him profoundly for what he and the crew of the trawler had done to rescue the *Miintinta* crew.

"Look, I'm a professional fisherman," replied Marshall. "We make our livelihood from the sea. If I ever get caught in the way that you were, I just hope to God that someone would do the same thing and come and get me."

Fifteen

Business Post Naiad

Bruce Guy and his crew considered Bass Strait their home ground when it came to offshore racing, and they were convinced they had seen the worst it could dish up. Only weeks before the 1998 Sydney to Hobart, *Business Post Naiad* had powered through a bitterly cold and arduous storm to register a surprise win in a 120-mile race across the Strait from Melbourne to Stanley, Tasmania.

"We weren't bad for what some people might have called a bunch of weekend sailors," said Rob Matthews. "The Stanley race was on the nose all the way, and it blew. It reminded us again that you have to treat Bass Strait with respect. If you don't, it can jump up and bite you." Matthews was probably the most experienced crewmember on board and had been sailing offshore for thirty-three of his forty-six years, clocking up a monumental 50,000 sea miles along the way, including nine Hobarts and a race around Australia.

Business Post Naiad was originally the successful New Zealand Admiral's Cup team yacht, *Swuzzlebubble*. Built in 1984 using the latest high-strength/low-weight composite construction technology and material, it came into Bruce Guy's hands after he purchased it from its Sydney owner in 1994. In 1998 Guy and a number of his Hobart race crew sailed into prominence when they won Tasmania's highest-profile race, the Three Peaks, a grueling ironman-style event requiring each yacht to race to three ports near mountains. Upon arrival, two of the crew must scale the peak before returning to the yacht and setting sail for the next port. It offers painful pleasure.

Guy was renowned for his meticulous race preparation. "The mast had been out of the yacht to be painted and rerigged," explained Matthews. "Every track worked—everything worked as it should. Nothing was left to chance, not even with the safety gear. It was an attitude that led to us having no concern about the Hobart race, no matter what the weather. We believed the yacht had seen everything when it came to the weather and could handle it."

Twenty-four hours into the race *Business Post Naiad* was 40 miles offshore, having covered 230 nautical miles with the assistance of the southerly current. The crew was justifiably ecstatic. Just after midday the wind was blowing a steady 20 to 30 knots and the sky was a beautiful deep blue. The yacht was sailing nicely under a No. 4 headsail and a double-reefed mainsail.

"We'd heard the forecast, 45 to 55 knots, and we all knew what a storm warning meant," said Matthews. "There was no concern. We'd also heard the warning put out by Telstra Control on *Young Endeavour*, reminding every skipper it was their responsibility when it came to continuing to race or retiring. Bruce, Keatsy, Steve Walker, and I were the sort of brain-trust, but we hadn't sat down and discussed it. We just thought, 'Righty-oh, 45 to 55 knots. We've all been here before. If it gets to 55 we might have to take things very carefully, perhaps even run off, maybe even go bare poles. We'll just hang around and wait for it to go and then start racing again.' We talked about the guys on other boats who hadn't seen Bass Strait in those conditions. There were some guys we'd spoken to in Sydney who were saying it was their first Hobart and that they were a little nervous. We'd all been there before, or thought we'd been there before."

Around 12:30 P.M. on December 27, the crew tucked a third reef into the mainsail. Thirty minutes later the rain arrived, and conditions began to deteriorate quickly. By 2 P.M. the winds were blowing 35 to 45 knots and showing every sign of getting stronger. The seas were worse than anything Matthews had ever seen. *Business Post Naiad* would soon be in the wrong place at the wrong time.

"The waves weren't all that high at that stage, but they had a very sharp face and an almost equally sharp back," said Matthews. "We were still able to sail OK; we'd sail up the face and drop the nose of the boat off over the back. The boat was handling it reasonably well, but it was starting to get a bit uncomfortable. When the wind got to about 45 knots we took the No. 4 off and just went under the main with three reefs. It was then that the wind and the seas got worse and worse. The wind went up to about 55, but the boat still seemed OK. We could see a break in the cloud out to the west and we thought, 'Well, you know, maybe this is it. The storm will all be over soon.' But then Keatsy came on deck from the nav station and said, 'We're going to get 24 hours of this shit now.'"

At around 3:30 that afternoon the top batten in the mainsail popped out. The crew flaked the mainsail and tied it down as neatly as they could, then put on the storm jib. The seas were getting rougher and the enormous waves were breaking in rapid succession. At the helm, Matthews was having considerable difficulty getting the bow to head up the crests of the waves. He was concerned that if the yacht went down the face of an especially large wave they might pitchpole—flip end-over-end.

"Every now and then the boat would get raked by one of these big breaking crests and would lie on its side and surf along, the bow being pressed down by the storm jib. The rain was driving. It made your face feel as if it was going to bleed. I had a couple of rain drops hit me in the eye a few times and blind me. It was at least half a minute until I got some sort of sight back. And the spume! It was even coming off the water out of the troughs of the waves—not just off the crests. It was being driven up and out of the troughs, a horizontal whiteout. It was hitting your face so hard there was no way you could look into it. We knew we had to do something to slow the boat and hopefully make it a little more comfortable. I wouldn't say that we were concerned, just cautious. We wanted to let the storm blow itself out. There was no panic on deck. Everybody knew exactly what everyone else was capable of doing.

"The storm jib blew out of the plastic foil on the forestay at one stage when we got knocked off by a big wave. Steve went up and put it back in. About ten minutes later it did it again. After the third time, Steve and Phil went up on the foredeck and spent an hour tying loops from the sail around the forestay. It was an amazing effort in those conditions."

In a few hours, the *Business Post Naiad* crew had gone from a fast, satisfying race into a gut-wrenching fight for survival. Steve Walker remembers looking up and seeing waves towering well above the 17-meter-high mast. At times visibility was down to 20 meters. Still, there was no talk of retiring. By late afternoon, though, as the winds peaked at 75 knots, the smallest of sails, the storm jib, was too much. *Business Post Naiad* was being belted so hard and tossed around so violently that even the crew below deck were in danger of injury from being thrown from their bunks. They realized that to run off down the face of the waves in those conditions would be calamitous: the yacht sooner or later would have been pitchpoled. They discussed setting a parachute anchor, or drogue, off the bow. Walker, being the on-board sailmaker, was trying to work out how he could fashion something from what was available. Meanwhile, they took down the storm jib and proceeded under bare poles. The yacht would be picked up and hurled forward by waves approaching from the aft starboard quarter, then forcibly pivoted to poke its bow up into the crests before they arrived.

Business Post Naiad hit more than 25 knots that afternoon but still appeared quite stable, even when beam on to the sea. The crew was far from happy having to "bare-pole it" in a race, but they understood it was their only option. Amid the chaos, Tony Guy, who had just handed over the helm to Matthews, decided he'd sit on deck and have a cigarette. To everyone's astonishment he managed to light the cigarette in 70 knots of wind and bulletlike rain.

"Hang on, here's another one!" Matthews shouted as a towering wave appeared from nowhere. The alarm in his voice told the crew how bad it was: a wave the height of a five-story building was beginning to break some 40 feet above them, and they were completely at its mercy. In an instant, the gargantuan curling crest extended over the 8-ton yacht, picked it up, tipped it on its side, and hurled it into the trough. Instinctively, the five crew on deck grabbed whatever they could to save themselves.

"The yacht landed on its roof and rolled back upright very quickly, almost instantly," recalls Matthews. "The tiller extension was ripped from my hand, and I thought there was no point in steering when we're upside down, anyway. The next thing I knew I was in the water alongside the yacht, on the windward side. There was a deathly calm because the wave had disappeared and the next wave hadn't arrived. My first reaction was to look straight up to see whether the rig had survived. It wasn't there. It was buckled and bent over the windward side. I looked around to see who was in the water with me and discovered there were five of us, all with our harnesses on, just bobbing around. Keatsy had rushed up on deck, worried about us because of what he had seen happen below. He helped us get back on deck, then we all set about getting rid of the rig before it could push a hole in the hull. It was broken into three pieces. Phil Skeggs saw it and said, 'This wasn't in the brochure.'"

Steve Walker was below deck during the roll and remembers the stove and oven breaking away from its mount and flying across the cabin. The ice chest disgorged its 50 prepacked frozen meals, and plates, cups, and saucers leaped out of lockers, spewing everywhere. Some of the floorboards flew out, and the anchor chain and anchor ropes tumbled from the lockers that were unceremoniously transformed into upturned bunks. The two aluminum- framed pilot berths were also broken.

"One of the windows—they were quite small—had broken and another was cracked," recalls Walker. "The bulkheads around the companionway had sprung away from the hull and the underside of the deck had delaminated. Water continued to pour in through the broken window when we were upright, so we just stuffed a couple of pillows in the gaps. Thank God we had pillows. So much for the people who laughed when they saw us taking pillows on board."

"I heard this tremendous roar, and next thing we were upside down," recalls Peter Keats. "It all went black in the cabin, absolutely pitch black. I thought, 'Oh, well, that's it—she's all over. We're finished.' At the same time you didn't have time to panic. It just happened, and then the boat came upright. I ended up on the floor with a heap of sails on top of me. I heard the guys call for help, and I flew up and found them all over the side. I can still remember the amazing roar of the storm while I was on deck. It sounded like an express train coming at me, or as if I'd been standing behind a jumbo jet as it was taking off."

Twenty minutes after the roll, at around 6:50 P.M., most of the crumpled mast had been dumped and the deck cleared. What was now little more than a hulk was being pounded regularly by the powerful broken crests of 60-foot waves. Each time one approached, those on deck would hang on, pinning faith in their safety harnesses but knowing this wave might be it. The weather didn't seem to be easing; in fact it appeared to be worsening.

The EPIRB was activated, and Keats grappled for the radio and issued a mayday. Fortunately, the backstay, which was the yacht's radio antenna, was lying on the deck and functioning, although with a considerably weaker signal. Geoff Ross's Beneteau 53, *Yendys*, acknowledged the mayday and relayed the message to Lew Carter aboard *Young Endeavour*. *Business Post Naiad*'s position was 42 miles into Bass Strait, south of Gabo Island. Keats turned his attention to the engine and after a few frustrating minutes managed to bring it to life. Now that the crew had regained some control over the vessel, and they quickly turned toward Gabo Island. Water continued to pour in, so the crew took turns with the bailing buckets.

"We were doing about five or six knots through the water, but it was only about two knots over the bottom according to the GPS, partly due to the current and certainly because of the waves," recalls Matthews. "The motor would scream its head off every time it went through the white water and tops of the waves because the propeller would just cavitate. We were still getting knocked sideways by breaking waves, and at times we actually surfed on our side for probably 200 meters. It was scary, really scary. We could hear Telstra Control on

Young Endeavour dealing with *Team Jaguar*, but they couldn't hear us. We called for further assistance through *Yendys*, asking for a boat to stand by. Keatsy also requested a chopper to take three off—I was apparently one of them because, for some reason, I couldn't move my arms."

After working on the *Team Jaguar* situation for some time, Telstra Control came back to *Business Post Naiad*. Matt Sherriff was violently ill, and although the crew was concerned, they took the opportunity to blame Keats's cooking. It hurt Keats to laugh at their humor. He had suffered two broken ribs when he crashed from the companionway stairs into the cabin.

"I didn't cancel the mayday," said Keats. "I was asked whether the mayday was still in existence and I said, 'Yes, the situation has stabilized. We are attempting to power back to wherever we can get to; Gabo or Eden. At best, you may reduce it to a Pan Pan but certainly no more than that—and I would request that if there are any boats in the vicinity we would like someone to stand by.' The request for the boat to stand by us was in case we were rolled again. I didn't really get a reply. I turned to Bruce soon after and said, 'I'm not looking forward to us trying to go through the night like we are—I'm concerned.' He agreed. I again tried to contact Telstra Control to see if we could get a chopper but couldn't get a reply. They may not have heard us." At that point Telstra Control had their hands full. The crew discussed what to do with the life rafts and decided to leave them where they were for the time being.

Later that night, somewhere between ten and eleven o'clock, a light plane roared out of the darkness and circled low overhead. The plane, homing in on the EPIRB, reported back to AusSAR that "Breakfast Toast Naiad" had been located. The humor, intentional or not, would have been lost on the *Naiad* crew.

Having regained use of his arms, Rob Matthews steered that evening in perpetual awe of the storm's ferocity. He had been sailing for thirty-seven years and had seen nothing like it. He tried to familiarize himself with the conditions and the motion of the yacht. He found the only way to judge the course was to read the angle of the wind on his face. The boom with the mainsail wrapped around it was lashed on the windward side of the cockpit behind him, providing a modicum of protection. Matthews was also trying to keep an eye on the dimly lit compass just four feet away, squinting to keep the stinging salt spray out of his eyes. Phil Skeggs came on deck, intending to relieve Matthews of the compass watch. The noise of the storm was so great that he had to scream out the heading.

Business Post Naiad had powered due north some 20 miles but was no nearer the coast. For a brief moment the clouds parted and the moon shed an eerie light on the mayhem. The moon disappeared as quickly as it had appeared, leaving the crew wishing it had taken with it the constant roar of the storm. Matthews was repeatedly calling out to Skeggs to hold on as each wave approached, but nothing could prepare them for the monster wave that suddenly whelmed them. It happened so quickly that Matthews's first recollection was being trapped underwater at the aft end of the cockpit, unable to move. The colossal wave had rolled the 40-foot yacht forward and upside down like a pebble.

"It was surreal, deathly quiet, because you could feel the yacht still surfing sideways," said Matthews. "All the time I was being slammed up under the side of the boat and my head was banging on the cockpit floor—above me. My life jacket and float coat were holding me up there. I knew exactly where I was because I could reach aft and feel the stern of the yacht. I was underwater and outside the aft lifelines, which are about a meter forward of the transom. Initially I didn't make any attempt to unhook my harness or try to swim out. I immediately had trouble when I eventually did try to release my harness clip. The boat was still being surfed sideways and all the while my head was slamming the cockpit floor. My harness strop was almost fully extended. There was just enough play in it to unclip. But each time I tried, the notch in the clip slotted over the stainless-steel plate on the front of my harness. It just jammed and I couldn't free it."

Matthews was almost out of oxygen and would likely have drowned but for another freak wave that lifted the stern just enough to let a puff of air dart under the cockpit floor. He pressed his nose against the floor and filled his lungs with the biggest gulp of air he could muster. Exhausted but breathing, he managed to free himself finally from the harness strop and pull himself to the back of the still-over-turned boat and up to the surface, where he srated calling to Skeggs. His main concern was that Skeggs might be similarly trapped in his harness, and he desperately wanted to dive back under the boat and search. But it was dark, he was fatigued from his own ordeal, and, apart from the time it would take to remove his buoyancy aids, there was the distinct chance he'd lose them altogether. Also, he didn't know where to start looking, and he could well have become trapped himself.

He remembered hearing of a singlehanded round-the-world race competitor who had survived by climbing onto his upturned yacht and attaching himself to the rudder. Matthews devised a plan. He would swim around to the side, try to stand on one of the wire lifelines, or side rails, and somehow launch himself toward his target. The odds were against him, but he had to try. As he swam to the side of the yacht, he stayed as close to it as possible so he wouldn't be washed away. He felt something brush against his leg underwater. It was a section of the broken mast that had been lashed to the deck. Matthews sat on it initially to rest then tried to stand on it and prepare for the leap, but he was too exhausted. All he could do was sit, hang on the best he could, and pray.

The sea was unrelenting, and an agonizing four to five minutes after the yacht overturned yet another behemoth of a wave came crashing toward *Business Post Naiad*. Matthews first heard it rumbling out of the gloom, then saw its churning white collar descending from above. It engulfed the boat, exerting enough force on the upturned keel to tip it up onto its side, where the full pendulum effect of the keel took over, whipping the boat upright.

"I don't know what I was hanging onto, possibly a stanchion, but suddenly I ended up on my feet in a squatting position from where I'd taken off; on the piece of cockpit floor that had been above my head when I was trapped. I can only assume that I was flicked through the air, did a back flip of sorts and ended up back on the deck. My lifeline harness that I'd unclipped was there in front of me, draped over the lifeline. I clipped myself on and stepped back inside the rail."

As Matthews regathered his senses he was confronted with the sight of Phil Skeggs, face down in the cockpit. His legs hung limply over the broken boom and protruded over the lifelines. Still held by his harness, Skeggs's body was wrapped in ropes. Matthews yelled for assistance from below. Crewmembers scrambled on deck and frantically cut away the harness and stray ropes and performed CPR and mouth-to-mouth resuscitation.

It was to no avail. Phil Skeggs was dead.

The massive wave had also wreaked havoc below deck. Half asleep, Steve Walker heard a loud swoosh, then an enormous roar, audible even above the noise of the diesel. With the aid of the faint light from their miners' headlamps, he and Bruce Guy had kicked out the stormboards in the companionway. This allowed more water in but only to the point where the air pressure equalized. A quick inspection of the keel revealed minimal damage. In the ghostly dim light a black figure appeared out of nowhere. It was Jim Rogers, covered in oil. He had been dozing alongside the motor for warmth when the yacht rolled.

The water was nearly knee-height in the cabin and was strewn with detritus: food, clothing, bottles, diesel, oil, and sails. Above the roar of the storm, the seven crewmembers trapped inside the overturned yacht could hear Matthews calling frantically for Skeggs. Bruce Guy suggested kicking a life raft out through the companionway to use if the yacht sank, but they decided the raft might stick in the companionway or the cockpit.

"The thought entered my mind that the yacht would not come back upright," recalls Keats. "She was floating so comfortably upside down due to the wide, flat deck. I was concerned because I couldn't see how we were going to get out. If the boat went down we were going to the grave with it."

When *Business Post Naiad* eventually came upright, a meter of water remained in the cabin.

"As the yacht righted, Bruce seemed to slip in the water and almost went under. He struggled to get up, and I went to help him. As

I grabbed him I could see he was in terrible pain, mainly from the left side of his chest. His eyes rolled back and he died immediately, there and then in my arms, of a massive heart attack. There was nowhere I could lay him because he would be underwater. All I could do was sit on a bunk edge and hold him in my lap—hold his head above the water and try to keep his air passage clear. I felt for his pulse and his breath but there was nothing. I sort of knew instinctively that he was dead, but I didn't want to give up on him. Jim and I held him and did what we could. At the same time we didn't realize that the other guys were trying to revive Phil up on deck."

The water in the hull surged toward the bow with every wave and threatened to submerge it. *Business Post Naiad* was within centimeters of sinking, and water was still flooding into the hull, sloshing into the cabin out of the cockpit. Someone found a stormboard and put it in place—a makeshift and temporary measure in a dire situation.

In the confusion, a life raft accidentally inflated as it was passed up from the cabin to the cockpit. Crewmembers wrestled with it until it was eventually pushed over the side and tethered to the yacht. Flares also arrived on deck, but no one on hand knew how to fire them. Peter Keats tried frantically to read the instructions through his salt-encrusted glasses, but his hands were covered in oil. When he managed to get one out of the pack he was unable to get the cap off.

"Eventually one of the guys got the first one going—an orange smoke flare—and gave it to me to hold," Keats recalls. "I then got hold of three parachute flares and let them go. I may as well have saved my energy. They went up fine and ignited, then disappeared to the east at an unbelievable speed because of the wind. They seemed to come back over us at a hundred miles an hour."

Because the batteries had been underwater and had short-circuited, the radios no longer worked. Hansen put some sails over the bow on a rope to act as a crude sea anchor. The second life raft, then on deck in its pack, was pushed back down below to protect it, but on the way it too was accidentally triggered. Four crewmembers struggled with the rapidly expanding rubber monster and ultimately got it on deck and over the side with the other raft.

Remembering that the bow ventilation port between the anchor locker and the forward cabin was open, Rob Matthews waded forward, smashed open the toilet door, and put the vent cover in place. That done, he rushed back to the raft. "We had thrown everything we thought we might need into one of the rafts—extra water, thermal rugs, some food, flares and things like that," he recalls. "When I went back on deck the raft was upside down and everything was lost."

With both bilge pumps clogged or broken, what was to be a three-hour bucket brigade against the incessantly rising water started. Two crewmembers handled the buckets below while two others on deck tipped the contents over the side. Peter Keats was on deck furiously bailing, soaking wet and freezing. He called for a jacket, but the only one they could find belonged to Bruce Guy. Once it was apparent that the buckets were stemming the tide, some of the crew moved Guy's body into an aft quarter berth. Neither Rob Matthews nor Peter Keats knew that Guy was dead.

The water level inside the cabin was brought down to a manageable level of around one meter, thus stabilizing the yacht. There was still the distinct possibility of another roll, but the weighted boat seemed to be handling the slamming waves a little better. The wind had lulled to 50 or 55 knots, which now felt like a pleasant afternoon breeze. The sails over the bow were holding *Business Post Naiad* up into the seas most of the time. There was no need for anyone to be on deck, so those who weren't bailing tried to rest. At around 3 A.M. another big wave swept across the yacht and submerged it, but this time it stayed upright. At one stage, well before daylight, one of the crew poked his head out of the companionway to check on the weather and saw something far more frightening. Both life rafts had gone. Their tether lines had either chafed through or parted.

"Some of the guys, particularly Keatsy, became pretty emotional about the loss of the rafts," recalls Rob Matthews, "but there was nothing we could do about it. We all knew that the only time you get into a life raft is when you step up to it. Our yacht had become our raft, and it was floating quite well. At dawn, Steve and I got up and went on deck to rig a red sail cover over the cabintop to make us more conspicuous, because we had a white boat, with a gray deck, on a gray sea, and white waves: we couldn't be seen too easily. We wanted to use the V-sheet, the orange distress sheet, but it had been washed out of its locker and lost. It was still blowing. There was still spume coming off the water, so I figured it was probably about 45 knots. I went back and rigged an oil can over the side, then punched a hole in it. It actually helped the situation. The oil drifting upwind on the surface of the sea did, to some extent, help smooth the seas as they came at us. It worked, but it wasn't enough.

"Steve went back down below, and I sat up there looking around for aircraft or something. At about 6 A.M. Matt Sherriff came up on deck and I said to him, 'I haven't seen Bruce up and about.'—I'd asked Steve during the night, 'Where's Bruce?' and he said, 'Oh, we've put him in a bunk.' I said 'Oh, right,' and thought no more about it.—Matt looked at me a little surprised and said, 'Oh, shit, mate, didn't you know? Bruce died last night.' That made me totally unstuck because I'd assumed he was down there in his bunk whacked and tired. It was seven hours after he died that I found out. I got really angry then, swearing and cursing and shouting about God knows what."

Around 7:30 A.M. on December 28 the crew spotted a light aircraft northwest and sent a red parachute flare arcing through the sky while igniting an orange smoke flare on deck. The plane turned and began circling the battered yacht, staying there an hour and acting as a beacon for the rescue chopper the crew prayed was on the way.

The NRMA Careflight helicopter out of Sydney arrived shortly after. At the controls was veteran pilot Dan Tyler; Graeme Fromberg was crewman, and Murray Traynor was the paramedic. They had been in Canberra on a medical mission late the previous day when they were "commandeered" by AusSAR and instructed to join the rescue effort as early as possible the next day. The only accommodation they could find at such a late hour was in the SouthCare headquarters at

Canberra airport. The four grabbed two fitful hours of sleep, two of them on the floor and two in beds, before a 4:30 A.M. launch for Merimbula. In Merimbula the Careflight team was initially asked to assist with a rescue of the Jarkan 40 *Midnight Special.*

"On the way out we heard a top cover plane flying around saying they'd just spotted a flare coming from one of the boats," recalls Murray Traynor. "They didn't know who it was but gave coordinates. We also heard that someone had completed the *Midnight Special* job. We were then only 7 to 10 minutes away from where the flare had gone off, so we diverted and came across *Business Post Naiad.* They were waving at us from the deck. Right from the start I didn't like the look of what I saw. The yacht was just flipped up onto its side by a massive wave. I'd never seen a wave that big in my life.

"Graeme and I spent some time just looking out the door, considering different ways we could extricate them. The first thing we decided was that we were not going to be able to pull them off the boat because it was being thrown everywhere. We couldn't tell which way the boat was going to go from one second to another. One of us suggested we try to get them to jump off the back of the boat and swim away from it, then I'd go down and we'd winch them straight out of the water. We went into a hover near the yacht and acted out what we wanted them to do: I'd come down the wire and I'd have this strop. I put it over Graeme's head and showed them what they were supposed to do. They seemed to acknowledge it."

Murray Traynor clipped onto the winch wire and began what was only his second, and certainly most dangerous, sea rescue. He knew that one mistake could result in the wire wrapping around a limb or even his neck. It required an exceptional team effort between pilot, winchman, and paramedic.

"We decided it would be safer if we looped one of the spinnaker sheets through my safety harness so we could double-end it back to the boat," recalls Rob Matthews. "I figured that the guys would be able to winch me back to the yacht if the chopper guys didn't get me. Anyway, I jumped off the back of the boat and this frogman came down and swam toward me. I unclipped my harness, put my arms up and the strop went over my head, then *whammo!* Next thing I'm being launched out of the water at a hundred miles an hour and up into this chopper.

"They whacked a headset on me and started firing questions, obviously wanting to see whether I was able to tell them what they needed to know. Making me do mental arithmetic about how many guys were on the boat and how many were dead. They could see Phil in the cockpit. They were asking, 'Is the guy in the bottom of the cockpit deceased?' I said, 'Yes, and there's another downstairs.' They wanted to make sure they got everyone accounted for. I also heard the pilot say, 'I think I'm only going to have enough fuel to get four on. We'll have to leave the rest until later.' The waves were still enormous, and that boat still looked like it could roll at any time.

"The other guys started arriving in the chopper. I have to say that the one guy in the team who doesn't get enough recognition is the winchman. You've got the pilot, who's just unbelievable, and the frogman who is outright mad, and then there's the winchman who is the integral part of the whole situation. He's the eyes and the ears of the chopper pilot. Things were obviously going well because after there were four of us on the chopper I heard the pilot say, 'These guys are good. Everything's going well. We're going to get them all. I had a big surge of relief—it was a fantastic feeling."

Although the rescue mission was progressing satisfactorily, it was still a hellish experience for the chopper crew. Tyler had the unenviable task holding the machine in hover against 45 to 50 knots of head wind. Traynor, dicing with death each time he winched down, was caught by two big waves. He had one crewmember in the strop ready to go when a mammoth wave appeared and broke directly over them. Two meters under, he paddled furiously back to the surface and blew the water out of his snorkel. But before he could take a breath, another wave pushed him under. He tried to relax, and within a second he and the crewmember were hurtling skyward.

"During the first few winches I wasn't aware there were two people dead on board the boat, so I didn't have that thought pressuring me," recalls Traynor. "The realization that someone might be dead didn't come until probably the fourth winch because I could see one person lying flat on the boat. I said to Graeme a couple of times when

I was back in the chopper, 'What's happening with that bloke on the deck?' and he said, 'It doesn't matter, just keep going down.' He thought I knew he was dead. I think it was the fourth winch when I stopped halfway down and looked at this bloke on the deck. I looked up at Graeme, shut my eyes, and crossed my arms across my chest. I signaled, asking if he wanted me to go and get him. He signaled 'Don't worry about it.' That's when I realized he was gone. I still didn't know there was a second person deceased on board.

"My biggest fear then was that I was going to have to go on board to get that person off. If I went aboard the boat, I would have had to come off the hook, which means my lifeline is gone. If the chopper had to fly away I'd be stuck out there, and I'm no boating person whatsoever. That was my biggest fear during the entire exercise."

Some 35 minutes after the rescue had begun there were seven depressed and badly beaten men aboard the Careflight helicopter. Dan Tyler turned it toward the coast, and at 9 A.M. on December 28 all seven were on dry land. A police launch left the next day, located *Business Post Naiad*, and towed it back into port with the bodies of Bruce Guy and Phil Skeggs on board.

Sixteen

Solo Globe Challenger

During the night of December 26, Tony Mowbray, owner of *Solo Globe Challenger*, received a phone call from a television reporter in his hometown of Newcastle who was preparing a story on the progress of the region's leading race entry. The reporter commented during the conversation that Mowbray seemed "pretty relaxed" about the forecast for 50-knot southwesterly winds the next day. Mowbray, having covered thousands of sea miles offshore in small yachts, replied, "Oh, well, you know, I've seen 50 knots plenty of times. I've crossed Bass Strait maybe thirty times." Twenty hours later Mowbray was shaking his head in disbelief as he tried to comprehend what was confronting him and his Cole 43.

Solo Globe Challenger is a comparatively slim yacht, but Mowbray saw it as a strong and very seaworthy design that would hold him in good stead on his proposed solo around-the-world voyage in 1999. His seven crew had similar faith. Until midday on December 27, they felt they were still competitive. They had been changing sails as required and were down to a storm jib. They were then about 30 miles into Bass Strait, not far from *Winston Churchill*, and encountering conditions Mowbray considered "fairly dangerous."

"We had probably 60 knots of wind and it was starting to get vicious. The seas were fairly short and sharp and close together, probably in the 20- to 30-foot range. Already the noise from the wind and the seas was amazing, just shrieking and roaring. You had to shout at the top of your voice to be heard by someone who was just a body's width away. At that point we pulled the storm jib off completely and proceeded to sail under bare poles. Ours is one of those boats where you can actually maintain a course under bare poles. We were getting up and over the waves, and it was certainly the safer option at that time. We had no desire to run away square with the waves."

Mowbray had not slept since the start of the race some twenty-four hours earlier, so when the 2:05 P.M. sked began he went below, climbed into the port quarter berth, and tuned into the airwaves while veteran Bob Snape reported the yacht's position and monitored developments. He listened keenly as *Sword of Orion* detailed the conditions they were experiencing, but he still felt confident that he had a solid boat and an excellent crew. Glen "Cyril" Picasso, a competent helmsman, was at the wheel, and three other crew were on deck with him.

The fresh on-deck watch was amazed at the speed with which the weather was going downhill. In just ninety minutes, conditions had gone from what some sailors might call "fresh," to "frightening," to nothing short of horrific. The wind seemingly rose in increments of five knots every fifteen minutes, and the waves more than doubled in height. At around 4 P.M. a 60-foot monster came roaring toward the yacht, picked it up, and threw it down on its port side. When the wave broke it dumped, forcing the boat over to about 145 to 150 degrees before sweeping it down the face for about twenty seconds.

In his bunk, Mowbray was taken completely unaware. "It was surreal. I was saying to myself, 'What the fuck is happening here?' It's a situation where you are totally out of control, you're in a washing machine, and someone's put it on bloody fast agitate and that's it, it's all over." The mast broke almost immediately, just above the boom and the sea engulfed the yacht, its force imploding the PVC skylight above Mowbray's bunk. Water poured into the nav station at the forward end of the quarter berth and swamped everything: GPS, radios, Satcom C, and mobile telephone. Bob Snape, who had been sitting there, ended up a sodden and bewildered tangle of arms and legs.

"I managed to struggle to the hatch and open it," recalls Mowbray. "I had four guys up on deck. One guy had been knocked unconscious but was coming around. The mast had come down over the port quarter and was hanging out over the port aft corner of the cockpit. His legs were pinned by the mast, so as the boat rode up and down over the waves the rig was sawing at his legs. Suddenly he was screaming like you wouldn't believe."

Mowbray's attention then turned to the water behind the yacht. Picasso, still attached by his safety harness, was being dragged along under the water. He said later that his life was flashing through his mind. He said to himself, "For Christ's sake, this harness better not break." His harness suddenly went limp and he stopped dead in the water. He put his hand up, touched the boat's stern, and grabbed the pushpit. Under the pressure of the moment, Mowbray uttered "one of the silliest things I've ever said: 'Cyril, for Christ's sake stop fucking around and get back on board.' Then I turned around and went to help the other guys. As I did, Cyril looked at me and said, 'Right, oh?' So that's what he did, climbed back on board, busted ribs and all."

Meanwhile, Keir Enderby was trapped by the rig and Tony Purkiss was also lying there with a broken leg and a terrible gash on his head. The able crewmembers did what they could to make the injured comfortable in the cockpit, but the yacht also needed attention. It had skewed off course and the smashed mast was now lying upwind. Each wave was slamming the broken and jagged aluminum spar into the side of the hull. The yacht was taking on a lot of water and showed signs of sinking by the stern. Cutting the rig away was paramount. Mowbray and three other crewmembers went forward to the mast, and within fifteen minutes removed the rig. Fortunately, none of it had snagged the rudder.

Snape had triggered both on-board EPIRBs and had started bailing. Two others manned the manual pumps, and after about forty-five minutes the tide of water inside the hull was well down. They tried to start the engine, but its response was spasmodic. It would run and then die, apparently because water had found its way into the fuel system via the fuel tank vent and sediment from the fuel filters had been stirred up. With the situation partially stabilized, some of the injured were transferred to bunks below, but Purkiss could not be moved without excruciating pain from his broken leg. He chose to remain in the cockpit.

As the only heavy-weather helmsman fit for action, Mowbray took the helm to guide the yacht down the waves. It was then about 5 P.M. and, with all communications lost, the crew were isolated in their little cocoon. Only their EPIRBs would be bouncing information back to AusSAR in Canberra. They had not yet prepared the life raft; Mowbray felt that should be a last, desperate alternative. During the night mammoth waves continued to pound them, tossing the 43-foot, nine-ton vessel like a cork. Caught on the northern side of the low and running downwind, they were moving with the worst of the storm and were destined to remain in foul weather for the next fifteen hours.

"We went into the night thinking the next wave could be the one that took us out," Mowbray recalls. "It was a very, very fearful situation. As far as I was concerned, death was right there in the water alongside us. You could sense it there. I was thinking, 'If I get out of this I'm going to be a lucky bloke.' We hadn't done anything special about preparing the life raft. It was still in place on deck near the mast. Actually, I've never been a great believer about getting into rafts; it's a bit like slashing your wrists before you die. It's the absolute last alternative. As we charged off into the night, we were tossed on our beam ends by a number of waves. In fact the waves did all sorts of things to us that night. One monster reared up behind and broke over the four of us in the cockpit. We sensed it was coming, and the others dropped to the floor to protect themselves. The white water threw me forward into the wheel. It was just an unbelievable wave.

"The whole boat was engulfed in white water, completely submerged. I was still on my feet, and the water was at chest level. I was looking ahead across all this white water while the boat careered down the face of the wave, completely hidden. All I could make out was the top of the bow pulpit. I yelled at the top of my voice, 'This is it! This is the one! We're gone!' I was thinking, 'When we hit the bottom of this bloody trough, the nose is going to keep going down and we're going to pitchpole.' Somehow, when we got to the bottom, the yacht stopped and we bobbed back up to the surface.

"There was one other wave I will never forget. It was huge, and the moment it hit it skewed us 90 degrees to our course. It picked us up, and the boat took off across its face like a surfboard. We were absolutely charging across the wave, literally thumping across the water like you do in a high-performance sailing dinghy.

"But we're in a 43-foot, 9-ton yacht. It's going whack, whack, whack across the wave, doing 15, maybe 20 knots, and I'm hanging onto the wheel, crouched down, waiting for the wave to break over us. I'm thinking, 'What do I do? Do I try and pull the boat away? Do I let it go straight ahead and try to steady it? Do I try and pull up through the back of it or what?' Then I realized the yacht was hanging in there. I decided to steer straight and let her go the way she wanted. This is all happening in a split second. I'm crouched down waiting for the water to swallow us—that's how big this bastard was—and then suddenly I'm thinking, 'God, I've got no water around. I've got my eyes and my mouth closed and there's no water. What's going on?' I opened my eyes and looked up and I could see the water curling over us. We were literally in the tube of the wave. It was phenomenal, unbelievable. You could see it breaking over us, and we were staying just ahead of the break. Next thing, of course, it caught up and *whumphh*, broke over us. Equally quickly, it was gone.

"I looked back upwind and could see white water for 400 meters. The amount of it was incredible. I made a few promises to myself. I decided that if I survived I was going to give up the plan to sail around the world. I'd imposed myself on my wife and children and my family and friends too much. You have to follow your passion, but there comes a point to back off."

At one stage the crew considered setting a sea anchor to slow the boat, but Mowbray's experience fighting a 50- to 60-knot Southern Ocean gale some years earlier assured him that what they were doing was safer.

"Throughout the night I kept wanting to see stars. We started seeing little patches of stars up there and I'd think, 'OK, please stay open, open up.' But they'd close over again. We just had to be patient. I steered the boat from five o'clock Sunday afternoon throughout the whole night. By the early hours of Monday morning I was absolutely ratshit. With my good helmsman injured, I could do nothing else. I started hallucinating at one stage and saw a monkey sitting on the broken stump of the mast. When I knew that it wasn't real, I told the guys I could see it. I said, 'I can see a monkey on the mast.' They just said, 'Can you? Oh yeah, there he is.'"

The two EPIRBs were still operating, but the crew didn't know if their signals were reaching AusSAR. They discussed how they might get off the boat, and concluded that they probably couldn't: it was dark, the seas were unforgiving, and the boat was being hurled around like a bucking bronco. Someone would almost certainly be killed. Mowbray had never contemplated abandoning his prized yacht, but that night admitted to himself that if his life could be assured by leaving the boat, he'd do it.

"By 1 A.M. I was shattered; unbelievably tired. I said to the guys, 'Have you got anything that can keep me awake?' and they came up with the idea of coffee. So Bob Snape made me three cups between 1 A.M. and about 4:30 A.M., so strong you could have stood the spoon up in them. They were like drinking bitumen. I hadn't drunk coffee for six years, but I did then. Each time I took a sip I'd go, 'Whoa, whoa,' and my mouth would take on the shape of a cat's bum. But I drank them—straight black. Anyhow it kept me going."

When dawn broke, a glimmer of black slowly turning to gray in the east, Mowbray noticed signs of the wind abating. It was down to around 45 knots, and the 50- to 60-foot seas that had hounded them all night had quelled to around 40 feet.

As the light improved, tired eyes again scanned the skies for any form of assistance, and around 7 A.M. the blissful sound of a He-limed helicopter filled their ears. They fired flares, and the big red and white Bell 412 turned their way. With no radio communications, the chopper crew indicated by hand that they intended to take every-one from the yacht. But Mowbray thought otherwise. He was con-vinced *Solo Globe Challenger* could be nursed back to port. He did, however, insist that the most seriously injured crew be lifted off.

Cam Robertson was the paramedic on the flight. They had been dispatched from Mallacoota at 6 A.M. and sent to investigate the *Solo Globe Challenger* EPIRB signal that AusSAR was registering.

Despite the huge seas and high winds, Robertson saw all three rescues as "pretty straightforward." He would be lowered into the water near the yacht, a crewmember would jump from the yacht, he would swim over, place the rescue strop around the crew, give the thumbs up, and head for the heavens. Amid the confusion, noise, and uncertainty about how much fuel the helicopter was carrying, one crewmember jumped into the water in haste and without a life jacket.

"It was Tony Purkiss, the guy with the broken leg," recalls Mowbray. "He believed that if you really seal up your wet weather gear tightly at the ankles and wrists and tie your hood down tight, there's enough air trapped inside your gear to float you for five minutes. So he put it to the test and it worked. When he was about to jump I saw that he still had his seaboots on, so I shouted, 'Get your boots off.' But he couldn't because of his broken leg. We all thought he'd go straight to the bottom, but he didn't.

"While they were getting lined up for one of the lifts I saw the chopper rear up into the air like a rocket. The next minute this huge wave came through. It would probably have wiped him out. That convinced me even more that those guys were absolute heroes. The guys in the choppers and the planes, and in particular the people who went into the drink from the choppers to rescue others—they're all superheroes."

Two crew with broken ribs remained on board, reluctant to be lifted lest they suffer further injury. Glen Picasso was prepared to go, but then "mateship" took over. "Glen actually appeared with his life jacket and started to walk toward the stern," said Mowbray. "He was ready to jump overboard and be lifted out. Then he stopped, looked at me, shook his head and said, 'I can't do it. I can't leave you guys.' He turned, went down below again, and closed the hatch."

With three rescued crew in its belly, the chopper headed for the coast some 60 miles away. *Solo Globe Challenger* continued its drift, the remaining crew determined to get it back to shore. Mowbray was severely fatigued but somehow mustered the energy to organize the building of a jury rig. Picasso took the helm so that Mowbray, Keith Molloy, and sixty-six-year-old Snape could go about the task. Enderby remained below because of the extent of his injuries.

The spinnaker pole became a makeshift mast, while the storm jib and trysail were hoisted to create a crude sail plan. The seas, rolling from the southwest, were still too big and dangerous to take beam-on, so the course was slightly east of north. To the best of the crew's knowledge, one of the two EPIRBs continued to transmit, telling the world the yacht was still afloat.

Conditions eased dramatically Monday afternoon, and *Solo Globe Challenger* assumed a more favorable course toward the coast. Picasso and Enderby, despite their injuries, worked tirelessly below deck to spur the motor back to life. The engine had so many problems with contaminated fuel, sediments, and water that the two crewmembers had to pull it apart piece by piece, examining, cleaning, and repairing where necessary. Unknown to them, the EPIRB they believed was transmitting had actually stopped, apparently because the antenna was damaged. That led SAR authorities in Canberra to fear that the yacht had sunk. A new search was established. Even local news reports in Newcastle suggested they might have joined the race's list of fatalities.

Soon after sunrise an Air Force Orion roared overhead and circled low, the flight crew trying to identify the yacht. They then dispatched smoke flares to check the wind speed and direction before dropping an emergency container into the ocean just ahead of the boat. It contained satchels of fresh water and a hand-held VHF. The remaining crewmembers aboard *Solo Globe Challenger* made contact with the twenty-six-year-old Orion captain, Paul Carpenter, who informed them that HMAS *Newcastle* was about 36 miles away and heading their way.

HMAS *Newcastle* had spent most of the night searching for *Solo Globe Challenger*, and the crew were extremely concerned because they knew that the yacht's EPIRB had stopped transmitting. Commander Steve Hamilton requested a special effort from all available on his undermanned ship to scan the ocean as they went into a search pattern 100 miles off the coast.

"We knew that the satellites had lost contact with the EPIRB, so we were more and more determined to find the yacht," recalls Hamilton. "We were frustrated by the fact that the seas were still around 25 feet—big enough to hide a boat from our eyes and radar. We centered our search around their last known position, not realizing that they had set a jury rig and were making ground north. Soon after daylight an Orion flew overhead and told us they had spotted the yacht 30 miles to the north."

Surmising that the Navy would want to take him and Enderby off, Picasso redoubled his efforts to start the engine and give Mowbray and the two remaining crew a better chance of reaching the coast. Only minutes before HMAS *Newcastle* appeared on the horizon to the south, the engine roared back to life.

"We had the hand-held VHF radio turned on," Mowbray recalls. "The next thing words burst from it that I'll never forget. '*Solo Globe Challenger*, this is the warship *Newcastle*.' I thought, 'you beauty, if these bastards can't save us, who will?' The ship came close to us and slowed. Then they sent two people—a male and a female—over to us in an inflatable boat. They came alongside and the young guy who was driving said, 'Good morning, sir,' and I said, 'Good morning to you, too.'

"'I'm instructed to remove all personnel from the vessel.'

"'Look, old mate, thanks very much for coming, but I really don't want to leave my boat.'

"'Oh, hang on a minute.' He had a bit of a chat into his mouthpiece, obviously talking to the skipper, then came back and asked, 'What would you like to do?'

"'Well, we've got two injured people here. We'd like to remove them if we may.'

"'That's fine.'"

Picasso and Enderby stepped gingerly into the inflatable and were whisked back to the ship. They were helped aboard and taken to the ship's small but impressive medical center, where the doctor treated them. As HMAS *Newcastle* turned toward Sydney, *Solo Globe*

Challenger was making about 5 knots toward Ulladulla under jury rig and motor. Before it disappeared, *Newcastle* advised that a fishing trawler had been sent out by an insurance company to tow the yacht into Eden.

At 4:30 the next morning, *Solo Globe Challenger* arrived in Eden at the end of a towline. Tony Mowbray still had his yacht and, possibly, his dream to sail nonstop around the world. It was a dream he'd renounced at the height of the storm, but the history of seafaring is littered with such promises, pledged in peril and broken when the weather turns fair.

"I think it's a bit like childbirth for a woman. You tend to forget the hard parts and want to do it again. There is one thing, though, that I certainly won't forget after going to hell and back. I'm not the sort of person who goes to sea undercooked; I'm always prepared for the worst, or at least I thought I was. I thought I knew where the top rung of the ladder was; now I know it's about 50 percent higher."

Seventeen
Winston Churchill, Part 2

O ver the course of six hours on December 27, the northeast corner of Bass Strait was a hellish place to be. Many of the 115 yachts in the race had been forced to retire through damage, injury to crew, or seasickness. Some crews chose to apply "prudent seamanship" and withdraw from the race, while others sought shelter in safe havens until the storm had passed. A minority, through desire or circumstance, continued racing toward Hobart.

Two yachts that the *Winston Churchill* crew were most keen to beat, Don Mickleborough's *Southerly* and Ian Kiernan's *Canon Maris*, were among the retirees late that afternoon. Two other seaworthy racers, Hugh Treharne's *Bright Morning Star* and Stephen Ainsworth's *Loki*, soon joined them. *Southerly* retired because of what, in hindsight, might have been a fortunate mistake. Mickleborough and his crew were unaware they were only about 48 miles from Eden when they decided their race was run. Had they known they were that far south, they might have continued deeper into the mayhem in Bass Strait.

Hugh Treharne had been aboard the Australian yacht *Too Impetuous* in the tragic 1979 Fastnet Race and ruefully remembers the conditions back then. "The Fastnet was like being in the fridge compared to this one. When a big wave poured over the top of *Bright Morning Star* [in the Sydney to Hobart], it was like being in a warm bath. The exposure to hypothermia in England was much worse: that's why they lost so many people. The conditions—wind and waves—were very similar, though. The only real difference was that in Bass Strait the seas were a lot more confused. My technique was to sail fast enough so I could poke the bow up into the waves and then through them. We were sailing with a deep reef in the main and no jib. The options were to run away with it and set either the trysail or storm jib or retire and go back to Eden under power.

"While I was trying to make up my mind, a huge wave arrived. I was looking a long way up at its crest—I had to stretch my neck. There was a lot of white water, a *lot* of white water coming at me, and the wave kept getting steeper and steeper. I braced myself by grabbing the wheel and leaning over it. There was nothing else to do. The moment it hit, the yacht was knocked over to 90 degrees with the mast in the water. I couldn't see for quite a few seconds. I was under green water. It wasn't just spray or a splash, it was hugely green. The water filled the mainsail and held the yacht down; it could have been 40 feet deep for all I know."

By the time *Bright Morning Star* righted, three crew in the cabin had suffered broken ribs. Treharne's brother, Ian, rushed on deck and worked with him to lower the mainsail. The engine was started. Eden would be *Bright Morning Star*'s new destination.

Michael "Zapper" Bell was one of three crewmembers on deck on Stephen Ainsworth's Swan 44, *Loki*. They were about 70 miles offshore and sailing under a storm jib when the wind instrument hit a staggering 74 knots. A rogue wave of enormous proportions loomed suddenly and broke above *Loki*. The yacht headed up the vertical wall of water and was then tossed back, landing upside down.

"What followed was the most amazing experience I've ever had at sea. There I was, underneath this upturned yacht in the most incredibly serene situation. I could have been swimming in the fish pond at home. In fact, it was like swimming in the Caribbean—the water was clear and warm. Everything was still and beautiful," he recalls. "My glasses were washed off my face, but I had time to reach out and grab them. I remember all the colored halyard tails and lines wafting through the water like sea snakes. I was surprised that I didn't feel panicked. I knew I had to release my safety harness at my chest to get out. I didn't gasp for breath or panic, I just made deliberate movements to escape. All of a sudden, the yacht righted itself with the rig and everything intact. All hell broke loose again. We were back into the real world. Not surprisingly, we decided that was enough. We set a sea anchor and ran under bare poles, still doing 7 knots. Some of the crew wanted us to head toward Eden, 70 miles upwind. 'Bugger that,' I said. 'We're heading for New Zealand. It might be 1,200 miles away, but I know I can catch a jet back to Australia from there. We are not going upwind in this.'"

Eventually, when the wind died and sea conditions improved, *Loki* made it back to port at Narooma, south of Sydney.

Initially, some good-natured father-and-son rivalry added spice to the battle between *Canon Maris* and *Winston Churchill*. John "Gibbo" Gibson, sixty-five, was aboard *Winston Churchill*, while his son, Jonathan, thirty-one, was with Ian Kiernan on *Canon Maris*. By the time the two yachts had entered Bass Strait, where they were both pounded by the storm, any competitive rivalry had dissolved.

At first Kiernan was reluctant to retire, confident the yacht was performing well. The wind direction caused him some consternation, however: it was heading west while the southern ocean was trying to squeeze through Bass Strait against a very strong current racing south. It was a deadly combination. Kiernan was standing in the companionway when a 30-foot-plus wave swept the spray dodger right off the boat. He wasn't prepared to sit still and watch his yacht be demolished or risk the safety of his crewmates, so he decided to retire. *Canon Maris* was then approximately 60 miles from Eden, but they thought they'd head for a port farther to the north—Ulladulla or even Sydney. Around 6:10 P.M. they set the spitfire jib, selected the new course, and began to extricate themselves from the worst of the storm.

The *Canon Maris* heard *Winston Churchill*'s mayday but didn't know the details. "When I heard Lew Carter mention over the radio that a search was underway and that there was no EPIRB signal, I started to think the yacht had gone down and taken the raft and all the crew with it," recalls Kiernan. "I couldn't say that, though. We had to keep a positive attitude—a stiff upper lip—for Gibbo's sake. He was hearing the reports, too, and while he appeared stoic about it all, he was deeply concerned. We kept telling him, 'Your dad will be all right, mate. They'll be OK. They'll be OK.' But in my heart of hearts I already thought they were all dead."

While race yachts continued to battle their way across Bass Strait and on toward Hobart, the nine sailors crammed into the two *Winston Churchill* life rafts began their own battle to survive what would be a traumatic night. In the four-person raft with Richard Winning and Bruce Gould were nineteen-year-old Hobart race novice Michael Rynan and Paul Lumtin. In the other raft with John "Steamer" Stanley, Jim Lawler, and John Gibson were Mike Bannister and John Dean. Winning's raft carried the yacht's single EPIRB required by race rules. The small lifeline between the two rafts soon broke. The crew of Stanley's raft set their drogue (a parachute-type sea anchor) to slow the rate of drift, but as it was let out it became tangled and wouldn't set properly. When it suddenly grabbed, John Gibson tried valiantly to hang on to it, but the thin line tore through his fingers, cutting them to the bone.

"My fingers immediately went numb," he recalls. "I knew straight away I'd done some severe damage. The fingers were bleeding, but I wasn't concerned that I was losing a significant amount of blood. There wasn't anything to wrap them, so I just left the wounds open and reckoned that salt water was the way to go."

The drogue was eventually set but lasted only fifteen minutes; the acceleration of the raft down the waves was too much for it and it broke free. "Suddenly, a big wave hit us and lifted my side of the raft," recalls Stanley. "My body went up but my feet were still pinned under the other guy's legs. I could only say, 'Oh, my God, my ankle's broken. That's not very good.' That meant both Gibbo and I were out of play." Unknown to Stanley, he had also torn tendons around both his artificial hips.

As with the other raft, the drogue attached to Winning's raft parted only minutes after the crew abandoned *Winston Churchill*. The four crewmembers decided their first job was to repair the tent flap on the canopy for better protection from the furious elements. Rain was still pouring down, and the 70-knot westerly showed no signs of easing. The flap fixed, they rummaged through the raft's ration pack. It was like a show bag at a fair and contained a small amount of basic food, water, medical supplies, and other rescue-and-survival support equipment, including an emergency pump for the raft, a knife, flares, and a reflector mirror to attract attention.

Young Endeavour was on its way to the rescue area on what had been a nightmarish passage dead downwind. The massive brigantine had skipped uncontrollably down the waves like a dinghy at least three times, and at one stage the pressure of water coming across the port side of the ship cracked the inch-thick plate glass in the steel-encased porthole. Most of the crewmembers were sick, and Audrey Brown had been hit by a flying object. Visibility was down to a measly 100 meters. *Young Endeavour* reported back to AMSA that there was still no sign of *Winston Churchill*.

Back on Bruce Gould's raft, the seas provided little relief for the four tightly packed occupants. Around dusk the raft flipped upside down. The crew couldn't undo the tent flap, which was tied with nylon rope. Their only choice was to cut their way out. After doing this, Winning took off his life jacket and swam to the surface. There was nothing to tether him with, so he just dived out and hung on. He grabbed onto a righting line and, with the help of the wind, managed to flick the raft back upright. The other crew quickly pulled him back in.

During the capsize, the antenna on the EPIRB broke in half, but morale remained high despite the conditions and the constant setbacks.

Around midnight yet another massive wave broke around the raft, capsizing it again. The raft was righted, but toward dawn the lower of the two chambers began to deflate. The crew worried that once the bottom chamber deflated, the canopy would start collapsing, as well. They consulted the instructions on how to inflate the raft manually, but the adapter had been lost during one of the roll-overs. Improvising, they pulled a nylon piece from the end of the pump hose, jammed that into the valve, and taped it up. It worked. Although the raft continued to be hurled about, now it remained upright. That crisis averted, a five-centimeter slit appeared in the floor. They were soon sitting in something akin to a toddler's wading pool.

"We don't know what caused the hole," recalls Gould. "It might have been the gas inflation bottle hanging off the raft, or the broken EPIRB antenna. We couldn't find a bailer, so we jammed a sponge in the hole. We had no bailer, but we had sixteen sponges. Fat lot of good they did: we ended up with anywhere between 6 inches [15 centimeters] and 2 feet [60 centimeters] of water in the raft the rest of the time. The level depended on how big the wave was that broke over us. After a while someone said, 'Hey, here's the bloody raft repair kit!' We ripped it open and read the instructions: 'rough the rubber surface, make sure it's clean and dry, and apply the patch.' We chucked the kit over the side."

The best bailing method they could devise involved seaboots and a plastic bag. One of the crewmembers had grabbed a *Winston Churchill* T-shirt as they were abandoning ship. The T-shirt brought another form of relief for the survivors on the raft — a hint of humor. All four debated whether the shirt from a sunken yacht brought good luck or bad. They decided, in a bid to appease the weather gods, to consign the shirt to the deep. It too was thrown from the raft.

The five crewmembers in the other *Winston Churchill* raft were in even graver danger. They were lying across the floor of the square raft like sardines—head to toe, toe to head—all the time being hurled about by the violent seas. "No one seemed worried," recalls Gibson. "The spirit in the raft was excellent. We were very concerned about John [Dean]'s obvious distress, not that he was complaining. Every now and then, when we were thrown around, there were significant exclamations—totally involuntary moans like, 'Oh, Christ!' We were trying to make him as comfortable as we could and keep away from his legs. We went through the bag of goodies we found and discussed some of the stuff that was in there. We found some fishing hooks, and I recall some jokes about what we were going to use for bait. Deanie and I were also saying how nice it would be to have some Scotch to mix with the water in the little plastic vials." With nightfall came the realization that rescue was highly unlikely before the next day. Waves buffeted the raft relentlessly, and then a monster wave flipped it upside down. They wound up standing on the inflated arch built into the raft to support the canopy. What was previously the raft floor was now the roof.

"We felt surprisingly comfortable, but we knew we were going to run out of oxygen," recalls Stanley. "You could just feel the air starting to get a bit tighter. Jim Lawler was next to the opening. He wanted to take his vest off to get out and do something to right the raft, but it was raging outside. We all decided it was too dangerous to go out for anyone to turn the thing up. If the raft were hit by one bad sea when someone was getting out, we would lose them."

"We had a calm discussion for about twenty minutes," recalls Gibson. "Certainly the comment was, 'Well, the damn thing's a lot more stable this way up than it is the other way.' It was certainly a lot quieter. Michael said words to the effect, 'We've got to get out and right this thing; otherwise we're going to be in terrible trouble.' I clearly recall saying to him, 'Michael, it's death out there.' When I said it, I thought to myself, 'Christ, that's a very dramatic thing to say; that's overstating the issue a bit.' But I really was very concerned because it was pitch black and there were very, very large waves coming through. Anyone outside would have to struggle to hang on to anything."

The five were standing in waist-deep water in pitch-blackness.

The men pulled out flashlights so they could inspect their upside-down world.

"It was definitely safer the way we were, so we decided to cut a small hole in the raft floor—now our roof—so we could breathe," explained Stanley. "There was a handle on the floor with reinforcing on either side of it. We did it longitudinally, 4 inches (10 centimeters). To do it the other way would have been better, but it would have been only 2 inches, and that wouldn't have let in enough air. When we made the cut the raft submerged about another inch in the water. That didn't matter. At least we had enough air to breathe."

They were "comfortable and quite happy" being upside down while their new "roof" was pushed up and down like a giant rubber bellow to circulate air into the raft. They drifted along for what seemed like a few hours until they heard another rogue wave roaring toward them. It was like being trapped in a railway tunnel with a locomotive coming at you without a light. The wave thundered in, picked up the raft, and hurled it upright. Bodies spilled everywhere and crashed on top of each other, and then the wave was gone. An immediate head count showed everyone to be present.

Marauding waves throughout the night rolled the raft thirty times or more. The floor started to split where the cut had been made, widening as the crew watched. In addition, the canopy was shredding. The men were hanging onto the inside rails of the raft, and when the top canopy shredded completely, they put their hands on the outside and hung onto the rails. Gibson had been in full sailing gear when he left the yacht (including his seaboots and complete harness) and had attached his safety harness to the roof arch. Others were wearing cumbersome life vests around their necks. Seasickness had thus far spared all five crewmembers.

Sometime in the early hours of December 28, the ultimate wave arrived.

"Normally we had some warning: we could hear them coming like breaking surf," recalls Stanley. "But this almighty wave gave no warning. Suddenly the five of us were just crashing. The raft was hurled from its crest and tumbled down its foaming face, 40, 50, 60 feet. I could only think about hanging on. I wrapped my arms around the roof frame and just hung on and held my breath until the wave went away. I knew that if I didn't hang on I was going to die. God knows how long it went on, but it felt like forever. When we finally stopped and I came up for air I was still hanging onto the roof frame but was on the outside of the raft. I yelled out 'Who's here?' The only reply came from Gibbo."

Stanley looked back to see a wide, white veil of water stretching some 350 meters. Amid the turbulence, a considerable distance away, he could see two people.

"I'm not sure who they were," he said, his voice full of emotion. "All I could do then was dive underneath the raft and get back up inside so I could grab the roof frame again and hang on. I said to Gibbo, 'Mate, we're by ourselves here. We can't do anything for those boys. The wind is going to blow us faster than they can swim, and we can't go back.' We could only hope that they could hang on till daybreak and be spotted by a search plane."

John Gibson has vivid memories of his experiences that night. "What little talk there was during the night was very positive, but at that stage everybody was semi-snoozing," he recalls. "We were just floating around and hanging on. My next recollection was my harness being taken up sharply—then all hell broke loose. I went on the most extraordinary ride of my life. I was obviously in white water and traveling at great speed with a huge sensation of sound. I was being dragged by my harness at terrific speed through white water and being hurled all over the place. I lost whatever handhold I had, and my body was being spun in all directions. I don't recall being scared. I remember thinking, 'This is the most extraordinary experience.' I don't remember having a problem breathing. I don't recall panicking. I recall this experience going on and on and on and on and on, and I just couldn't believe it.

"I just went with it. I didn't fight it. It went on for a remarkably long time. I also had a sense of falling. I knew I was in fast water. I knew I was in white water yet, I didn't feel I was going to drown. But I didn't know what was going to happen. I was trying to somehow or other go with it, not fight it, and at the same time try and work out what the hell was going to happen next, but at no stage did I think I was going to die.

"Then it all stopped. It just stopped. *It just stopped*, and it was dark. There was white water all around me and the raft was still. There wasn't a sound. I looked around, but no one was there. I heard a voice coming from outside the raft. It was John [Stanley]. He said, 'Who's here?' I answered, 'It's Gibbo.' He popped up inside the raft. He'd obviously been flicked outside the raft but had somehow hung on. I don't know how he did it.

"We turned around to try to see what was happening. I thought I'd lost both my contact lenses because my vision was restricted. I was aware of white water, but on recollection I still must have had my right lens in because I was able to see a strobe light come on. I knew exactly who it was—Jim Lawler—because he was the only person who had one. I had one as well, so I activated mine and held it up. I thought, 'Well, he can see that I'm still alive,' but he was a long way back. Then I heard voices. I couldn't tell you what they were saying, but I might have heard words to the effect of 'Where are you?' or 'Who's there?'—something like that. I'm sure I heard 'Who's there?' or 'Where are you, Mike?' I don't recall, exactly. They were human voices in the dark, in the white water further away."

Through a miracle, divine intervention, or sheer guts and determination, Stanley and Gibson somehow continued to defy the odds that night and hang on. Stanley said they were rolled at least five more times before daybreak.

The conditions the two rafts were experiencing by midmorning on December 28 were horrifying. But, after having battled through such meteorological malevolence overnight, the scene was improving for the *Winston Churchill* survivors. Bruce Gould remembers the winds easing to around 30 knots and moving around to the southwest, and while the waves were still huge and breaking regularly, they too had decreased in size. Inflating the raft and bailing out the water kept the men amused during a fairly uneventful day. Most of the time Winning positioned himself at the small entrance to the raft canopy so he could scour the skies for search aircraft. "I kept seeing ships and submarines and hearing aircraft all day. I wasn't hallucinating. I think it was just wishful thinking."

At around 3 in the afternoon they heard, then spotted, a plane. By the time a flare was found, unwrapped, and lit, the plane had gone. The already frustrated raft occupants watched the plane disappear toward the horizon. About twenty minutes later, it reappeared, apparently flying a planned search grid. A red phosphorescent flare, Gould and Winning's last, rocketed into the gray sky. Anxious seconds passed while the men watched for a sign that it had been seen. The twin-engine plane, an AusSAR civilian search aircraft, began a gentle turn that gradually became more and more positive. It was turning back, but it didn't come to them. It kept circling, going around their position twice.

The plane spotters were frantically trying to locate the source of the flare. It was a small black spot with a tinge of orange somewhere on the surface of the wild ocean a few hundred feet below. Finally they spotted the life raft and turned the aircraft for an approach. They radioed AusSAR with a message that wives, families, fellow sailors, and news media across Australia had hoped to hear for nearly twenty-four hours: a life raft with occupants had been sighted some 80 miles off the coast. About twenty minutes after the plane spotted them, the four survivors heard the "sweetest sound you could ever want to hear—a bloody big chopper coming at us."

If rescuing people equaled a good day at the office, paramedic Cam Robertson and the rest of the team aboard the Helimed 1 chopper out of La Trobe were going gangbusters. They had already found *Solo Globe Challenger* that morning and successfully completed the mission. Then they were assigned to search for and identify some of the many EPIRBs still transmitting. By midafternoon, things seemed to be quieting down, until AusSAR contacted them to ask them to investigate a flare from a one-person life raft sighted about 80 miles offshore. Pilot Stef Sincich acknowledged the request and turned the powerful red and white chopper toward the target.

"We located it without a problem," said Robertson. "We looked at the raft and discussed the fact that it wasn't a one-man raft, it was bigger, but we still didn't know where it had come from or who might be aboard. The guys winched me down and I finned over to the raft and stuck my head in. I couldn't believe my eyes. There were four blokes inside, and they were very pleased to see me. The noise of the chopper was really loud, so I yelled out and asked if there were any injuries. They all seemed OK. I told the guy closest to the door—it turned out to be Richard Winning—that I'd take him out first. I asked him if he would get in the water so I could get the strop around him, and he said he would. I told the other guys to collapse the canopy and get on top of it so the raft would be more stable if it got into the downwash from the chopper."

"Everything went smoothly," recalls Robertson. "Just as we got clear of the water, I yelled across to my first guy, asking if he was OK. He was. I also asked what yacht they were from and he said *Winston Churchill.* I couldn't believe it. I was shocked. It was a very special moment for me because a lot of people involved in the search thought *Winston Churchill* was lost and doubted we'd find any survivors. In no time we had all four in the chopper. It was a great feeling to know that we had got those guys. Sometimes you think it's a privilege to rescue people, and that time it really was."

"It wasn't until we were up in the helicopter and could look down at the sea that we really appreciated what we'd been through," recalls Gould. "It was a white mass of waves. It was an absolute shemozzle. We also realized how hard it had been for the poor guys in the search aircraft to find us."

The four survivors inquired after their five other crewmates. They were told they hadn't been found, news that concerned them. But the fact that they'd survived suggested to them that the others could be safe and still in a raft somewhere nearby.

John "Steamer" Stanley and John Gibson had hoped to see search aircraft during the morning of December 28. Their raft had disintegrated to a flimsy black ring drifting on the savage black ocean. Many hours had passed since the yacht sank, so the search area was now huge, and the low cloud base limited visibility to little more than a few kilometers at best. Also, flares and other emergency equipment were lost during their numerous capsizes. They estimated they were at least 50 miles from where the yacht had sunk. As the day dragged on, they began to think it was almost impossible that the other three crewmembers had survived. They were still hopeful of being rescued and knew there was an EPIRB in the other raft that would have alerted the searchers. What they didn't know, of course, was that the antenna had broken and the device wasn't transmitting correctly.

"We had to do something about staying with the raft because all we had left was a ring," recalls Gibson. "If you leaned on any section of the ring, it would submerge and the whole thing would flip over. We had to be very careful about what we were doing. We worked out a system whereby we could control what was happening, bearing in mind that John [Stanley] had very restricted mobility. The raft had lost its shape. It seemed to take whatever shape it wanted. You couldn't put your foot from one side to the other. We worked out that if we positioned ourselves opposite each other, and John put his good foot in my crotch and pushed against me, we could move our shoulders sort of above the wall of the raft and lock ourselves in. We were parallel to the arch, so we could also hang onto that for support. Our bodies gave us some buoyancy with our backs pushed against the rubber. We took that position in the early hours of the morning and held it until we were pulled out at 11 o'clock that night.

"All I can say about the arrangement is that John now owes me a few beers because he got the good end of the deal. His foot was wedged hard against my balls, and I can tell you that when it was all over my whole crotch was black. My balls were up underneath my eyes. We were hallucinating all the time. I remember thinking there was definitely a section of the raft that had a soft floor and that I could walk round and put my feet on it. Then I hallucinated about a solid floor. There was a corridor that I went down and I could simply stand there. It was the most blissful feeling. We both saw buckets of ships and sailing boats; cutters and schooners. We went past millions of them.

"John saw exactly the same. There were vessels with lights on that went past us. I also spent lots of time with some of the lovely things in my life, particularly on the romantic side. I revisited all the beautiful women I've known. I spent hours with them. It was a lot of fun and certainly helped pass the time, I won't elaborate except to say it was much better than counting sheep. I also thought about Jane, my wife of three years—beautiful, lovely thoughts. There was some conversation with John—he's a great talker—and there were long hours of silence. I felt it was important to have some sort of dialogue. I knew John was in pain, and I was quite concerned about him."

Sometime during the afternoon a beautiful albatross landed in the water near the raft and looked sadly at the two forlorn sailors. It then flew over and sat right beside Gibson. Both agreed it was a good luck sign.

"We just lay there for a long time in silence. I remember thinking to myself, 'Jesus I'd better try and liven this up a bit,' so I said to John [Stanley], 'Do you reckon we're on a steamer path here, a ship's path here?' He said, 'No, Gibbo.' Then we just lay there in the water with the raft going splish, splosh, splash, splat.

"After a while I asked, 'Steamer, do you think any of the Hobart boats would come out here?'

"'No, Mate.'

"'Steamer, where do you think we are?'

"'I reckon we're about 90 miles east of Eden.'

"'Well, Steamer, there are no boats.'

"'No, Gibbo.'

"'No yachts.'

"'No, Gibbo.'

"'We're 90 miles off.'

"'That's right, Gibbo.'

"'Mate, who gets to eat who first?' There was no answer. Not even a grunt.

"We continued to drift along, and I started looking at my hands. They were both oozing blood. Steamer looked at them and then we looked at each other. We didn't say anything, but we were both thinking the same thing—old Jaws sniffing along behind the blood trail toward us. It was another part of the equation that we weren't ready for. We just dismissed that one altogether. The cold started to move through my body; muscle contractions, shudders, and shakes. I distinctly remember as I attempted to shuffle my shoulders back up—to try and keep as much of my upper body out of the water as I could—that the effort needed to push against John for leverage was growing all the time. It was getting harder to do."

"Gibbo was trying to have a chat all the time—probably because he's a lawyer," Stanley recalls. "But he never complained about his hands, not once. I suppose I didn't complain about my ankle, either. Gibbo had lost his contact lenses and couldn't see, so I was his spotter for planes."

Around four or five o'clock in the afternoon, Stanley and Gibson were convinced they had seen a fishing vessel, a big commercial trawler. They were also hearing aircraft. Finally, more than twenty-four hours after *Winston Churchill* sank, came their first real hope for salvation. Stanley heard, then spotted, a plane north of the raft. He waved frantically but wasn't seen. About twenty minutes later the plane returned but once again missed the raft. Stanley's efforts were rewarded sometime later. He saw a large aircraft at a low altitude coming straight at them, and he shouted to Gibson to give him the yellow life vest. Stanley grabbed it and waved it in large, sweeping arcs over his head. He hoped the bright vest would contrast better against the sea than the black raft. He kept waving furiously as the plane went past and was overjoyed to see the wing light flash.

They were little more than two yellow pin pricks in an expanse of bubbling sea, but about an hour later the plane returned, accompanied by a helicopter, and both flew straight past them. Stanley and Gibson had not been spotted. The chopper was on its way to rescue the four others.

Darkness closed in on Stanley and Gibson for the second night. They had no food or water yet still managed to hang on. At that moment, new hope burst from the sky. The pair were roused from their near comatose state at the sound of a search plane. It emerged from the blackness, its navigation lights flashing brightly. Gibson aimed a strobe light and Stanley a Mag light at the plane, which flew overhead for about ten minutes, indicating to them they'd been spotted. As comforting as that sight was, Stanley and Gibson still had no idea how or when they would be rescued.

Above the roar of the storm, Steamer and Gibbo began to hear the deep-throated engines of a large helicopter approaching. It became louder and louder. A lumbering Navy Sea Hawk chopper emerged from the clouds, its search lights blazing. The two sailors were elated.

The frigate HMAS *Newcastle*, staffed by a skeleton crew, was in the area and proved to be Stanley and Gibson's springboard back to civilization. It also provided an offshore refueling point for the Sea Hawk helicopter piloted by Lieutenant Nick Trimmer. He and his crew, Lieutenant Commander Rick Neville, Lieutenant Aaron "Wal" Abbott, and Leading Seaman Shane Pashley, had been searching offshore almost all day for disabled yachts and for Glyn Charles, who was missing from *Sword of Orion*.

"It was dark, and we were heading back to Merimbula," recalls Pashley. "We heard an Air Force PC-3 Orion on the air. He was obviously searching using infrared. We heard him advise AusSAR that they had seen a light, a strobe in the water, and someone was shining a torch at them. Obviously it wasn't just an abandoned life raft: someone was alive in the water. He couldn't get a good enough ID on it with his infrared. He had also dropped a couple of flares in the water near the target. We judged the target was abeam of our track into Merimbula, probably about twenty miles to the south. We waited to hear if any other aircraft were around, and when it was obvious that there was nothing available, we advised the PC-3 we'd have a look. When we got closer to the search area, the PC-3 dropped a couple of flares in the water for us, close to the life raft. Through the murk we could see the torch. It was still a few hundred yards away and hard to see. But it was there."

The crew aboard the Sea Hawk now had to work out the most effective rescue strategy. They knew the two stranded sailors had been in the water for some time, possibly were injured, and most definitely were fatigued. This ruled out dropping the strop into the water and letting them fend for themselves. The only option was to winch Pashley down. He landed in the water and went straight under before popping up and flipping into the raft. Not realizing the raft was bottomless, he went straight under again. Pashley was doing his first nighttime sea rescue in conditions he didn't want to know about. He was also concerned about the threat of a shark attack.

"He was an agile bloke and jumped over the top of the raft—straight into the water," recalls Stanley. "I had to shout to him, 'Watch out, mate—we haven't got a floor. Be careful!' I told him to take Gibbo first because of his hands, and away they went. All of a sudden I saw the pair of them take off sideways, really hard and fast. I thought the pilot must have wanted to move them that way before he started lifting them. Regardless, I have to say that the guy who grabbed Gibbo, and the pilot, did a magnificent job."

"Just as I got the strop over the first man, the aircraft had an auto hover failure and slid away a bit," Pashley recalls. "The wire just went tight and literally tore us sideways out of the raft. It felt like you'd tied a rope around yourself, attached it to a car, and then the car took off at high speed. Gibbo went sort of backwards and sideways while I went forward and over him. That's when the knife in the leg of my wetsuit caught on the side of the raft and carved into my knee—it subsequently needed surgery. At that time, though, I could have lost my whole leg and probably not realized it. I also knew then that if either of us had any of the wire wrapped around us at that moment, we would have lost a body part. It's fine wire and would have ripped a limb off pretty quickly."

With the chopper now on manual hover, Gibson and Pashley were winched out of the water. Gibson was placed on the floor of the chopper, covered in a space blanket, and given some water and a quick check. Then it was John Stanley's turn, but as Pashley prepared to go down he was advised the plan had changed. The chopper crew felt it would be too dangerous lowering Pashley again and thought that two men on the winch would work better. Pashley drove the winch while Abbott guided the aircraft into position using the thumb control beside the door.

"I was surprised to see that the guy didn't come back down on the cable to get me," Stanley recalls. "They lowered a ring to me, instead. I thought they must have assumed I was OK. He landed the ring right beside me and I put it on. I got my arms and shoulders through it, but while I did that I must have tangled a rope from the life raft into the ring with me. He started lifting and all of a sudden I looked down and said to myself, the life raft's coming with me. I must have a rope tangled. I got to about 25 feet and thought, 'Oh, no, this is going to be danger- ous!' So I just put my hands in the air and bailed out, straight back into the water. The next thing the guy landed the ring about two feet away from me. I climbed back into it again. I remembered having watched these rescue procedures before; you don't put your hand onto the wire but lock your hands underneath the strop."

Stanley and Gibson were in remarkably good condition con- sidering their thirty-hour ordeal. They told the Navy crew everything they could about what had happened with their three mates the pre- vious night in the hope that they might still be found alive. Pashley and Abbott talked to the two nonstop, knowing it was vital to keep them awake and alert to minimize any shock that might set in before they were in doctors' hands.

Mallacoota, a tiny town on the south side of the New South Wales–Victorian border was, as the first four survivors of the *Win- ston Churchill* found out, a town with exceptional community spirit and a determined will to help. From the moment the sailors were helped from the rescue chopper, still wet and bedraggled, they were made to feel safe and comfortable. A local resident was allocated to each survivor, with the role of comforting and caring for them. The Red Cross and local Volunteer Coast Guard group were also on hand to help.

"They were just unbelievable," said Gould. "The hospitality, the way that community pulled together, they were just fantastic. They took our names and telephone numbers so they could call our wives and reassure them we were OK while we were checked over and then taken to shower. Dry clothes arrived for each of us. Noth- ing was a problem."

The joy of speaking with loved ones on the telephone was followed later that evening with the news that the second raft had been found.

"We assumed, obviously being optimistic after our rescue, that all five of them would be on board," said Gould. "We didn't know how or when they would be picked up or where they would be taken, so we had a beer in celebration and then—because we could hardly keep our eyes open—went to bed. The sweetest thing on earth that night, after being jammed into a life raft with three others for so long, was to be able to stretch out my 6-foot, 3-inch body in a bloody big bed."

Richard Winning rose early next morning to do a national television interview. While on air he was asked how he felt about losing three crewmates from the *Winston Churchill*. He hadn't heard the news. Mike Bannister and John Dean, two of his closest friends since they sailed dinghies as ten-year-olds off Vaucluse, on Sydney Harbour, were gone. Jim Lawler, a friend in more recent times, was also gone. Winning bowed his head, deeply shocked and choked with emotion, and walked away from the interview.

Part Three

Eighteen

Racing to the Finish

M any people have struggled to comprehend how the fifty-fourth Sydney to Hobart could start so innocently then metamorphose within thirty-six hours into one of the world's worst ocean racing disasters. By the time the hurricane had cut its catastrophic swathe across the northeast corner of Bass Strait, television viewers from Tasmania to Greenland were witnessing a horror story unfold. Graphic television pictures, newspaper photographs, and interviews with survivors presented the perils of ocean yacht racing as it had never been seen before.

Even as the massive rescue effort continued and the race went on—much to the surprise of those who did not understand the dynamics of the sport. Some uninformed sectors of the media called for the race to be stopped. Such suggestions were likely from people who hadn't considered the full situation. Perhaps they thought it was akin to car racing, where if it rained too hard and the track became slippery, flags were waved and cars pulled into the pits. In reality, even if the race had been stopped, there were many yachts still 50 to 100 miles from safety. They would have battled life-threatening seas and wild winds for a day or more to return to port. For some, friendlier skies lay ahead, not astern.

The diligent staff at AMSA's Rescue Control Center in Canberra were running on coffee and adrenaline. The second day of operation became a blur. The usual overnight workforce of five had soon quadrupled to twenty, and as each staff member arrived they were briefed and sent to fill another gap in the rescue coordination. Some would not leave their post for the next fourteen to sixteen hours. In a "normal" environment, the Reserve Control Center would not be dealing with more than two incidents at a time. Here they saw up to seventeen.

AMSA's public relations service was also under severe pressure as calls from families and friends of competitors plus countless media inquiries from all over the world flooded in. David Gray, Brian Hill, and Robin Poke handled some three hundred calls each in the space of forty-eight hours. They did live television broadcasts across Australia and to the United States, and even did interviews to remote parts of Europe. Uncertainty and confusion reigned: most of the yachts had lost their communications and locating them was exceedingly difficult at times. Often the RCC had to rely solely on analog mobile phones on aircraft.

Assistant Operations Manager Steve Francis had difficulties gauging, then keeping up with, the dynamics of the operation. At one point the RCC was dealing with five beacons and 406 beacon alerts simultaneously. When a helicopter with a homing capability was sent out, its on-board system was instantly overloaded, unable to cope with the volume of alerts. The search-and-rescue effort covered some 10,000 square miles and involved five civilian helicopters, thirty-eight twin-engine fixed-wing aircraft, two Royal Australian Navy Sea Kings, and two Sea Hawk helicopters, plus HMAS *Newcastle;* and from the Royal Australian Air Force, two PC-3 long-range Orions and two C130 Hercules aircraft.

While the weather continued to improve on December 28, it was not without incident. At one stage, helicopters and aircraft were alerted that they might be rescuing one of their own—the NRMA Care Flight chopper piloted by Terry Sommers had an engine malfunction 80 miles offshore. Sommers advised the top cover SAR aircraft that they had a problem and were returning to the coast. Assistance was immediately arranged, but they returned safely.

With CYC commodore Hugo van Kretschmar competing in the race aboard the yacht *Assassin*, former commodore Peter Bush became the club's official spokesman. Bush was a veteran of fourteen Sydney to Hobart races and was in regular contact from his Sydney home with club officials, monitoring the progress of the race the first night out. Suspecting the fleet was going to cop some bad weather, he took a nap, then headed to the club at 2:30 A.M. so he could monitor the 0300 hours sked. Bush finally left the club more than forty hours later. At around 12:30 on the afternoon of December 27 he heard *Rager* on the single-sideband radio in the sailing office report that they were in extreme winds of 70-odd knots. The club was soon inundated with phone calls from relatives and friends of competitors. Droves of media also began arriving, determined to get a more powerful story than their competition. Bush was feeling the heat, so he arranged to stage a media briefing every two hours.

Around noon on December 28 *Assassin* returned to Sydney, having retired from the race. Bush had briefed van Kretschmar of developments by mobile phone while he was still at sea so he'd be more prepared for the media firing squad awaiting him dockside. Van Kretschmar soon realized he should go to Hobart to take control of proceedings on behalf of the club. The media followed, always seeking answers. He held press conferences to update the media on each drama. He also found himself having to defend the sport and the CYC.

By midnight on December 27, thirty nine yachts had retired, most heading into Eden. Seriously damaged boats, some with just the twisted remnants of a tall spar, made a sad sight. At times ambulances seemed to be running a shuttle service. More yachts continued to wend their way into port that night while others that had miraculously managed to escape the most explosive forces of the cyclone raced on toward Hobart.

The two fastest yachts, *Sayonara* and *Brindabella*, avoided much of the storm's fury, but they still had their share of frightening moments. Amid the terror and tragedy there were moments of humor.

"Our mastman, Paddy Broughton, was wearing a hydrostatic life jacket—one that automatically inflates after a few seconds of total immersion in water," recalls *Brindabella* crewman Andrew Jackson. "Because there was so much water going over the boat Paddy decided the best thing he could do to keep the water away from the automatic inflation device was to put it on under his wet-weather jacket and harness. At one point in Bass Strait, Paddy went up to the bow to haul in the No. 5 jib. Next thing, the boat stuck its bow through this dirty, big wave and the jib started being washed over the side. The wave was so big Paddy was underwater.

"When the water cleared Paddy was still there, flat on his back over the spinnaker pole on the foredeck and restrained by his harness. Next thing he started grabbing at his chest in apparent pain, then before we knew it he had pulled out his knife and started stabbing himself in the chest, or at least it appeared that way to us. So much water had got inside his wet-weather gear it had activated the life jacket inflation device. His safety harness wouldn't let the jacket expand, so his chest was being crushed. He had grabbed his knife to stab the jacket to deflate it."

Radio problems prevented *Brindabella*'s crew from learning fully of the devastation behind them. The *Sayonara* crew had a fair idea, but they were still battling their own predicament. Larry Ellison and his twenty-two crewmembers ran into unexpected trouble when they reached the northeastern corner of Tasmania, where a huge high-pressure system filling in against the low had again turned mountainous. With little warning they lost their secondary forestay; stanchions were being ripped free—the boat was coming apart piece by piece. Crewmembers were flung about like rag dolls and were suffering from injuries as well as fatigue. Crewmember Phil Kieley was hurled through the air and snared his ankle as he went. "When I landed and looked down I thought my seaboot had come off because it was hanging out sideways from under the leg of my wet-weather trousers. Then I realized my foot was still in it. There was so much happening around me it took a moment to realize my ankle was broken." *Sayonara* eventually tacked in toward the Tasmanian coast, hitting the waves at a better angle and skillfully managing to stave off disaster.

The crew of *Foxtel-Titan Ford* were more than sixty miles off-shore when they were forced to go under bare poles for more than five hours. To head for shelter on the mainland may have been more dangerous than to continue across Bass Strait. The crew were painfully aware that the boat was untried since its bottom had been rebuilt and the keel replaced. Their insurance came in the form of boatbuilder and crewmember Andrew Miller who, at the height of the storm, kept pulling up floorboards "to inspect the workmanship." Co-owner Peter Sorensen swore he was scaling snowcapped mountains, not waves.

In the middle of the furor another of the owners, radio show host Stan Zemanek, was doing live radio reports while confined to his bunk with broken ribs and other injuries. Though he had been sailing for forty-two years he was a Hobart race debutant, and he vowed to his listeners that he would not be going a second time.

"We had a skeleton crew up on deck and all the time those of us below could hear them shouting '*In-coming, in-coming!*' as though we were in Vietnam," Zemanek recalls. "We could only sit down below in this confined space and listen to the yacht being pounded. There was certainly a time when I thought, 'This is it, it's all over, and we're going to die.' I started to think about my wife and my kids and all the family, thinking all the time that maybe I would never see them again. I'm not too proud to say I was praying, and I'm sure everybody else on the boat was doing exactly the same thing. When you're sitting out there helpless, like you're a cork in a bathtub, you have to rely on that spiritual belief. We all tend to believe we're big rough and tough sailors who can handle anything, but in the true scheme of things, when push comes to shove, when you're faced with the realities of life and you know this could be your last moment on earth, you start to think of family, and friends, and God. You also tell yourself you'd better start making amends."

For the third owner, and *Foxtel-Titan Ford*'s navigator, Julie

Hodder, the fear of flying off waves was tempered by the reality of what has happening to other members of the fleet—and by an especially eerie experience. *Foxtel-Titan Ford* sailed through the eye of the storm, going in a matter of minutes from 70- to 80-knot wind to none. Unsure what to do, they waited a few minutes, put up the mainsail with one reef in it, then hesitantly set the storm jib. Twenty minutes later the "eye" blinked and the storm slammed them again— but this time it was only 40 to 50 knots. Hodder was in charge of the radio and the infirmary downstairs, dishing out seasick tablets, bandages, and whatever else was required to the three injured crewmembers. She also bailed furiously, helping Tony Poole, and radioed information to Telstra Control on board *Young Endeavour*.

She and the other crewmembers were concerned about *Winston Churchill's* position and condition. They knew almost everyone on board. Ian Kiernan and the crew aboard *Canon Maris* were also distressed as they made their way back up the coast toward Sydney. Every possible radio frequency was being monitored in the hope that his crewman Jonathan Gibson's father, John, who was aboard *Winston Churchill*, had been found. When the news came through John was alive, young "Gibbo" grabbed the whiskey bottle from the shelf and quaffed a quarter of the contents in one hit.

Hobart was in mourning when the world's greatest maxi yacht, *Sayonara*, sliced its way up the Derwent River around eight on the morning of December 29. For fifty-three years the great race had brought national and international focus on this capital of Australia's island state, but this year it was attention burdened with sorrow. It was the height of summer, but there was a distinct chill in the air as the white-hulled sloop broke through the finish line off Battery Point, immediately adjacent to the city's waterfront. And while the usual fleet of small craft was on hand to escort the first yacht into port, the elation that often accompanied the moment was nonexistent. Officials canceled the massive welcome—including daytime fireworks and a trophy presentation—as a mark of respect for those who had lost their lives. Aboard *Sayonara*, some of the world's most seasoned and professional sailors were shaking their heads in disbelief. Some just slumped to the deck.

The five thousand people who crammed the wharves seemed undecided whether it was proper to celebrate *Sayonara*'s arrival. As the yacht docked alongside the pontoon specially prepared for the welcome, Larry Ellison stepped ashore and was greeted by the waiting media throng. Immediately above him, colorful flags hung at half-mast. Ellison, his eyes reddened by tears and salt spray, spoke about his experiences.

"Never again. Not if I live to be a thousand years old will I do a Hobart race. This is not what it's supposed to be about. Difficult yes, dangerous no, life threatening—definitely not." After suggesting he might quit the sport, he said there was only one word to describe the race—"nightmare." "It was by far the toughest race I've ever done in my life. It was horrible. The crew work was inspirational. Very bad things could have happened to us out there, and these guys got us through. Guys were knocked down but they just kept getting back up and getting back to work. They kept doing what had to be done to keep the boat in one piece—and keep all of us alive. It was truly extraordinary. Anyone who signs up for this race expects a difficult race, but no one expects a dangerous race. The seas were enormous, and the wind made sounds I've never heard before."

World champion yachtsman Chris Dickson sat on the edge of the yacht, staring into space and listening to what Ellison was saying. His wife of a week, Sue, comforted him. "That's as tough as it gets," said Dickson. "Being here first sure is nice, but being here at all is the big thing. Every member of the crew is thinking about those who are still out there and not thinking too much about how we have done."

Lachlan Murdoch was equally contemplative. "I think a lot of the guys in this crew have very strong mixed feelings about even finishing in this race at all. You needed to be out there to know just how bad it was. Imagine any disaster movie you have seen before, then double it or treble it."

Navigator Mark Rudiger, winner of the previous Whitbread round-the-world race with the team led by American Paul Cayard, echoed the sentiments expressed by Murdoch. "The Sydney to Hobart lived up to all the fears I ever held about this race and then some. I was hoping I'd get away with an easy one, but I didn't. At times it was worse than the Whitbread. It didn't last as long, fortunately, but at its peak the wind and waves we saw coming across Bass Strait were the worst I have ever encountered."

From the time *Sayonara* arrived until the last yacht crossed the line at dusk on January 1, the normally boisterous dockside scenes in Hobart were replaced by a respectful silence. Most activity centered around the major television networks who had descended on the city, bringing satellite dishes, broadcast vans, and spotlights.

Brindabella crossed the finish line almost three hours after *Sayonara*, followed by the battle-scarred remnants of what had been a strong 115-yacht fleet. With each arrival came incredible stories of survival, of unbridled courage, and of how fate had intervened. It was not until these crews got to the dock, saw family and friends, and heard of the death and carnage in their wake that they could completely comprehend the magnitude of events. One of the most remarkable achievements was that of David Pescud and his team of disabled sailors aboard *Aspect Computing*, which placed first in their division. The crew's motto was "Carpe Diem"—seize the day. Events in Bass Strait galvanized friendships, and there was none greater than that of two *Aspect Computing* crewmembers, the race's youngest competitor, twelve-year-old Travis Foley, a dyslexic from Mudgee in New South Wales, and his blind crewmate, Mooloolaba's Paul Borge.

The bond was apparent when the two went to the podium to join Pescud in collecting their prize for being first in PHS Division. Young Foley was Borge's "eyes" onshore as they went forward to be saluted by the large dockside crowd. Borge already had twenty-eight-year-old Danny Kane to help him on the yacht over the previous twelve months. Kane was partially paralyzed after a stroke four years earlier. During the race Foley became part of that special team. "I was helping Paul whenever I could," said young Foley, "showing him where things were and helping him get into his wet-weather gear. This whole crew are now my best friends." Foley, who was doing his first ocean race, admitted he was scared, but added he'd do it again.

At the other end of the spectrum was eighty-one-year-old Papa Tom—Sir Thomas Davis—former Prime Minister of the Cook Islands. He was the champion among the crew of twenty-six aboard the 83-foot *Nokia*. Despite the horrors he'd faced and the protestations of his friends, Papa Tom was happy he had accepted skipper David Witt's invitation to join the yacht. With his medical background, he became crew doctor, and at the height of the storm he was belowdecks caring for the injured. He remarked he was by no means cured of ocean racing, but he was cured of the Sydney to Hobart.

The tragedies that had crushed the race also overshadowed an incredible achievement by the overall race winners, Sydney's Ed Psaltis and Bob Thomas with their 35-footer, *AFR Midnight Rambler*. This relatively small and lightweight yacht was tenth into Hobart, beating many larger yachts home. Declared the race winner on handicap, *Midnight Rambler* became the smallest yacht in a decade to take the major prize. It was Psaltis's seventeenth attempt to win the classic, his previous best placing being eighth with the even smaller *Nuzulu* in 1991.

"If there was an element of luck, then it was that we got the worst of the weather during the daylight hours," he said. "We could see the most dangerous of the waves coming at us and because of that we had the best possible opportunity of getting the yacht over them. I guess you could say we didn't get 'That Wave,' the really big one that wiped out so many others. If it had been dark, it might have been a different story."

On January 1, 1999, a large crowd, weighed with sadness, watched in silence as six floral wreaths were cast onto the waters off Constitution Dock in Hobart in memory of those who would not race again.

Epilogue

Sailing has always been my passion, and since I left school that passion has also been my career. The 1998 race was the thirtieth Sydney–Hobart I covered. Along the way I had also managed three starts and three finishes in the classic. Being in Hobart in 1998 to report on the finish for television and newspapers stretched me—like so many of the race competitors—to the absolute limit of my emotional capacity. Suddenly my sport and my life had come face to face with fatalities.

For me, being ashore and understanding from some tough sailing experiences just how horrendous things were in Bass Strait, then trying to relay that in a composed fashion to the world, was not a pleasant experience. People had already died, and I knew more would die. At the same time I was trying to cope with my own emotional burden. Search-and-rescue personnel were out searching for my friends. Were they dead or alive?

I also had to field a flood of telephone calls from anxious wives and friends whom I had to reassure, encouraging them to have faith in their loved ones' survival. It felt almost as tough as being in the race. Those people desperately needed to know if their husband, father, sister, son, or brother was coming home.

To speak with Robyn Rynan on the telephone that third night and confirm for her that her young son Michael, who was aboard

Winston Churchill, had been found alive in a life raft was a bitter-sweet experience. I will never forget her torrent of tears, wavering voice and sobbing sighs of relief. For me it brought a realization of what family bonds are all about. At the same time, there was the thought of what other families, those who didn't know the fate of their loved ones, must be going through.

I am regularly asked why we go ocean racing. Since this tragedy, one of the most appropriate answers I've found is in Sharon Green's great book of her sailing photographs, *Ultimate Sailing.*

> *It is a romantic sport . . . not carried out against the elements, but because of them.*

Honor Roll

Following is what is undoubtedly a partial list of the search-and-rescue crews, organizations, and companies that helped save so many lives in the 1998 Sydney–Hobart race.

Air Services Australia Helimed 1 Air Ambulance

Captain Peter Leigh
Captain Howard Bosse
Captain Stefan Sincich
Air Crewman Steve Collins
Air Crewman Stephen Simpson
Air Crewman David Sullivan
Paramedic Cam Robertson
Paramedic Peter Davidson
Paramedic Terry Houge
Observer John Sloyan
Observer John Bailey
Senior Base Engineer Russell Gallattly
Operational Logistics Officer Wendy
    Civetta

SAR Observer Eddie Wright
Aviation Manager Ken Laycock

NRMA Careflight

Pilot Dan Tyler
Pilot Terry Summers
Pilot Richard Nest
Aircrewman Graeme Fromberg
Aircrewman Steve Johnston
Dr. Richard Cracknell
Dr. Ken Harrison
Dr. Arthas Flabouris
SCAT Paramedic Murray
    Traynor
SCAT Paramedic Steve Martz
SCAT Paramedic Ian Spencer
Engineer Mark Cruse

Coordinator John Hoad

Coordinator Ian Badham

Victoria Police Air Wing

Senior Constable David Key, Rescue Crewman

Senior Constable Darryl Jones, Pilot

Senior Constable Barry Barclay, Winch Operator

Senior Constable Trevor Rim, Rescue Crewman

Senior Constable Keith Fisher, Winch Operator

Constable Chris Jameson, Pilot

WESTPAC Lifesaver Rescue Helicopter, Illawarra Branch

Chief Pilot Jon Klopper

Rescue Crewman Peter Mangles

Air Crewman Douglas Smith

Air Crewman Matt Scott

Air Crewman Roger Graham

ACT Ambulance Service Southcare

Pilot Ray Stone

Pilot Simon Lovell

Acting Base Manager Pilot Ron Maurer

Crewman Mark Delf

Crewman Matthew Smith

Crewman George Casey

Base Engineer Colin Hobbs

Paramedic Michael Abigail

Paramedic Paul Bibo

Paramedic Michelle Blewitt

Paramedic Paul Brooke

Paramedic David Dutton

Paramedic Grant Hogan

Paramedic Kristy McAlister

Paramedic Stephen Mitchell

Duty Superintendent David Foot

Duty Superintendent David Holdom

Acting Superintendent Andrew Edwards

Director of ACT Ambulance Service Ken Paulsen

Chief Executive Officer Emergency Services Bureau Mike Castle

Young Endeavor

Royal Australian Navy Crew

LCDR Neil Galletly RAN, Commanding Officer

LEUT Brenton Witt RAN

LEUT Ian Heldon RAN

LEUT Nathan Jacobsen RAN

LEUT Debra Dunne RAN

CPOCSM(AC) John Crawford

CPOMT Gregory Goddard

POMT Paul Baker

LSCK Angela Miranda

ABWTR Sally Kingston

Supernumeraries

LCDR Ron Matsen RANR

LSPH Stephen Coates

Kirsty Boazman

CYC Radio Operators

Lew Carter

Michael Brown

Audrey Brown

Youth Crew

Benita Ainsworth

Kathy Baker
Meretta Boyer
Katy Glenda
Catherine Habermann
Louise Keogh
Amelia Mills
Alethea Mouhtouris
Clare Omodei
Michelle Redden
Desiree Wilson
Timothy Davies
Richard Evans
Steven Hammond
Benjamin Harzer
Matthew Hosie
Jason Ives
John Moir
Steven Roberts
Angus Stevenson
Chris Daley

The New South Wales, Victoria, and Tasmania Police Forces

Eden

Sergeant Keith Tillman
Senior Constable Bradley Ross
Senior Constable Craig Baker
Senior Constable Nick Markulin
Merimbula
Sergeant Colin Bell

Bega

Sergeant Mark Welsby
Batemans Bay
Superintendent John Ambler
Inspector Rick Mawdsley

Water Police Launch *Nemesis* and Crew

RAN Sea King Helicopters (HS817 Squadron)

SHARK 05

LEUT Alan Moore, Aircraft Captain and First Pilot
COMMANDER George Sydney, Commanding Officer HS 817 squadron, Second Pilot
LEUT Philip "Wacka" Payne, Observer, Tactical Navigator
Petty Officer Kerwyn Ballico, Aircrewman

SHARK 20

LCDR Paul "Tanzi" Lea, Aircraft Captain and First Pilot
LEUT Chris "Ox" Money, Second Pilot
LEUT David Hutchinson, Observer, Tactical Navigator
Petty Officer Brian "Dixie" Lee, Air Crewman
Duty Officer at HS 817
LEUT Scott Booker, Royal Navy Exchange Pilot
Maintenance Personnel HS817 SQN
LEUT Andrew Watson, Observer
CPOATA Mario Cinello
CPOATA Tony Bouckaert
POATA Rohan Denman
LSATA Edson Flores, Observer
LSATV William Miles, Observer
ABATA Kieran Molloy
ABATV Jonathan Kick, Observer

RAN Sea Hawk Helicopters

TIGER 75,
HMAS Melbourne

LCDR Richard Neville
LEUT Nick Trimmer
LEUT Aaron "Wal" Abbott
LEUT Richard Allen
POA Shane Pashley, HS816
 Squadron
CPOATV David John Larter
POATA Laurie Tomasinni
LSATV Zoran Dimov

TIGER 70,
HMAS Newcastle

LCDR Adrian Lister
LEUT Mick Curtis
LEUT Marc Pavillard
LSA David Oxley
POATV Jamie Edwards
POATV Henry Wakeford
ABATA Anthony Devenish-Meares

RAAF PC-3 Orion (No. 92 Wing)

FLTLT Paul Carpenter
FLTLT Mark Ellis
PLTOFF Mathew Taylor
FSGT Mark Wilson
FSGT Michael Makin
SGT Mark Koschenow
FLTLT Richard Wolf
PLTOFF Cecelia O'Leary
FLGOFF Andrew Gerkens
WOFF Mark Styles
FSGT Murray Walters

SGT Scot Bugg
SGT Shaun McConville
FLTLT Christopher Gall
CAPT Christian Martin
WOFF Christopher Kennedy
WOFF Andrew Ortlepp
FLTLT John Flynn
FLGOFF Simon Van Der
 Wijngaart
FLTLT Kevin Mulgrew
FLGOFF Colin Gray
SGT Andrew Kassebaum
WOFF Adam Tucker
WOFF Wayne Newberry
SQNLDR V Ludwig
SQNLDR G Roberts
SQLDR G Zidicky
FLTLT P Hay
FSGT Larry McLoud
SGT Jamie Burgess
SGT Peter Drury
SGT Gordon Tusti
CPL Ralph Bobart
CPL Paul Bonnar
CPL Scott Brady
CPL Barry Ramsbotham
LAC Michael Horner
LAC Adam Pannel
WOFF Pete Harte
SGT Garry Wood
SGT Mark Borchard
SGT Kim Nagel
CPL Vaughan Wilds
CPL Antony Hawkes
CPL Shane Drew
CPL Mark Bridewell
LAC Aaron Agnew

RAAF C-130 Hercules (37th Squadron)

HMAS Newcastle

CMDR S. R. Hamilton
(Commanding Officer)
LCDR B. J. Wheeler
(Executive Officer)
LCDR M. Richardson
(Marine Engineering Officer)
LEUT L. D. Van Stralen
LEUT C. Dummett
LEUT L. Brick
LEUT N. Brett
LEUT M. Harris
LEUT A. Cox
LEUT N. N. Marshall
SBLT A. Banks
CPOB P. R. Kiely
CPOET D. A. Stratford
CPOSN D. J. Russell
CPOMT A. E. Vernon
CPOMT P. T. O'Keefe
POB P. L. Wood
POSY R. M. H. Tadin
PORS S. B. Dummett
POCSS P. Hassall
POSN M. Hancock
POET R. M. Glover
POET G. L. Cruickshank
POMT A. W. Sims
POMT A. Bowman
POMT D. B. McCelland
POMT M. J. Jakes
LSBM S. A. Nesbitt
LSBM(SE) M. J. Golding
LSBM(FF) S. R. Cannan
LSPT D. A. Hunt

LSCSO R. P. Pringle
LSSIG K. Viant
LSRO S. D. Golder
LSRO D. C. McLeod
LSMED G. J. Davis
LSET D. Fielding
LSET J. G. Seguin
LSET M. P. Weidenhoffer
LSET D. Levett
LSMT G. Santini
LSMT J. Strange
LSMT G. Criado
LSMT P. Armour
LSMT D. Plummer
ABBM D. A. Low
ABBM D. J. Brearly
ABBM R. L. Fealy
ABBM P. W. Beckwith
ABCSO C. W. Woodland
SMNCSO P. A. Keitly
ABCSO D. A. Wruck
ABCSO J. D. Allen
ABCSO D. C. Seaman
SMNCSO S. S. Allan
ABSIG J. Upton
ABSIG G. Judd
ABSIG L. Hillier
ABRO M. T. Dwyer
ABRO P. A. Hunter
ABWTR P. Aldridge
ABSN A. Corr
ABSTD R. Furner
ABSTD M. Walker
ABCK J. Holmes
ABCK G. Janes
ABET G. A. O'Connor
ABET S. Sandwell

ABMT P. Marriott
ABMT A. Walsh
ABMT G. Beech
ABMT P. Williams
ABMT N. Thomas
SMNMT D. Goodbun
ABMT S. Atkins

ABC TV Helicopter

Gary Ticehurst
Peter Sinclair

IBIS Air

Air Sapphire

Air Ambulance VIC

Southern Region SLSA

Direct Air

Tasmanian Aero Club

Nation Wide

Joyce Aviation

Australasian Jet

Australian Aerial Patrol

General Flying Services

South East Aviation

Brindella Airlines

Airtex

Tasair

Vee H Aviation

Vessel *Josephine Jean*

Owner Lockie Marshall
Skipper Olli Hrcinsson and Crew

Vessel *Moira Elizabeth*

Owner Joe Pirrello
Skipper Tom Bibby and Crew

Publisher's Afterword

On June 1, 1999, the Cruising Yacht Club of Australia released the "Report, Findings and Recommendations of the 1998 Sydney to Hobart Race Review Committee." The report's key findings—summarized by Peter Bush, the committee chair, included the following:

- No one cause can be identified as being responsible for the 1998 Sydney Hobart Yacht race fleet becoming involved in multiple incidents on 27 and 28 December 1998. As a result, there is no single change that can be identified for the future running of the Race that could preclude the repeat of such incidents. However, there is a series of incremental changes, that while on their own may appear of little significance, will together have a substantive and lasting impact on the organisation, running and safety of the event. These changes include a range of issues such as administration (processes and procedures), safety (education and equipment), communications and weather (forecasting and education).

- The Race Committee has the power under the "Racing Rules of Sailing 1997–2000" (RRS) published by the Australian Yachting Federation (AYF) to abandon the race. The Committee did not exercise this power. It was the Com-

mittee's view that Rule 4 ("Decision to Race") should
remain in each skipper's hands, particularly because of the
fact that each yacht was in the best position to evaluate its
own circumstances fully in the conditions.

- The competitors, while concerned about the 1998 SHYR
  itself, and being keen to pursue improvements, generally
  believe that the rules, safety regulations and safety equipment with which they raced, met their needs in the conditions. From interviews of 28 yachts, it is clear that skippers
  and crews do not see a single (or several) reason(s) for the
  incidents occurring and certainly see no basis to apportion
  blame to any particular group—organisers, Bureau of Meteorology (BOM), Search and Rescue (SAR) authorities etc.
  Furthermore, they do not see as a result, any need for wide
  sweeping changes to safety regulations and equipment.

- Yachts that experienced problems or encountered difficulties, and even those that continued racing reported that
  "exceptional" waves were responsible for inflicting the damage or causing severe knockdowns. These waves were always
  a minimum of 20% and up to 100% bigger than the prevailing seas and always came from a direction other than the
  prevailing wave pattern.

- Although the precise location, timing and depth of the low
  pressure system were not accurately forecast, the key issue
  relating to the weather was the gap in knowledge between
  the BOM's forecasts and the way they were understood
  by the sailors. The Bureau assumed that its forecast winds
  would be interpreted as being up to 40% more than stated
  and seas up to 86% bigger. The fleet reported expecting
  winds and seas to be "as forecast" or a bit stronger/bigger.

- There is no evidence that any particular style or design
  of boat fared better or worse in the conditions. The age of
  yacht, age of design, construction method, construction
  material, high or low stability, heavy or light displacement
  or rig type were not determining factors. Whether or not a
  yacht was hit by an extreme wave was a matter of chance.

- The level of crew experience exceeded the requirements pre-
  scribed by race authorities and the AYF. However, many

crews, despite having high levels of ocean racing experience, were poorly informed on aspects of safety equipment use and search and rescue techniques.

- After the 1993 SHYR, when only 38 out of 104 starters completed the race, the CYCA circulated a questionnaire to competitors. The results found safety equipment was satisfactory, but recommended that a series of actions be taken by the Club. These included the improvement of some safety equipment and the skill level and education of sailors in the use of safety equipment and heavy weather sailing. While some of the issues identified in the survey were addressed and implemented, many of the same issues emerged again during the investigations into the 1998 Race. These particularly relate to training and education. The CYCA should have pursued these issues more rigorously.

The review committee recommended a number of changes for the race beginning in 1999. These include

- Compulsory reporting of strong winds (above 40 knots) and high waves by competing yachts

- Compulsory assessment and report from each skipper prior to entering the Bass Strait as to the boat and crew's capability of continuing

- Broadcast of additional "layman's" weather forecasts to the fleet

- Increase in the requirements for crew experience and an increase in minimum age of crew to 18

- Introduction of mandatory offshore qualifying races

- Compulsory attendance for at least 30 percent of a yacht's crew at weather, safety, and search-and-rescue seminars

- Compulsory use of the highly accurate 406-MHz Emergency Position-Indicating Radio Beacons (EPIRBs)

- Upgraded personal safety equipment

- Improved race communications

- Handheld VHF radio carried aboard each boat as a last communications resort during a search-and-rescue operation

    Every competing boat will be required to obtain an International Measurement System certificate of stability compliance whether the boat races under IMS, the Channel Handicap System, or the Performance Handicap Rating System (PHRS).

About the Author

Sailing has been Rob Mundle's life—his sporting passion and his career. Equally, the Sydney to Hobart has been part of that life. He has covered the annual classic on thirty occasions and has competed three times.

Born in Sydney, he was the first cadet journalist employed in the Sydney office of the national daily newspaper, the *Australian*, in its first year of publication, 1964. After training as a general reporter, he created the ideal situation by combining his career with his sport. He is widely recognized today as a leading media authority on sailing.

As a sailing competitor he has won local, state, and Australian championships and has contested many of the major offshore events overseas. He was responsible for the introduction and successful marketing and promotion of the Laser and J/24 classes in Australia.

In the 1980s he established a new career in television as a reporter, commentator, and, at one stage, a prime-time news weatherman. He has reported on five America's Cup matches (including the live international coverage of Australia's historic win in 1983), three Olympics, and numerous other major sporting events. In 1993 he wrote the biography, *Sir James Hardy, An Adventurous Life*.

Today Rob Mundle runs a media services and event promotion company, while continuing to contribute to newspapers and magazines around the world.